Client/Server Computing

James Martin/McGraw-Hill Productivity Series

McGraw-Hill and world-renowned computer/communication technology expert James Martin team up to provide IS managers with the information they need to meet the application development challenges of the 1990s.

Organizations worldwide are under great pressure to achieve strategic corporate objectives, meet increasing global competition, get products to market faster, respond faster to competitive challenges, increase the quality of products and services, and reduce cost. Traditional IS technologies are no longer adequate to meet these challenges. IS managers need to learn a new set of technologies that can be used to rebuild the enterprise information system.

This unique series has been designed to present a comprehensive view of the new technologies that are required to rebuild the business. These technologies include business process redesign, client/server computing, downsizing, open systems, client/server development tools, CASE tools, relational database management systems, object-oriented techniques, and rapid prototyping methodologies. The Series provides a consistent view of how these technologies can be used within an integrated framework to meet the strategic needs of the organization.

Client/Server Computing

Dawna Travis Dewire

McGraw-Hill, Inc.

New York San Francisco Washington, D.C. Auckland Bogotá
Caracas Lisbon London Madrid Mexico City Milan
Montreal New Delhi San Juan Singapore
Sydney Tokyo Toronto

Library of Congress Cataloging-in-Publication Data

Dewire, Dawna Travis.
    Client/server computing / Dawna Travis Dewire.
        p.   cm. — (James Martin/McGraw-Hill productivity series)
    ISBN 0-07-016732-X
    1. Client/server computing. I. Title. II. Series.
QA76.9.C55D48   1993
004'.36—dc20   92-9429
                                                              CIP

        4 5 6 7 8 9 0   DOC/DOC   9 9 8 7 6 5 4

ISBN 0-07-016732-X

*The sponsoring editor for this book was Neil Levine, the editing supervi-
sor was Jane Palmieri, and the production supervisor was Donald
Schmidt. It was set in Century Schoolbook by Decision Tree Associates.*

Printed and bound by R. R. Donnelley & Sons Company.

To Andy

ABOUT THE AUTHOR

Dawna Travis Dewire (Wellesley, Massachusetts) has more than 20 years of experience as a programmer, analyst, systems architect, consultant, instructor, and writer. As a contributing editor to the James Martin Report, Inc., she was responsible for preparing such end-user-oriented volumes as *Query, Reporting and Graphics, Decision Support and Financial Analysis,* and *Text Management.* She is an adjunct lecturer at Babson College in Wellesley, Massachusetts, and is president of Decision Tree Associates. She is the author of *Building Applications for Distributed Environments* and *Text Management,* both to be published by McGraw-Hill.

Contents

Part 2 The Client

Chapter 5. Client Hardware and Software

Chapter 6. Client Software Products

Chapter 7. Client Requirements

Part 3 The Server

Chapter 8. Server Hardware

Chapter 9. Server Environment

List of Figures

Chapter 1. Overview of Client/Server Computing

Chapter 2. Evolution of Client/Server Computing

Chapter 3. Overview of Client/Server Applications

Chapter 4. Understanding Client/Server Computing

Chapter 5. Client Hardware and Software

Chapter 6. Client Software Products

Chapter 7. Client Requirements

Chapter 8. Server Hardware

Chapter 9. Server Environment

Chapter 10. Server Operating Systems

Chapter 11. Server Requirements

Chapter 12. Server Data Management and Access Tools

Chapter 13. Overview of Networking

Chapter 14. LAN Hardware and Software

Chapter 15. Development Methodology

Chapter 16. Application Development Tools

Chapter 17. Managing the Production Environment

Chapter 18. Production Requirements

Chapter 19. Hardware and Software Trends

Foreword

The new James Martin/McGraw-Hill Productivity Series provides Information Systems professionals with the objective information they need to deal with the rapid changes in computer technology. The Series offers insight into how new technologies can be used effectively to meet strategic corporate objectives and reduce costs.

Downsizing and client/server computing have become the hottest topics in the computer industry. Managers expect downsizing and client/server computing to provide the following benefits:

- Meet the strategic needs of the organization
- Provide transparent access to data anywhere in the organization
- Establish flexible, scalable, and expandable computer architectures
- Substantially reduce the cost of computing
- Provide greater ease of use and higher end-user productivity
- Support connectivity, portability, and compliance with industry standards

The new architectures, methodologies, and tools described in this first book in the Series enable IS professionals to develop client/server applications much faster and at lower cost than with traditional techniques. The resulting applications support requirements for portability, interoperability, and interconnectivity across multiple target environments. Topics discussed in this book include:

- Many mainframe computers are becoming obsolete and are being replaced by low-cost networks of micros and powerful servers that manage the data. This process, called downsizing, can result in a 10:1 reduction in computing costs while improving performance and flexibility.
- Mainframe-based applications are being migrated to a distributed client/server environment.

- New software development tools are available that can be used to build applications for a distributed client/server environment at low cost.
- Hand-generation of computer software using source languages, such as COBOL and C, is being replaced by automated tools that generate immediately executable code for the entire application.
- Older software development tools based on structured techniques, such as CASE tools, are being replaced by client/server development tools that are based on object-oriented techniques and the event/response model. Client/server tools are less costly, require less training, and impose less cultural change than conventionally structured tools.
- Client/server development tools are moving toward support of open system standards, including SQL, RDA, OSF/DCE, OSF/DME, POSIX, and GOSIP.

IS managers need to learn how to re-tool IS to take advantage of this new technology. Using the new architectures, methodologies and tools described in this book, IS managers can respond to corporate requirements to generate a bottom-line contribution to the business, meet strategic objectives, and be more responsive with fewer resources.

James Martin

Preface

Every decade has its star technologies. The 1970s had Management Information Systems (MIS) and the use of terminals for screen input/output—the birth of online systems. The 1980s gave us Decision Support Systems (DSS), Executive Information Systems (EIS), and the microcomputer. The 1990s have already given us more powerful mainframes, midrange, and micros; laptop and notebook micros; GUIs; textbase management technology; client/server computing; and wireless networks. In each decade, the software supported the business worker with tools that were "user friendly." The hardware gave each worker more horsepower or allowed more workers to use the same horsepower.

Each of these revolutions carried with it marketing hype: how much money would be saved, how much more productive the worker would be, how critical it was that the worker have access to data (which leads to needing to access *more* data), how important sharing data was. Every product description included the right words for the times: MIS, DSS, EIS, client/server. Early vendors in each revolution spent a great deal of sales time educating.

Many industry analysts forecast that most applications will be client/server based by 1995. This major paradigm shift in computing is attributed to its significant benefits such as:

- **Cost savings**. Client/server computing allows organizations to leverage existing hardware and, in some cases, software.
- **Data accessibility**. Business users have access to data anywhere in the network via an easy-to-use interface.
- **Adaptable Environments**. Due to its modular nature, client/server computing allows organizations to easily port applications, enhance existing technologies, and integrate new technologies.

What exactly is client/server computing? It involves splitting an application into tasks and putting each task on the platform where it can be handled the most efficiently. This usually means putting the processing for the presentation on the user's machine (the client) and the data management and storage on a server. Depending on the application and the software used, all data processing may occur on the client or be split between the client and the server. The server is connected to its clients via a network.

Client/server architectures can be as straightforward as a standalone LAN-based server with micro clients. There might be a communication line to a host (mainframe or midrange) for data feeds, but the host is not accessible to the users for interactive data access. More complicated are systems with communication links from servers to interconnected hosts which give users access to data on any of the connected machines. As the configuration expands to a geographically disbursed heterogenous network of different hardware, software, operating systems, LAN operating environments, and database management systems, the chances for incompatibility increase exponentially.

We are led to believe that implementing client/server applications is a snap. An organization purchases the new tools and some additional hardware (or upgrades existing hardware) and trains some of their best IS professionals to handle the new technology. These new technology leaders spend a couple of months working on new applications and voila! Client/Server Applications. This scenario has not turned out to be true.

As is the case with any new technology, the first steps into a new arena require care, patience, money, and managed expectations. Just as the leap from DP/MIS into DSS/EIS required a change in corporate culture and new skills for IS professionals and business users, so does the leap into client/server technology. When data is to be shared among business units, data definitions and availability must be agreed upon and understood. It is essential that all groups are working with the same data models. While this is obviously necessary, it is a major stumbling block for success with Decision Support and EIS systems. When data is readily accessible, the ownership of data becomes a sensitive topic—*I don't want anyone else to see it before I say so*—and security takes on a whole new level of importance. When the interface is jazzy and easy to use, business workers are more likely to enjoy using it and, therefore, will use it.

Client/server computing is significant to both business users and IS organizations. Information management is improved with centralized validation and access rules. Easy access to data improves users' productivity. By separating the front-end and back-end processing, changes to the back-end processes do not require modification to the front-end processes. IS professionals can develop applications on their desktop machine, which frees up mainframe resources and reduces development time. Organizations can *rightsize* applications to the platform that provides the most benefits.

However, client/server architecture is not necessarily right for all applications (or organizations, for that matter). Support is required from many vendors (hardware, software, and network—often more than two of each). Hardware reliability becomes a major issue—if the server goes down, so does the system. Security of the hardware and of the data (since access is easier, the data is vulnerable to fraudulent uses) add a new level of complexity. Because client/server applications rely on communication networks for data retrieval, response times may increase due to network traffic. With application software spread throughout an organization, maintaining and updating software require new methodologies and controls. Client/server computing changes the organization's structure and the change is often disruptive. IS professionals need to be trained in the new technology. Users become responsible for the maintenance of their system and have to be trained to perform duties formerly performed by IS.

The first vendors of client/server products (which were mostly database products) have spent a great deal of time and effort to communicate the merits of the technology. The maturity of network software, robustness of midrange computers, acceptance of UNIX, increased software offerings for client/server development, proven productivity with GUIs, and easy-to-use tools for developing GUIs have brought client/server technology within reach of most organizations.

This book is intended to educate. The view of client/server computing expressed in this book is based on research and hands-on experience. The intent is to provide a framework for the reader's leap into this new technology. Some questions will be answered and more questions will, no doubt, be raised. As is true of any new technology, more than one product is right for an organization and there will be a few more introduced at the next trade show. The question for today is not *Whether we should try on this new technology for size*—the obvious answer is YES! The question is *What mix of products feels right for us and which vendors will be able to help us benefit from this new technology now and grow with us in the future?*

This book is in six parts. Part 1 is an introduction to client/server computing. It covers the evolution that has brought us to this leading-edge technology and the benefits that can be gained by its use. It also covers the strengths and limitations of the technology.

The next three parts deal with the components of client/server computing individually. Each part dicusses the hardware and software used for that particular component and its requirements. The layers of software in each component are discussed and the major software packages for the component are reviewed.

Part 5 deals with the issues of developing and installing client/server applications. Different development methodologies and application development tools are reviewed. Tools that manage a multivendor environment are examined. The unique production requirements for client/server computing are detailed.

Part 6 looks at the expected trends for this new technology, such as mobile computing, workgroup computing, and the impact of object technology.

The text is followed by two reference lists and an index. One is a list of abbreviations used in the book. The other is a list of all the trademarks and registered trademarks used in this book. They are listed alphabetically, not in the order of appearance.

Dawna Travis Dewire

Acknowledgments

Special thanks to James Martin and Pieter Mimno for giving me the opportunity to write this book on the computer technology I so strongly support and for their continued support and encouragement.

Thanks to Marcia Pomerance of Wilde Communications for her expertise, advice, and support, as well as her attention to detail.

And a very special thanks to Andy, Travis, and Gregory for giving me the time and support necessary to complete the book.

Introduction to Client/Server Computing

It has been called the wave of the future—the computing paradigm of the 1990s. Client/server technology has caught the interest of large and small organizations.

This new technology is the result of the advances in hardware and the newest evolution of software products. It has become a popular strategy for companies trying to minimize costs while improving control and customer service.

Client/server applications have three elements: a client, a server, and a network. Each of these has a hardware component and several software components. It sounds simple enough, doesn't it?

However, client/server applications rarely confine themselves to their own network. In addition, clients in the same network can use different software. Servers in the network can use different operating systems and server database software. When client/server applications need to go outside their own network, the environment must be able to communicate with the accessed environment, accept data, and then transport it back to its own environment.

There are many types of client/server applications, ranging from simple to complex, each with their own requirements for the individual components of the architecture. Organizations starting with the simplistic must plan for future growth when deciding how to configure their architecture.

Much of the software and hardware used for client/server

computing was not designed with the security and reliability necessary for applications that run the business. As client/server computing evolves, the integrity and reliability of its components is improving, but this is not happening overnight and not with all product offerings.

The goals of client/server computing are to allow every network node to be accessible, as needed by an application, and to allow all software components to work together. When these two conditions are met, the environment can be successful and the benefits of client/server computing, such as cost savings, increased productivity, flexibility, and resource utilization, can be realized.

These goals can be achieved in part by adhering to industry standards and creating open systems. However, some of the components of client/server computing have multiple standards to choose from, others have none.

All would agree, it is the best of times, it is the worst of times.

Overview of
Client/Server Computing

Dallas-based American Airlines Decision Technologies cut their computing budget by 90 percent—from $5 million to under $500,000— as the result of an 18-month project that created an open systems network. Built with $4.5 million worth of multivendor UNIX-based hardware and software, it increased productivity of the company's analysts and paid for itself in one year. The company develops systems for companies such as American Airlines, Lufthansa German Airlines, Ryder Truck Rental, Inc., and Royal Caribbean Cruise Lines.

Consolidated Insurance Group in Wilmington, Delaware, reduced capital expenses from $1 million to $300,000 and operating expenses from $2.5 million to $500,000 in the first year after replacing its headquarters-based IBM 3090 mainframe and support staff of 30 with seven micro-based servers supported by a staff of 10.

When United Airlines Inc. converted to a client/server environment from a mainframe computer environment, the company saved millions in computer costs and improved flight schedules for its pilots and flight attendants, which is predicted to save nearly $1.5 million a year.

How are these organizations achieving such savings? Client/server computing.

1.1 What Is Client/Server Computing?

Client/server computing uses local processing power—the power of the desktop platform. A simple definition of client/server computing is

3

that *server* software accepts requests for data from *client* software and returns the results to the client. The client manipulates the data and presents the results to the user or, acting as a server (or an agent), sends the results to the client (server) that requested it. To make it sound more technical: most of the application processing is done on a programmable desktop computer, which obtains application services (such as database services) from another computer in a master/slave configuration.

The emphasis of client/server computing is not hardware. The hardware components have been around for quite a while. While the hardware does indeed deserve some attention, the major focus of this book will be the technology that makes client/server computing possible—the software.

Client/server computing provides Information Systems (IS) professionals with options by allowing applications to be segmented into tasks. Each task can be run on a different platform, under a different operating system and with a different network protocol. Each task can be developed and maintained separately, accelerating application development. Data can be placed closer to the user. Users can access their data with a comfortable interface and tools for manipulating that data into meaningful information. Suddenly users are able to do more for themselves, rely less on IS for assistance, and receive quick turnaround time for applications requested of IS. The end result is more efficient use of existing equipment, increased effectiveness of future spending, and more productive workers.

Application processing performed on more than one machine in a network may be either distributed computing or cooperative processing. Distributed computing partitions the data between two or more computers, which may be geographically dispersed. The user has transparent access to the data. Cooperative processing splits an application's functions (processing) between two or more computers in a peer-to-peer relationship. Most client/server network structures are based on distributed access, not distributed computing. Client/server architecture uses a master/slave configuration where processing may be performed by both the master and the slave.

The use of open systems (hardware, software, operating systems, databases, and networks) enhances client/server computing. By adhering to standards, open hardware and software can provide interoperability and portability. Open systems offer IS greater flexibility in linking divergent technologies. However, in some cases there are multiple standards and in others, none at all.

While this new technology seems very straightforward, it is actually more complex than the technology it is replacing. Even if all the pieces adhere to standards, multiple components must be integrated and managed. The network and all its nodes are treated as "the computer." Departmental LAN-based systems become part of the enterprise-wide network. Before changes are made to departmental systems, impact on the enterprise-wide system must be identified and resolved.

Before an organization ventures into the world of client/server computing, an application's functions should be reviewed. This breakdown parallels the division of duties in client/server computing.

1.1.1 Application Tasks

An application can be broken into six tasks:

- **User interface**, what the user actually sees
- **Presentation logic**, what happens when the user interacts with the form on the screen
- **Application logic**
- **Data requests and results acceptance**
- **Data integrity**, such as validation, security, completeness
- **Physical data management**, such as update, retrieval, deletion, and addition

When applications are entirely mainframe based, the mainframe file management system handles the physical data management. The programs in the application handle the other components. Early online systems did not actually change this division of duties even though the user interfaced with the application via a screen.

The acceptance of database management systems (DBMSs) began to change the division of duties by including some data integrity functionality within the physical data management software. This integration allowed early query languages to access data for retrieval without compromising its integrity. IS no longer had to develop and maintain data-retrieval programs. Query languages have since evolved to support update, create, retrieve, and delete functions, all under the security of the DBMS, as illustrated in Figure 1.1.

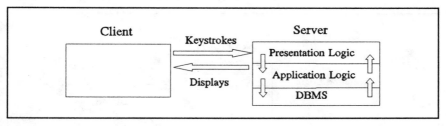

Figure 1.1 Query language architecture

One of the first products to utilize a micro-based windowing environment as an interface to a host computer was EASEL, from Easel Corp. IBM 3270/5250 screens were replaced with EASEL-developed displays (on a micro) that were easier to use and more pleasant to work with. The success of EASEL-based systems and the growing acceptance of Microsoft Windows spawned the birth of graphical user interfaces (GUIs).

GUIs require a great deal of processing power to create the screen the user sees. Since the processing costs on a micro are lower than a host (mainframe or midrange), presentation processing is best done by the desktop machine, freeing up host resources for other processing requirements and requiring no changes to the host application. As application tasks were split between the host and the screen-generating desktop machine, illustrated in Figure 1.2, the idea of client/server computing was born.

The first generation of client/server applications operated in a file server environment, which handles data in database structures or as complete files. File servers allow more than one worker to access the same document, although not at the same time. They allow a document file or data to be accessed from anywhere in the network. When a user needs data elements from a file, the server transmits sectors of the index file, together with the entire file, even if only a few records are required. As each record is received, the micro checks it to see if it meets the query criteria.

A file is locked once it is sent to a user machine—even if only parts of it are sent. Early versions of file servers did not differentiate between a browse access and an update access. Current LAN software recognizes the difference, eliminating some access bottlenecks.

Organizations quickly outgrew file management systems. It is inefficient to send an entire file and related indexes when the user only needs a few records, or possibly only one record. LAN-based DBMS products support multiple accesses to the same database and can send individual records (and just fields in some cases) instead of files. This minimizes the overhead of sending large amounts of unused data across

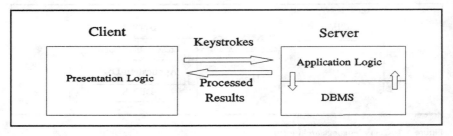

Figure 1.2 Original client/server applications

communications lines. Now, only the fields of the records that meet the query criteria are sent over the lines.

Once this split occurred, client/server computing evolved into a simple model in which the server served data, and the clients did everything else. The processing of the data and the presentation of the data was in the domain of the client. The only application processing that a server performed was to process a request for data and return the results. Since validation routines and security checks were embedded in the DBMS software, these processes were handled by the server as part of the data management function.

As the software became more robust and the power of the desktop machines increased, some of the data validation was moved to the client. It made sense to move the error-checking and validation routines to the client—the user received quick turnaround for errors and omissions and the host did not receive faulty requests.

In addition, some portions of the application processing were moved from the client to the server, especially number-crunching activities such as sorting processes and large consolidations, as well as stored procedures and triggers. The distribution of processing between the client and server is accommodated by the client/server model, as illustrated in Figure 1.3. When to make this split and how to make this split continues to be up to the developer. Some products that facilitate building client/server applications can easily incorporate this split—some even do the partitioning automatically. Otherwise, the split must be coded into the client/server application. (The production headache caused by having application logic distributed throughout the network instead of centralized on the host is discussed in Chapter 18, Production Requirements.)

As the client/server model evolved, organizations began to look at client/server computing as a way to implement systems at a lower cost. Just as organizations considered midrange computers as an option to mainframes, they began looking at micro environments as alternatives to midrange and mainframe platforms. The integration provided by LANs made the client/server option even more appealing.

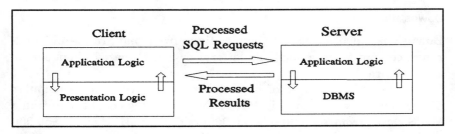

Figure 1.3 Distribution of processing in client/server model

1.1.2 Rightsizing

As client/server technology evolves, the battle cry is now rightsizing— design new applications for the platform they are best suited for, as opposed to using a default placement.

An application should run in the environment that is most efficient for that application. The client/server model allows applications to be split into tasks and those tasks performed on individual platforms. Developers review all the tasks within an application and determine whether each task is best suited for processing on the server or on the client.

In some cases, tasks that involve a great deal of number-crunching are performed on the server and only the results transmitted to the client. In other cases, the workload of the server or the trade-offs between server MIPS (millions of instructions per second) and client MIPS, together with the communication time and network costs, may not warrant the use of the server for data intensive, number-crunching tasks.

Determining how the tasks are split can be the major factor in the success or failure of a client/server application. And if the first client/server application is a failure, for whatever reason, it may be a long time before there is a second.

Some variations on this theme are:

- **Downsizing.** A host-based application is downsized when it is re-engineered to run in a smaller or LAN-based environment.
- **Upsizing.** Applications that have outgrown their environment are re-engineered to run in a larger environment.
- **Smartsizing.** In contrast to rightsizing, which is technology based, smartsizing affects the entire organizational structure and involves re-engineering and redesigning the business process, as well as the information systems that support the process.

Downsizing

Downsizing involves porting applications from mainframe and mid-range computers to a smaller platform or a LAN-based client/server architecture.

One potential benefit of downsizing is lowered costs. Computer power is usually measured in MIPS. Currently, the cost of mainframe MIPS varies from $75,000 to $150,000; midrange MIPS about $50,000 and desktop micro MIPS about $300. A micro that can perform as a LAN server ranges from $1,000 to $3,000 per MIPS. As technology improves, the costs of LAN servers and micros continue to drop. The midrange and mainframe (host) technologies are improving at a slower rate. Their costs are dropping at an even slower rate.

However, the cost benefit is not as straightforward as it appears. Host MIPS are used more efficiently and the processor has a higher utilization rate. Hosts automatically provide services (such as backup, recovery, and security) that must be added to LAN servers. Host software costs more than micro software, but more copies of micro software are required. Mainframes require special rooms, operators, and systems programmers. Micros sit on a desk. LAN servers use existing office space and require no specialized environment.

Another way to look at the cost benefit is to recognize where most of an organization's MIPS are today—on the desktop! And most of those MIPS aren't fully utilized. Figure 1.4 illustrates the relationship between the number of LAN-connected micros and the number of business micros. Gartner Group (Stamford, Connecticut) predicts that by 1996 there will be nearly five million LANs and 75 percent of all

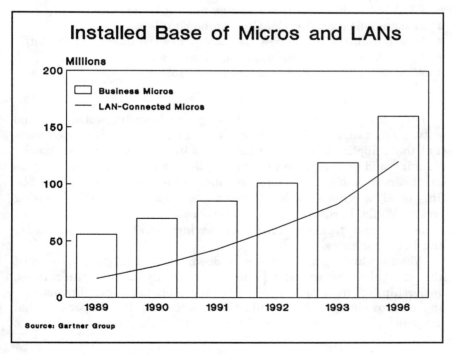

Figure 1.4 Growth in installed micros and LANs

business micros will be connected to a LAN.

By using the existing desktop MIPS, organizations can postpone or eliminate hardware acquisitions. Many of these desktop machines are already linked to a central machine using terminal emulation software, so the network is already in place.

Other potential benefits of downsizing are improved response time, decreased systems development time, increased flexibility, greater control, and implementation of strategic changes in workflow processes. In addition, mainframe applications downsized to a desktop/LAN environment allow data to be accessed by other applications. However, the decision to downsize should be made on an application-by-application basis. Downsizing the wrong application could put an organization at risk.

According to Theodore P. Klein, president of the Boston-based consulting firm Boston Systems Group, Inc., an organization must answer the following questions when evaluating applications for downsizing:

- Is the application departmental, divisional, or enterprise-wide?
- What is the database size and how must it be accessed?
- Is the application functionally autonomous?
- How familiar with the new technology are the users and IS staff?
- Is the data in the application highly confidential?
- What level of system downtime can be tolerated?

Downsizing is not as easy as buying and installing hardware and software that support client/server computing. The larger environments that these applications run on have built-in features, such as capacity planning and performance monitoring, that are still in their infancy in client/server platforms. As a result, client/server environments must be fine-tuned to reduce bottlenecks and make optimal use of processing cycles. While hardware and software cost savings may be almost immediate and dramatic, processing savings will be slower to realize and less impressive.

When evaluating applications for downsizing, an organization must also recognize the political issues involved. In many organizations, ownership of information systems represents power. Downsizing applications changes the organizational structure. It is important that the political issues be planned for and dealt with.

Upsizing

Even as companies are downsizing from their glass-housed mainframes to distributed LAN-based systems, they are planning for the future by ensuring that these new systems are expandable. When an application outgrows the current environment, the capacity of the environment should be increased or the application should be ported to a larger environment with no disruption to users.

Environments can be expanded in many ways, which include:

- Increasing memory and storage on the server
- Swapping a more powerful processor into the server
- Adding processors to the server
- Upgrading to more robust network software

For expansion to occur with a minimum of disruption to the users, open systems (hardware and software) should be used whenever possible.

Smartsizing

Smartsizing is based on re-engineering the business processes themselves, in contrast to downsizing, which re-implements existing automated systems on smaller or LAN-based platforms. Downsizing focuses on cost savings and increasing current productivity. While the code for the application may be streamlined, little or no thought is given to the process itself.

Smartsizing implies that information technology can make the business process more efficient and increase profits. Business re-engineering focuses on using technology to streamline internal workflow tasks, such as order entry and customer billing. Information technology can be used to increase customer satisfaction. Products can be developed and brought to market faster using information technology.

1.2 Benefits of Client/Server Computing

There is little disagreement that the implementation of client/server computing can result in current and future savings, but this new technology usually cannot be justified on cost/benefit analysis alone. The other major benefits are intangible and hard to quantify.

1.2.1 Dollar Savings

The examples cited earlier in this chapter indicate the magnitude of savings that can be realized by migrating host-based applications to a client/server environment. Mainframe environments are costly to maintain—the hardware, software, and staff required to maintain and develop applications are very expensive. Fewer staff are required to maintain client/server platforms and maintenance contracts (if there are any) are moderate in cost.

Significant cost savings on hardware and network expenditures relative to mainframe-based environments can be identified. When more power is required of a server, it can easily be expanded instead of replaced, as is often required in mainframe-based environments. Maintenance costs for a server are negligible compared to the costs for mainframe maintenance. Networks are now providing mainframe-like security at much lower costs.

Client/server technology allows organizations to protect current investments by using existing equipment and protect future investments by using scalable, expandable products. The days of buying a new mainframe to replace an existing one are just about gone.

Client/server-based applications can be developed in less time than mainframe-based applications. Since front-end and back-end processes are separate, they can be developed and maintained separately. Client/server applications are usually developed on the client machine, freeing up mainframe resources for processing. Security and business rules are written as stored procedures within the server database software, stored separately from the applications programs, and maintained separately. Once these common business rules and procedures are programmed into the server software (coded and verified once), developers can focus on solving application-specific business problems.

1.2.2 Increased Productivity

Both users and developers are more productive using client/server tools. Users are more involved in the development process and in control of the application, once it is operational. They have transparent access to the data they need to do their jobs and have a standard, easy-to-use interface to that data.

End User Productivity

Flexible data access for end users was first provided by fourth-generation languages (4GLs), although early versions only provided access to their own proprietary databases. Later versions included transparent access to other data sources as well. But the interface was command-line driven. The user had to know the commands and their arguments. Although the languages were not procedural, they had an inherent degree of syntax.

The ease-of-use promoted by client/server computing is obtained through the use of windowing environments such as DOS-based Microsoft Windows 3.x, IBM's OS/2-based Presentation Manager, and UNIX-based Motif and OpenLook. These graphical user interfaces are mouse driven; take advantage of color; and present groups of data in boxes, tasks in windows, and choices in menus or icons. (Note: DOS will be used to represent all of the versions of DOS, such as Microsoft MS-DOS, IBM PC-DOS, and DR DOS from Novell).

Studies have shown that users can be more productive using a GUI-based application as compared to a character-based application. A study conducted by Mercer Management Consulting (formerly Temple, Barker & Sloane, Inc.), a market-research firm based in Lexington, Massachusetts, found that experienced GUI users were 58 percent more productive than experienced character-based user interface (CUI) users. Novice users of GUIs were 48 percent more productive than novice CUI users. Despite the fact that these tests were run in a laboratory setting using only word processing and spreadsheet software, the statistics support the claim of increased productivity through the use of GUIs.

The sales literature for just about every software product today claims that it incorporates a GUI, or that one is under development. Marketing literature may talk about the product as having a window interface, which turns out to use boxes with text and menus or lists that can overlay one another and whose interface is still keyboard driven—not exactly what most users think of when they visualize a window interface.

But the key to increased productivity goes is more than the interface itself. Increased productivity also is the result of the close fit between the system design and the way users actually do their jobs. The benefit comes from users being able to easily access data stored in a variety of formats without needing to know anything about those formats. And using the same, easy-to-use interface to get to all that data certainly does help.

Developer Productivity

Developers can be more productive using client/server development tools. Applications may be designed, implemented, and tested in a client/server environment much faster than in a mainframe environment. Not because they are simpler—most of them are not—but because the development environment and the tools themselves are easier to use and automate many of the development steps.

Most client/server development tools make use of object-oriented technology. Most of the user objects, including those controlled by Windows, can be customized and used in multiple applications. The GUI for an application is easily designed and modified. Some products have a point-and-click intelligent interface to SQL, reducing the code the developer must actually produce.

The development platform is the desktop machine. All phases of application development—designing (in some cases), coding, testing, executing, and maintaining—can be performed from the desktop machine. The finished product can be ported to a more appropriate environment, if necessary. The desktop environment offers the developer a GUI interface, local autonomy, and subsecond response. The platform is also appropriate for building iterative prototypes of the application.

1.2.3 Flexibility and Scalability

By segmenting the application tasks, an organization can easily migrate to new technologies or enhance existing technologies with little or no interruption. An application does not have to be redesigned to use a new interface software or be moved to a new platform. An upgrade to a server should have little impact on the applications themselves.

Client/server computing is modular. Adding new components or replacing existing ones is as straightforward as adding or replacing components in a stereo system. Organizations can easily upgrade components or migrate to a newer technology without changing the specifications of the application.

Data access is as easy as providing address links to the GUI platform (assuming the data structure is accessible). Users can choose their own presentation interface: a GUI, such as Windows or Motif, character-based screens or a spreadsheet format. Users have more control over how they work with their applications and their data.

As industry standards evolve, applications that run in mixed environments and across different platforms will become commonplace. Applications will be easily ported from one environment to another, either up, down, or peer-to-peer. If applications outgrow their current environment, migration can be as easy as plugging in a more powerful server that supports the same software. Support for symmetric multiprocessing by the server operating system will also provide a growth path to more powerful servers. A new client for an application can be added by simply adding their network address to the Access Control List for that application. If an application doesn't need the horsepower of its current environment, it can be downsized to a smaller environment. The process of adding a network to the overall network structure is straightforward.

In today's competitive climate, it is imperative that an organization be able to move quickly—to take advantage of a business opportunity, to react to a competitor's move, to be the first to market with a new product or service. One reason micros have been successful is that micro tools allow management to react. Mainframe-based application development and maintenance does not lend itself to quick response. A simple data dump requires that someone in IS write a program, which accounts for why many IS departments still have a backlog of requests.

1.2.4 Resource Utilization

A basic tenet of client/server computing is effective use of computing power. In a balanced client/server network, the processing power at every node in the network is efficiently used. By focusing client machines on user interfaces and application processing, and servers on data storage and retrieval, computing resources are leveraged—reaping obvious cost benefits.

The first client/server implementation in an organization may not require new equipment. One of the important features of client/server computing is being able to link existing hardware and applications. It allows an organization to use the equipment they already have more effectively. Perhaps a midrange machine can be used as a server if the application processing is offloaded to the micro front-ends.

Server 32-bit operating systems, such as UNIX, Microsoft's Windows New Technology, and IBM's OS/2 2.0, will improve performance of the servers, permitting them to perform more data manipulation and data management functions. Routines that are shared or that should be optimized can be pre-compiled and stored on the server. These stored procedures would then be called by applications as needed and the compiled code executed.

Client/server architecture is designed to use LAN technology efficiently, minimizing any potential bottlenecks. The client generates the request and checks it for syntax accuracy. The completed and checked SQL request is sent to the server. The server processes the request and returns only those records or fields that match the request. Since the request is more accurate when sent and only the requested data is returned, network traffic is minimized. By reducing the amount of traffic required for data requests, the network is freed up to support applications that require the transmission of large files, such as images and text. Since most client/server environments use a LAN, the term LAN operating system will mean (in this book) a network—LAN or otherwise—operating system.

Network bottlenecks can be reduced further by separation of duties. Local processing can focus on supporting the user, remote processing aimed at number crunching. Products, such as Ellipse from Cooperative Solutions, automatically assign processes (which can be overridden by the developer) to the client or the server to maintain load balancing.

1.2.5 Centralized Control

We have come full circle in the architecture of IS facilities. The centralized facilities of the 1960s and 1970s became decentralized without network links. Data was transmitted via a channel or data feed. Data was not easily shared and compliance with control standards and procedures was difficult to enforce. Client/server computing allows today's IS facilities to combine the best of both centralized and decentralized architectures.

This split is illustrated in Figure 1.5. The decentralized portion of the computer system consists of the processing done on the client and is the responsibility of the business end user. The centralized portion of the system consists of the processing performed on the server and is the responsibility of IS professionals, as are the links to the server. The

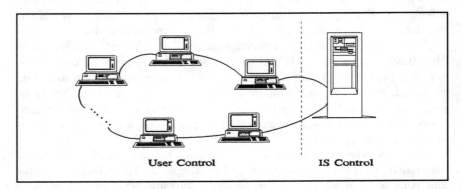

User Control   IS Control

Figure 1.5 Centralized and decentralized control

server maintains an intelligent database with rules and security checks coded into the server. The end result: IS gets centralized control over the data and users focus on their business requirements.

The rules governing the management of all the organization's data are located at one source and controlled from that source—the server. All access to data goes through that source, and, therefore, must pass through the stored business rules and security checks. Any controls that are the responsibility of the local facility can be implemented as rules on the local server.

Backup and recovery procedures are centralized. To ensure that the server is always operating, procedures, such as uninterruptible power supply, shadow system, mirrored data, and fault-tolerant processing, can be in place.

The client/server model permits IS to recover much of the control that was lost when micros began appearing in the organization. Users purchased micros and expected IS to make them work. Users didn't think about backing up their files until it was too late. Data was keyed into spreadsheet software from host-generated reports. Numbers on micro-generated reports didn't always agree. Users argued that they needed the speed of the micro and its friendly interface to solve business problems.

IS can now give users the speed and the friendly interface they require, as well as reliable data that is accessible from anywhere in the internetwork. Security of data is back in the hands of IS. Software distributions and version compatibility are handled reliably by IS—not by sneakernets.

1.2.6 Open Systems

For client/server computing to be effective, multiple environments must be supported. When applications are rightsized, it is important that there be connectivity among the components of the platform. There must be support for multiple hardware vendors, multiple GUI platforms, multiple operating systems, multiple DBMSs, multiple communication protocols, and multiple LAN operating systems. Management of the network can become the weak link in the configuration. Tools that allow the systems administrator to manage the network (configuration, console, problems, modification) and monitor its performance must be developed.

The benefits of open systems—interoperability and portability—result from adherence to standards. However, there are multiple standards in some areas and none in others. It is up to organizations to make a strategic decision on which standards they will adopt and establish those standards throughout the organization.

Evolution of
Client/Server Computing

The use of computers by organizations has always been an evolutionary process. A review of technology and its uses ten years ago, five years ago, and as recently as one year ago can provide some startling insight into what might be expected in the next wave of technology. And the change brought on by this evolution makes it feel more like a revolution. Sometimes the new leader in technology stays in power for quite a while and sometimes is quickly replaced by a new leader.

2.1 Hardware Trends

Terminals replaced punch cards, micros emulating terminal processing replaced terminals. Midrange computers replaced mainframes, LAN-based networks—and client/server computing—are replacing midrange and mainframe machines.

The evolution toward client/server computing has been driven by business needs, as well as the increasing costs for host (mainframe and midrange) MIPS and maintenance, the decreasing costs and increasing power of micros, and the increased reliability of LANs.

Inexpensive UNIX RISC (reduced instruction set computing) systems have been rated over mainframes for performance and value with factors ranging from two-to-one to nearly ten-to-one. Their price/performance ratio has improved annually by almost 50 percent—

compared with close to a 10 percent improvement for mainframes. In addition, large disk subsystems available for UNIX-based machines cost about a tenth of their mainframe-based cousins. As the acceptance of UNIX grows, so does the software available for the platform, most notably DBMS products. One of UNIX's weak areas has been in its lack of support for the high level of throughput necessary for online transaction processing (OLTP). UNIX System V Release 4 from UNIX Systems Laboratories (USL) addresses this weakness, improving the viability of UNIX as an option for OLTP applications.

In addition, mainframes are expensive to maintain. The annual maintenance contracts with hardware vendors and annual fees for software can run into the millions of dollars. According to Computer Economics Corp., based in Carlsbad, California, the annual cost of support (hardware, software, personnel support, and miscellaneous) for mainframe MIPS is about $80,000. RISC MIPS run about $2,500 and micro LAN MIPS about $1,000.

Part of the rise in client/server interest has been fueled by the potential compute power that is available in the number of micros and workstations that sit on workers' desks. When one considers how much of the day these machines are idle or underutilized, it is no wonder that organizations see great dollar benefits in client/server computing. With client/server computing, organizations can make greater and more effective use of these desktop machines (which are already paid for!). The machines are ideally suited to support the user by providing the resources for generating GUIs, the easy-to-use interfaces users are demanding. A host machine just cannot support multiple resource-demanding GUI-based environments.

2.1.1 Power

The power of desktop machines (micros and workstations) has grown exponentially, from 8 MIPS on a 386-based computer to 80 MIPS on a 486. As the power of the micro has increased, the cost of providing that power has decreased. In the meantime, the power of host machines has grown at a slower rate than its cost. Consequently, organizations are trying to use the host for applications that require the processing power only a host can provide.

2.1.2 Chips

Machines used for servers are typically built with mass-produced chips, such as Intel 386 and 486 processors, Motorola 68030 processors, and

Year	Type	Transistors	Speed-MHz
1989	Intel i486	1 million	25-50
1992	Intel i586	4 million	75-100
1995	Intel i686	22 million	150
1998	Intel i786	100 million	250

Figure 2.1 Capacities of processors

such as Intel 386 and 486 processors, Motorola 68030 processors, and RISC-chip processors. These mass-produced chips are cheaper and more powerful than those used in mainframe and midrange computers. According to Intel, the projected MIPS rating for the Intel 586 processor equals the MIPS rating of the new IBM mainframe Summit architecture.

The power of these processor chips is growing rapidly. The Intel family of processors, which is compatible with the IBM PS/2, is evolving as shown in Figure 2.1. The speed of the chip is actually faster than the cycle time indicated. Currently, most microprocessors execute about one instruction for every five chip cycles, so a 25 MHz chip operates at about 5 MIPS. Newer chips can operate at one instruction per cycle, so a 25 MHz chip could operate at 25 MIPS. The IBM POWER chip used to drive the IBM RS/6000 does a look-ahead (like a mainframe, it fetches instructions before they are required) allowing a 33 MHz chip to operate at 56 MIPS. It is conceivable that a future 150 MHz chip could operate at nearly 500 MIPS.

2.1.3 Memory

The capacity of memory chips has been quadrupling every three years. The evolution started with a 1 megabit chip in 1986. By 1992 standard chips stored 16 megabits. By the year 2000, don't be surprised at one billion-bit chips.

The amount of storage and memory that micros and workstations are able to support has also increased dramatically. Extended memory and expanded memory have raised the primary memory ceiling to 16 Mbytes. A 40-Mbyte hard drive is standard on an entry-level micro. Machines that are designed to be used as servers use disk arrays, which are multiple disk drivers that are treated as a single logical drive by the processor. The future integration of CD ROM storage into business applications puts an almost unlimited amount of data in reach for end users.

2.2 Software Trends

Vendors of database products, such as Sybase, Oracle, Ingres, and Informix, have gained early client/server computing market shares. These database products are successful not because they were written to support this new technology, but because they support distributed data and use SQL, the standard data access language for client/server applications. Because they were recognized as important data sources, third-party front-end interface products have been written that access data stored in the formats of these leading database products.

2.2.1 Relational Databases

So much attention is paid to relational databases when client/server is discussed, the naive user might assume that all data resides in relational database structures. If that was the case, client/server data management would not be the headache it is. In reality, most of an organization's data is legacy data: data from applications written before databases were in vogue, or data from applications that use first-generation database products such as IMS, IDMS, and Model 204. This data must also be transparently accessible by users applying the same easy-to-use methods.

Instead of relational structures, applications may use structures, such as hierarchical, inverted, specialized structures for managing text and images, and object-oriented and CASE (computer-aided software engineering) repositories. Each structure is appropriate for a particular class of data and can co-exist in the data structures of an organization. IBM's Information Warehouse implies that there can be only one structure under the control of a resource manager. It just isn't so. Multiple structures with multiple management technique must be supported and integrated.

2.2.2 GUIs

The development and acceptance of GUIs—such as Microsoft Windows 3.0 and 3.1, IBM's Presentation Manager, Open Software Foundation's Motif, and USL's OpenLook—has had a major impact on the acceptance of client/server computing. In the first six weeks of release, Microsoft shipped 3 million copies of Windows 3.1. (Note: Windows 3.x will refer to Windows 3.0 and 3.1, and Windows will refer to any version of Microsoft Windows.)

Graphical user interface platforms do more than provide a presentation layer to applications. They provide an operating environment on top of the operating system of the desktop machine. For example, Windows 3.1 expands the memory management of the operating system with its own memory management and simulates a multitasking environment, using task-switching techniques to keep one process at a time moving forward. One process is kept in background, and the other in foreground.

2.2.3 Multithreaded Processing

A thread is a process or an execution. Because it is a single-threaded operating system, DOS can execute only one process (thread) at a time. Multithreaded software, such as the OS/2 operating system and the Microsoft LAN Manager network operating system, supports multiple threads of execution and allows the threads to communicate with each other. One thread could be controlling the printer, one the keyboard I/O, and another executing application code. Multithreaded support allows the software to make more efficient use of the hardware. Multithreading is covered in Section 8.3, Features of Server Machines.

2.2.4 Continuing Evolution

Client/server computing has been predicted to be the "wave of the future" since 1990. The delay has been attributed to the lack of robust client/server-oriented application development tools. That is finally beginning to change. Organizations are using products, such as PowerBuilder from Powersoft Corporation, SYBASE SQL Toolset, and Ellipse from Cooperative Solutions, to take advantage—successfully—of this new technology.

Things continue to change. Server operating systems are beginning to incorporate some network operating system functions. Server data management software is getting smarter. Products that generate GUIs have some intelligence about interfaces, SQL, and transaction processing. CASE vendors are beginning to address this new paradigm. 4GL vendors are building GUIs to their products and building gateways to major server data management software. In short, computer hardware and software vendors are paying attention to what business end users want and need and are addressing the need to integrate those wants and needs with IS's responsibilities to the organization.

2.3 Evolution of Operating Systems

The first generation of operating systems managed the various components of the hardware and ran one batch job after another. The next generation of operating systems used partitioning to improve resource utilization. The central processing unit (CPU) divided its time between partitions, each partition running a different batch job or active program. CPU resources could be balanced between partitions. Printing and spooling operations could be run in background.

Online transaction systems, the next generation, required more sophisticated capabilities from operating systems. The major hardware vendors [IBM, Digital, Hewlett-Packard (HP)] differentiated themselves by their operating systems. MVS from IBM uses partitioning and requires a teleprocessing (TP) monitor for processing of transactions. Under Digital's VMS, a TP is not required because the CPU can support many different processes at once. However, since a TP has multithreading capability, Digital recommends a TP for large online transaction processing systems. Otherwise, large amounts of memory would be required to handle the transaction processing. HP's MPE operating system does not require a TP monitor because it has built-in multithreading support.

When the IBM System 36/38 minicomputer (predecessors to the AS/400) was introduced, IBM surprised the industry by including a DBMS as part of the operating system—not as an extra component. The industry began to question the positioning of DBMSs. Should data management services be separate from operating systems or be a service provided by the operating system?

The question was answered by the next evolution of technology, which included the overwhelming acceptance of the micro, and the slow—but steady—gain in the popularity of UNIX, an off-the-shelf operating system that provides little security, has a primitive file system, and no built-in DBMS. But it's portable and not proprietary.

Operating systems have two components: a shell, which the users interact with; and a kernel, which controls the hardware components (such as memory, disk, CPU, and peripherals). The UNIX kernel is written in the C language and, therefore, can be implemented on any CPU that has a C compiler, making it portable across a wide variety of hardware architectures. Following the success of Apple's mouse-driven interface, graphical shells were developed for the UNIX world, including Motif, OpenLook, and NeXTStep from NeXT, Inc. These rounded out the software offerings for the UNIX world and, in effect, validated the UNIX operating system as a viable choice for business applications.

Micro operating systems have evolved from 8-bit file handlers to 32-bit multitasking systems. Operating systems are no longer bounded by a DOS-imposed 640-kbyte memory limitation. The newer operating systems are beginning to include host-like features such as virtual memory, communications support, multithreading, and a GUI front-end.

As micro operating systems evolve, there should be some common capabilities. These include:

- Portability in the underlying kernel and application programming interfaces (APIs) that sit above it
- Further use of 32-bit architectures (CISC and RISC)
- Support for symmetric multiprocessing hardware
- Extensions for multimedia and pen-based computing
- Compliance with POSIX (Portable Operating System Interface for UNIX)

2.4 Networking Trends

The earliest micro LANs were easy to install. Telephone wires (unshielded twisted pair) were strung between the micros or coaxial cable was installed behind a wall. Each micro needed a LAN adapter card on its main bus, which translated requests into network packets and vice versa. These early networks were used primarily to share devices such as laser printers and plotters. The network software was installed on a micro that was hooked to the shared devices. This machine became known as the server.

The next logical step was to allow users to share data. Early implementations transferred data as complete files. When a user requested information from a file, the whole file was sent over the network to their machine. The file was locked and was not available to any other user. Software advances modified the procedure so that files were accessed for query only, thereby not locking other users out. However, complete files were still sent over the network. Software advances have now taken the locking down to the record level, eliminating the need to send entire files over the network.

The network is the least widely understood component of client/server computing. Many users and developers understand and are comfortable with the front-end and back-end hardware and software—but how the data goes back and forth on the cables correctly is somewhat of a mystery. Gone are the days when the only questions were "What is the baud rate?" and "Is it full- or half-duplex?"

Many books have been written about networks. Most are too technical for the average business user or IS professional. But when implementing client/server technology, it is important to have an understanding of the mechanics of networking.

A network is an interprocess communication system that lets data and messages be transferred between processes (and threads of processes). A network architecture has rules (called protocols) for how transfers occur within that architecture. Different hardware and software can communicate as long as they use the same protocols and data formats.

Most client/server implementations are LAN-based. LANs can use different cabling wire and can be laid out differently—both affecting how signals travel on the LAN. If a LAN is totally self-contained, networking is very straightforward. Complications arise when LANs are connected to other LANs, either through hardware devices, such as bridges, routers, and gateways, or through a backbone network. This can result in dissimilar LANs connected to one another, such as connecting a Token Ring running LAN Manager from Microsoft to an Ethernet running NetWare from Novell.

Networks have operating system software and management software. The network operating system manages the communication services of the server and shields the application programs from direct communication with the server. The network operating system is installed on the server machines but a portion of it runs on each connected client machine as well. Each network operating system has its own protocol.

Management of interconnected LANs is complicated by the multiple protocols, multiple operating systems and multiple hardware platforms that must be supported. It is further complicated by the fact that these nodes are usually geographically dispersed. Most LAN management products focus on providing reliable service and minimizing traffic bottlenecks and downtime.

Network-related issues are covered in more detail in Part 4, Networking and LANs.

2.5 Business Considerations

Another driving force for this technology is the vast amount of data that organizations are capturing. This data must be managed and shared. Departments need more than one database. Each database could be of a different structure (hierarchical, relational, network, inverted) and use different software. It is also conceivable that the data might be distributed over several machines. The idea of an information warehouse is fitting, and leave it to IBM to trademark the name!

Increased computer power and computer literacy generates requests for more applications which, in turn, create more data to manage and share. In addition, organizations are no longer dealing with well-defined, well-behaved structured data. They are dealing with voice, scanned images, text, and graphic images—all of which require large amounts of storage and use formats that are difficult to organize.

As more systems are built to support decision makers, additional information about production data must be captured and maintained. Because this data must be reviewed before the user can decide how to manipulate it, the data is difficult to proceduralize and storage is difficult to optimize for retrieval.

There is also the ongoing effort by organizations to cut costs while improving worker productivity and customer service. By offloading processing from mainframes to micro-based LANs, organizations can postpone the purchase of another mainframe or the upgrade to an existing mainframe. Applications rightsized to the client/server paradigm require fewer hardware and software dollars and reduced maintenance time. The use of client/server computing can improve worker productivity, response time for requests, and, as a by-product, customer service.

Overview of
Client/Server Applications

A client/server application has three components: a client, a server, and a network. Each of these components has a hardware and a software component. Their interaction is illustrated in Figure 3.1.

3.1 Components of Client/Server Applications

Client/server computing uses a divide-and-conquer approach, as shown in Figure 3.2. Servers perform the routine, behind-the-scenes tasks. Clients, the front-ends, get the glory. To many users, the client is "the system."

For most applications, this division of labor is straightforward. The data management software on the server is responsible for keeping the data "safe and sound." The application itself deals with the customized procedural logic and the interaction with the user. The server doesn't care what interface the client application uses. The server views clients in terms of connections, sessions, and requests.

Connections are established according to a communications protocol. But there is no single communications protocol. Communications channels can be synchronous or asynchronous, dictating whether a client can make more than one request at a time. The client/server model assumes a many-to-one relationship (many clients to one server). However, some organizations have applications where clients need to maintain concurrent connections with more than one server, which is a many-to-many relationship.

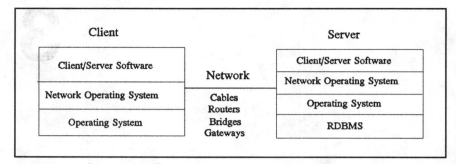

Figure 3.1 Components of client/server computing

3.1.1 The Client

The client hardware is the desktop machine that runs client software. It could be a micro or a workstation. The client hardware has to be robust enough to support the presentation requirements and the client-based processing of the application.

The client software formulates data requests and passes the requests to the network software. This software sends the requests to the server, accepts the results from the server and passes the results back to the client software. The client software may perform some application logic on the results of the request before passing it on to the presentation component of the software.

The presentation component produces the interface that the user views and interacts with. It is often, but not always, a graphical user interface. GUIs provide a graphic-oriented presentation front-end to applications and provide (or simulate) multitasking processing (the ability to run two or more applications at the same time). The major windowing environments are Windows from Microsoft, Presentation

Client Functions	Server Services
GUI	File, print, database server
Distributed application processing	Distributed application processing
Local application	E-mail
E-mail	Communications
Terminal emulation	Network management
	Resource management
	Configuration management

Figure 3.2 Client/server division of duties

Manager from IBM, Motif from Open System Foundation (OSF), and OpenLook from USL.

For those who have not seen or used a windowed environment: Using a mouse as a pointing device, users select options by positioning the cursor on the item of choice and clicking (pressing a button on the mouse). Options are displayed as icons (a small picture that illustrates the choice) or lists. If a user must choose from a valid list of values, a scrollable list box appears, the user scrolls through the list until the choice is highlighted and then clicks. The user can toggle between multiple tasks and/or programs. Each task/program is in its own window and the windows can be positioned by the user so that they are side-by-side or overlayed. Every effort is made to reduce keyboard use. The interface hides most, if not all, of the requirements for data retrieval and system administration from the user.

There is also an operating system running on the client hardware, which may or may not be the same as the server's operating system. The client operating system must be robust enough to support the presentation processing and application logic processing required for the applications. Each of the major windowing environments was designed for a particular operating system. Windows runs under DOS, Presentation Manager under OS/2, and Motif and OpenLook under UNIX.

There is also communications software running on the client hardware. The client-based network software handles the transmissions of requests and receives the results of the requests. However, individual network operating systems do not support all available client and server operating systems.

The client may also be executing runtime support for applications generated with client/server development tools. Using the development tool, the application logic is specified and partially executable code is generated. The generated code is executed by the client's runtime version of the software.

In some cases, a client is actually a server acting as a client (then the server is called an agent) by requesting data from another server.

3.1.2 The Server

A server is the machine that runs data management software that has been designed for server functionality. Compared to a desktop micro, server hardware has increased memory capabilities; increased storage capabilities; increased processing power, including, in some cases, parallel processors; improved cycle times; and improved reliability with built-in reliability features, such as uninterruptible power supply, fault tolerance, and disk mirroring.

When evaluating server hardware, the following measures should be kept in mind:

- **Reliability.** How often does it fail? What is the mean time between failures?
- **Availability.** How quickly does the system come back into service after a failure? To assure high availability, some systems have self-healing routines, continuous processors, fault-tolerant hardware, alarms to highlight problems before they become serious and continuous functioning (although more slowly) in a reduced configuration. Some can be rebooted from remote sites.
- **Flexibility and scalability.** How easily can the server be expanded as processing needs grow?

A server has operating system software, data management software, and a portion of the network software. The operating system has to interact reliably with network software and be robust enough to handle server technology.

The data management software responds to requests for data—retrieves, updates, and stores data. Relational databases have become the *de facto* standard structure and SQL the *de facto* standard data access language. Gateways to non-relational data sources are offered by most major vendors of server DBMS software, as well as third-party vendors. Server DBMS software incorporates many of the services taken for granted in mainframe-based applications, such as backup and recovery routines and testing and diagnostic tools.

Two of the keys to successful client/server applications are the separation of presentation management from other application services and the distribution of application logic between the client and the server. In most cases, the distribution of application logic is determined by the developer when the application is designed or installed. In some cases, this split can be determined by the application software, based on current resources, at runtime.

3.1.3 The Network

The network hardware is the cabling, the communication cards, and the devices that link the server and the clients. Connections must allow servers to access other servers and for users (clients) to access data on any network node. The connection devices, such as routers and wire hubs, are beginning to incorporate network software, which frees up server processing. The most common communications-related services to be migrated to hubs are messaging and routing capabilities.

The communication and data flow over the network is managed and maintained by network software. The network operating system manages the network-related input/output processes of the server. Each network operating system has its own protocol, which is a set of rules that define the formats, order of the data exchange, and any actions that are to be taken on the transmission or receipt of data.

Network technology is not well understood by business end users and many IS professionals. This is partly due to the fact that it is largely invisible—the wiring is in the wall and function boxes are usually in a closet. The people who deal with the network software directly are those in charge of network management.

However, this area causes most of the problems in client/server configurations. Hardware failures (a broken cable), network incompatibilities (among network, client, and server software), and bottlenecks in the network all result in unacceptable response time.

3.2 Classes of Client/Server Applications

Client/server applications can be categorized by class, based on where most of the processing is done, as illustrated in Figure 3.3. Each class requires different hardware and software capabilities on the client, the server, and the network.

3.2.1 Host-Based Processing

The most basic class of client/server applications has a presentation layer running on the desktop machine with all the application processing running on the server/host. The presentation layer provides the user with an easy-to-use interface. The processing power of the desktop machine is used to produce this interface, which requires a great deal of machine resources.

Host-based processing applications require less functionality on the client than the other classes of client/server applications. Because the server/host application is interacting with the client software in the same manner as the application interfaced with a non-intelligent terminal, these applications also need less coordination.

The rationale behind this class of client/server applications is that application users are more productive working with the easy-to-use graphical front-end. Existing equipment (desktop micros) is used to provide this increased productivity. However, host-based processing does not permit organizations to re-think the business process. Any inefficiencies in the host-based application—and by implication, the business process itself—are still there.

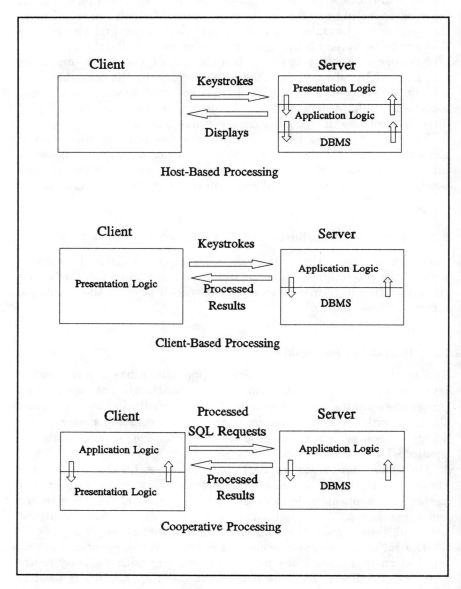

Figure 3.3 Classes of client/server applications

3.2.2 Client-Based Processing

The client-based processing class of client/server applications puts all the application logic on the client machine, with the exception of data validation routines, which are coded into the DBMS on the server. These applications have been designed to take advantage of the new technology and architectures, instead of just simulating host/terminal interactions, as is the case with host-based processing applications.

This type of environment requires coordination between the platforms and the software running on the platforms. The use of the network becomes more sophisticated. More planning for the entire information structure is required. Users can access data on any node. Many of the host functions, such as security and reliability, must be built into these new client/server applications. Networks, software, and hardware from a variety of vendors need to communicate.

Most current client/server applications would be considered client-based processing applications.

3.2.3 Cooperative Processing

The third class of client/server applications uses a fully cooperative peer-to-peer processing approach. In a true cooperative approach, all components of the system are equal and can request or provide services to each other. The processing is performed wherever computing resources (devices, CPU, and memory) are available. A single system could act as a client for other servers and a server for other clients.

Data manipulation may be performed on both the client and the server, whichever is more appropriate. For example, to produce a report, the data sort might be performed on the server and the sorted data passed to the client. The client formats the data and executes any run-time calculations, such as row totals or column computations.

Application data may exist on both the client and the server. Local data, as well as server data, might be used in generating a report. Cooperative processing requires a great deal of coordination and there are many integrity and control issues that must be dealt with.

Client-based processing applications do some cooperative processing because data validation, stored procedures, and triggers may be executed on the server. Validation logic performed on the client optimizes server resources. When data is checked for completeness and accuracy before it gets to the server, the server handles only valid data requests. In addition, the transaction or request is sent over the network only once, minimizing network traffic.

3.3 Categories of Client/Server Applications

Client/server applications can also be categorized by their support function. The architecture of client/server computing promotes group interaction, whether it is messages, mail, shared data, or shared applications. Users can be "closer" to one another. Users of an application can be anywhere on the network.

3.3.1 Office Systems

Client/server computing provides a framework for electronic communication, as illustrated in Figure 3.4. Users on LAN C can communicate with users on LAN A or LAN B even though they are

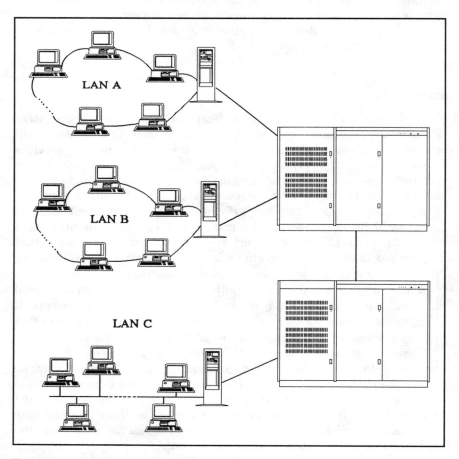

Figure 3.4 The foundation for electronic communication

Businesses are trying to improve interpersonal communications, both internally and externally. Many organizations are using their linked LANs as a network for enterprise-wide mail systems and workgroup applications. These applications could be electronic mail (E-mail) and access to a bulletin board or groupware software, such as Notes from Lotus Development Corp.

In LAN-based E-mail systems, the server maintains the directory, or address book, of users' addresses. The directory may also include user information, such as preferred word processor and spreadsheet. This allows the E-mail software to translate messages to the user's preferred format. The server also stores and routes the actual message files.

The two major LAN mail products are Microsoft's Mail 3.0 and Lotus's cc:Mail. Each uses a different architecture to support the OSI standards for electronic mail transport (X.400) and directory services (X.500). Microsoft uses its own system-level Messaging Application Programming Interface (MAPI), which allows diverse applications to be mail-enabled.

Lotus (and the other trustee companies, Apple, Borland, and Novell) supports Vendor Independent Messaging (VIM) application programming interface (API), which is at the program-level interface and is not tied to any operating system. VIM is in its infancy and the four trustees have announced it will be included in future releases of their products (cc:Mail and Notes; System 7; Object Exchange architecture; and NetWare Global Messaging and NetWare Message Handling System, respectively). IBM has announced that it will support VIM in its office product strategy.

Microsoft Mail, which runs under DOS, Windows, or Macintosh, supports Windows clients, which can work with any mail server across the enterprise network. Messages are encoded for storage and transit. Microsoft's Object Linking and Embedding technology can be used to incorporate graphics or data into a mail message. Microsoft also offers Mail Gateways that permit Microsoft Mail networks to link transparently to other mail networks, such as MCI Mail, SMTP, FAX, 3+Mail, Novell's Message Handling System, and IBM's Professional Office System (PROFS) and SNADS. A gateway is also provided for Apple's AppleTalk networks.

cc:Mail from Lotus consists of a front-end application and a back-end services provider. cc:Mail runs under DOS, Windows, OS/2, and Macintosh and can run in terminate-and-stay-resident (TSR) mode. Third-party application software can be launched from within text and E-mail documents. Facsimiles (FAXs) can be viewed as incoming mail messages.

Notes, a user-friendly groupware product, provides an environment for building information-sharing applications on networks. It is document-oriented and supports compound documents (many kinds of information from many sources). It can handle structured data as well as unstructured data. It supports distributed databases and has built-in robust security. Business users can build their own applications based on an organizational Notes system.

In some organizations, E-mail is also being used to download application revisions, as well as software upgrades. Recognizing this need for more controlled software distribution, Lotus is developing a product, code-named Lynx, that will manage the distribution of software revisions and upgrades.

When evaluating LAN-based E-mail packages, organizations have to take into account the features users are already using, such as calendaring, and decide if they should be available on the LAN-based system. Another issue is whether LAN-based systems can link to host systems, such as IBM's PROFS or Digital's ALL-IN-1. This would allow mail messages generated by the LAN-based system to be easily transmitted to the host-based E-mail system.

Mail-enabling products are being developed with message handling functions, which make sending mail as easy as saving a file. It is not farfetched to expect a word processing package (running in unattended mode) to request current data from a spreadsheet package on another node in the network, incorporate the requested data into a template document, and send the resulting document to appropriate personnel.

Developments in this area will integrate voice mail and support workflow processes. Messaging-enabled workflow applications use messages as agents to carry out tasks, which are programmed into the application.

3.3.2 Front-Ends to Existing Systems

Another category of client/server applications consists of screen-emulation systems (screen-scrapers), which convert existing character-based screens to GUI screens. No changes are made to the existing application on the server, which is most likely a host. The benefits of these systems are ease of use and increased worker productivity.

These applications fall into the host-processing class of client/server applications. They provide a fairly low-risk avenue into this new technology. However, many companies find that it doesn't take them far enough for true cost savings and resource offloading. It doesn't allow them to redesign the business process. It simply automates what already exists instead of determining and implementing the best way to handle the process.

Existing products facilitate building front-ends to existing systems. They capture the 3270/5250 data stream and map it onto a client-based display panel. Such products are discussed in Section 6.2, Converting 3270/5250 Screens.

3.3.3 Database Access

Client/server applications are being written to provide a GUI for accessing corporate data, as illustrated in Figure 3.5. These query-oriented applications provide a single window to the data of the organization. In some cases these applications are read-only, in others they are read-write. The benefits of these systems are also ease of use and increased worker productivity. The productivity for these systems is not measured by how easily a worker deals with an application, as is the case with screen-emulation systems. Productivity with these systems is measured by how easily workers can access the data they need to do their job. The system should provide transparent and consistent access to data wherever it is located.

Some of the tools for this category of client/server applications are offered by server DBMS vendors. These tools work best with the vendor's DBMS, although links are usually provided to some other data sources. Tools from non-server DBMS vendors usually access a wider variety of data sources. These products are discussed in Section 6.3, Database Access Tools.

3.3.4 Transaction-Processing Applications

Typical transaction-processing applications, also known as mission-critical applications, include order entry, inventory, and point-of-sale systems. A mission-critical application must run continuously. If it is

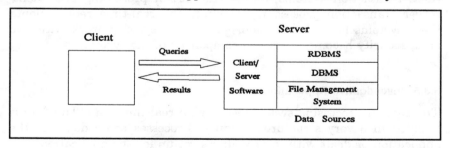

Figure 3.5 Query-oriented applications

unavailable, even for a brief moment, the organization will experience severe repercussions. Examples of mission-critical applications are stock exchange systems, air traffic control networks, financial trading systems, and airline reservation systems.

Business-critical applications are essential to the business but brief interruptions can be tolerated. The loss in access is traded against the cost of increased reliability and availability.

A transaction is two or more operations performed as a group. Transactions are generated at the client and sent to the server for processing. That server may, in turn, send one or more operations to other servers. For a transaction to be considered complete, ALL operations must be successfully performed. If ANY operation of a transaction cannot be completed, the operations that have taken effect must be reversed using a process called commit and rollback. For reliability and data integrity, the data server software should use a two-phase commit procedure, discussed in more detail in Chapter 11, Server Requirements.

While executing the steps of a transaction, the system keeps before and after images of the data. When the transaction is successfully completed (this may include printing a document), the system commits all the changes permanently. If the transaction is not successfully completed (all steps committed), the system uses the images to restore (rollback) the database to its state prior to execution. This function is mandatory for transaction processing systems to keep the database in a consistent state between transactions.

Commit and rollback facilities are aimed at recovering from data errors or software malfunctions. The effects of hardware malfunctions, such as power outages or hardware failure, can be minimized by using such safeguards as an uninterruptible power supply and disk mirroring.

The hardware for transaction processing applications in client/server environments must be reliable and available and the performance of the hardware and the network must be optimal. The terminology for these transaction systems, online transaction processing and client/server transaction processing, reinforce the real-time requirements these systems have. In addition, since these systems work with live data, security becomes a critical component of the system.

3.3.5 Investigative Applications

Transaction processing systems work with real-time data. The data is handled in a very structured manner. Processes are coded into the application or dealt with in procedures set up for the application.

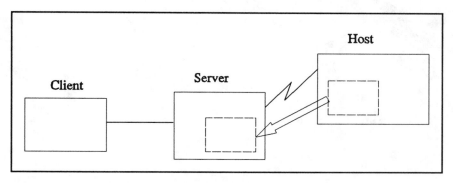

Figure 3.6 Snapshots of data for investigative applications

In contrast, investigative applications are designed to support decision makers and are not usually based on real-time data. In fact, the data may be a (replicated) subset of the live data, as illustrated in Figure 3.6. These applications, usually a series of queries, provide some manipulation capabilities using SQL functions, such as totaling and averaging. Some client/server query tools have strong reporting capabilities and provide other manipulation capabilities. These applications also allow the user to download the retrieved data into a spreadsheet format for further processing.

These types of investigative applications are often called Decision Support Systems (DSS) or Executive Information Systems (EIS) by the client/server literature and the press. However, these labels are inventive marketing. Current tools do not provide the robust functionality required for a true DSS development tool, such as Express from Information Resources, Inc. and System W from Comshare Inc. EIS development tools provide functionality, such as toggling between graphics and data displays, that is not yet present in most client/server tools.

What these tools do provide is flexibility. The user can access data using a natural table-oriented paradigm and a very easy-to-use interface. With the click of a mouse button, that data can be moved to a variety of personal productivity tools, such as graphics, spreadsheets, and modeling tools.

Understanding
Client/Server Computing

Client/server computing has many facets. It is comprised of three distinct and very different components. However, client/server computing is so loosely defined that it can easily take on the characteristics of the component most familiar to the definer, often a vendor of hardware or software for that component.

4.1 Dispelling the Myths

Many myths surround client/server computing. Some are promoted by marketing literature. Others are promoted by the press, more by omission than inclusion.

4.1.1 Client/Server Computing Is Easily Implemented

Implementing any technology that requires integration of hardware and software from multiple vendors is not easy. Implementing client/server computing is no different.

To many mainframe-oriented IS professionals, client/server computing is part of the micro world. Without understanding the capabilities of the micro and its related software and how the mainframe capabilities can complement them, applications cannot be designed to take advantage of both.

Micro-oriented professionals need to understand why it is important that a server include host-like functions, such as backup and recovery, security, reliability capabilities, and network management. They need to understand the impact of sharing data and services within a large network. Their focus has been on providing services to users. That focus must be expanded to include protection for the system and its data.

Even if the developers understand the host capabilities that should be included *and* the micro capabilities that should be included, there is still the network to be dealt with. It has the most parts, is the least understood, and requires the most technical expertise. Hardware vendors who always blamed the software and software vendors who always blamed the hardware have a new scapegoat.

In the name of progress, some micro applications are being forced to fit into a client/server architecture, when they belong entirely in the micro world. The same holds true for mainframe applications. It is critical that an organization review the placement of each application with an open mind, and that the review be based on business reasons, not personal or technical reasons.

The client/server environment ties together all the components of an organization's computer-based information structure, which usually consists of many heterogenous platforms, software, and networks. For a client/server application to be successful, these diverse components must work together reliably. Developing and running client/server applications is not a plug-and-go operation.

4.1.2 Current Desktop Machines Are Sufficient

Organizations cannot always use their existing desktop hardware to support a client/server environment. The AT and 286 class machines do not have the power required for this environment and will have to be upgraded or replaced. Most client software requires at least a 386 machine (ideally 33 MHz) with a minimum of 2-Mbytes memory and 40 Mbytes of hard disk capacity.

If the client/server application is just providing a GUI to an existing mainframe application, a basics-only client machine will suffice. As the applications get more complex, the capabilities of the desktop machine must be reviewed. If a great deal of processing must be done on the client machine, that machine needs more memory, greater hard disk capacity, increased memory caching, and, possibly, a faster cycle speed.

4.1.3 Minimal Training Is Required

Marketing literature gives organizations the impression that they can train a few of their best IS professionals in client/server technology and be off and running. But how is "best" defined when skills are needed in so many new areas? Now IS needs experts in networks, network software, client software, and server software. In addition, they have to maintain this new environment in geographically dispersed locations. The design, installation, and management of LANs alone require experts who understand the interdependencies among hardware, software, and networks. If ever there was a need for cross-training, client/server computing is it.

And what about the people who don't adapt well to these new skills?

4.1.4 All Data Are Relational

Relational DBMS vendors continue to push relational technology as the only structure required to manage all the data in an organization. Since it is based on SQL access, client/server technology assumes any data needed by a user can be accessed via SQL requests or through a translator that accepts SQL statements and converts them to another access language.

But what about the data sources that aren't reachable through one of those methods? There are still a lot of legacy systems with file structures, not database structures. And new structures are being introduced, such as object-oriented databases.

Relational data structures require that the user understand the data and know something about relational technology. They have to understand what a *join* is, how to do one, and when to do one. They have to understand how the data is split among the tables in the database. Intelligent databases can relieve the user of this requirement but not all server databases are intelligent databases. Intelligent SQL interfaces can also relieve the user of the requirement to understand relational technology. Using a point-and-click interface, the user builds the SQL statement. The interface can decide how to join multiple tables and optimize the statement. But this intelligence is not present in all SQL interfaces.

In an attempt to cut costs, many technical questions get overlooked. This is especially true of client/server computing. The client/server relational orientation forces SQL into applications where it might not be the ideal structure.

4.1.5 Development Time Is Shorter

Compared to host-based applications, client/server applications are typically smaller in scope and designed for smaller user communities. The automated development tools for building client/server applications are easy to use and shorten development time. These tools were designed, from scratch, specifically for the client/server environment. In addition, many of these tools are based on object technology. As a result, development should be relatively easy and short.

But the question is—shorter compared to what? Any tool that promotes prototyping is going to shorten development time. Any tool that sidesteps some of the rigid system development life cycle and gets the user more actively involved in the design process is going to shorten the development time. 4GLs have claimed shorter development times since their introduction, and for applications that fit a 4GL-type environment, that has proven to be true.

Be careful when using productivity as a benefit without actually giving quantifiable measures. If the development of typical client/server applications will take 50 percent less time than their mainframe counterparts, state it as such. Build the learning curve, integration issues, system tuning, and debugging into time estimates. Be sure to manage management's perception of what shorter really is.

4.2 Obstacles—Upfront and Hidden

Client/server computing is not the easy task that marketing literature would have us believe. There are some very real, and painful, hurdles on the road to success.

4.2.1 Costs

Potential cost savings prompt organizations to consider client/server computing. The combined base price of hardware (machines and network) and software for client/server systems is often a tenth of the cost of host machines and software.

Conservative figures for the cost per MIPS (millions of instructions per second) are:

- IBM mainframes—about $100,000
- Midrange—about $50,000 (includes some bandwidth processors)
- Desktop—about $300

However, the impression that the existing equipment on the desktop can support client/server applications without modifications is misleading. To run Windows efficiently, you need a 386 machine with a minimum of 2-Mbyte memory running at 20 MHz for tolerable response times. Many industry observers recommend 4 Mbytes of memory, 33 MHz, a 40-Mbyte hard drive, and a VGA monitor. The machine also needs to have room for the communication connection boards and be easily upgradeable to the next generation of processor chip.

In addition, for smaller systems, the cost of the network operating system and the cost of the server database could be more than the cost of the server hardware itself.

Training costs and long learning curves must be anticipated. The client/server environment seems simple and straightforward, and yet requires experts in mainframe, midrange, micro, and LAN technologies. It requires people who can imagine the big picture and integrate all the pieces to support that image. Even with advanced, easy-to-use development tools, IS professionals constantly switch from user details to machine details. It takes tremendous skill to manage the whole process: the user expectations, the learning curve, the frustrating prototype cycle, and the management of multiple vendors. Communication is as critical on the human side as it is on the hardware side. Everyone must work as a team.

Conversion costs can be misleading. There are few products that can convert 3GL code, such as COBOL, into C, one of the preferred languages for client/server computing. After programmers are trained, the application has to be written in the newer language, which will no doubt take longer than estimated due to the learning curve. The new application code must be thoroughly tested to ensure an accurate conversion. The existing application most likely used character-based screens, which have to be converted to GUI screens or new screens developed for client users. If the database was converted from an older DBMS, such as IMS or IDMS, to a relational data manager, all I/O statements must be re-written.

4.2.2 Mixed Platforms

In the past, most large organizations operated homogeneous centralized mainframe and midrange processors and terminal networks. Each was managed separately with independent systems and protocols.

Today's organizations have at least two micro operating systems, multiple network operating systems, a variety of network topologies and different mainframe and midrange platforms and data sources. A representative system configuration is illustrated in Figure 4.1. The systems are geographically dispersed. The earlier problem of reading EBCDIC data on an ASCII machine are trivial compared to today's connectivity issues.

On the client side, there is a battle between Microsoft's Windows and IBM's OS/2 for GUI platform supremacy. The battleground is complicated by the Intel vs. Apple advocates. On the server side, the contest is between OS/2, UNIX, and the yet-to-be released Microsoft Windows New Technology. And then there is the network battleground: Ethernet or Token Ring topology; Novell's NetWare, Microsoft's LAN Manager, or Banyan's VINES network operating systems. Let's not forget the software necessary to manage the network. And don't forget, there are the server databases—SYBASE/Microsoft SQL Server, Gupta's SQLBase, Tandem's NonStop SQL, and ORACLE Server, just to name a few.

The goal of client/server computing is to have all these hardware and software platforms working together. It is not an easy task.

4.2.3 Maintenance

Maintenance is the bane of every IS organization. It is costly and time consuming. Client/server computing might shorten the backlog but it won't do away with maintenance. A recent study by the Boston-based Boston Systems Group, Inc. found that their clients were spending $1.20 on client/server application maintenance for every $1 they were spending on host application maintenance.

Client/server applications are modular in nature. The process of updating application code is more straightforward than it is in host-based systems, primarily due to the use of object paradigms. The modularity of client/server computing and the use of object technology make the maintenance task (the coding and testing) easier.

However, consider this new wrinkle to maintenance: if some of the application logic is processed on the client and there are hundreds of clients in the network, any updates to the application logic have to be distributed to all those clients without impacting processing. Procedures (preferably automatic ones) have to be in place to ensure that desktop clients and servers are using the correct versions of application software and platform software. Some of the client/server application development products, such as Ellipse from Cooperative Solutions and PowerBuilder from Powersoft, include procedures for managing version control.

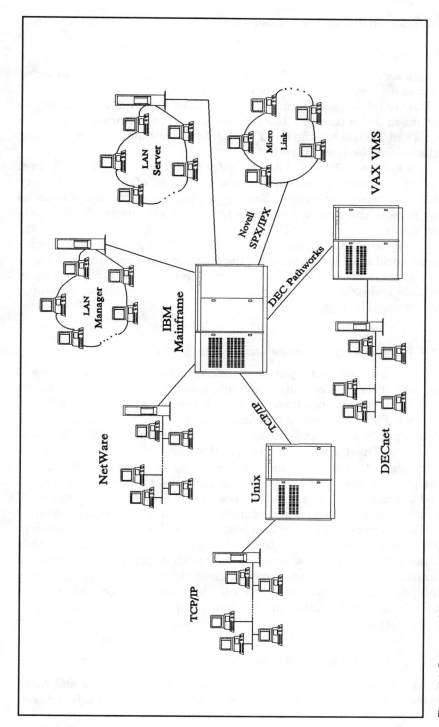

Figure 4.1 Representative system configuration

49

4.2.4 Reliability

When a server goes down, the organization does not wait for the vendor to come and repair it—they fix it themselves.

How reliable the environment needs to be is part of the planning—how much down time can the organization afford? Hardware must be stable and include backup units, fault tolerant systems, and monitoring software for the system itself.

The system software (database software, communication software, and the operating system—maybe more than one of each) must be very robust and easily integrated. Backup and recovery procedures must be easy to use. The network needs to be able to reroute traffic if a node goes down.

The backup and recovery procedures taken for granted in the mainframe world must be provided for the client/server environment. These procedures include two-phase commits for transactions that span multiple nodes, commit and rollback procedures, exception handling, and transaction logs.

4.2.5 Restructuring Corporate Architecture

Client/server computing puts computing management in the hands of the user group, while control and administration is still in the hands of IS. These two groups have not been known to work well together in the past. For client/server computing to work, both end users and IS must begin to look at computing power as a resource to solve business problems. The focus has to be on the business problems, not the technology. IS professionals are beginning to report to functional managers on the same level as the business users. Business users also need to understand why centralization is still important, why IS should be responsible for control and administration of the computer resource.

Client/server technology also restructures the workflow processing, partly by placing it closer to the work node. By building a totally automated information system for the workflow process, organizations eliminate the delays and errors created when data is manually manipulated. The use of electronic data interchange (EDI) is an example of a modification in workflow processing.

4.3 Open Systems and Standards

To IS professionals, open systems mean network protocols and APIs. To business end users, open systems mean easy access to information.

However, vendors often define open systems based on the capabilities of their technology.

Client/server computing and open systems are often discussed together as if they were the same. Client/server computing offers organizations the ability to distribute computing, storage, and other resources as dictated by business needs. Standards-based open systems provide the necessary flexibility and interoperability for maximum benefits.

The Institute of Electrical and Electronic Engineers (IEEE) Technical Committee on Open Systems offers the following definition of open systems:

> A comprehensive and consistent set of international information technology standards and functional standards profiles that specify interfaces, services, and supporting formats to accomplish interoperability and portability of applications, data and people.

4.3.1 Standards Areas

Standards address four areas of client/server computing:

- **Platforms.** These standards are developed by hardware and software vendors, usually in response to *de facto* standards, such as Intel chips, UNIX, and DOS with Windows.
- **Networks.** Industry-standard networking protocols such as OSI and TCP/IP are being used instead of vendor-specific networking protocols.
- **Middleware.** This new term, used to classify the software that sits between the application and the operating system, includes GUIs, databases, E-mail systems, software development tools (such as CASE), and IS management tools (such as encryption and recovery routines).
- **Applications.** Organizations decide on standard applications to facilitate work group interaction and work-product compatibility.

Standards specifications should be developed by consensus and be publicly available. For a standard to be effective, its specification must be widely accepted (used). It is difficult to predict which specification will gain wide acceptance (and therefore be considered a standard). Consider those organizations that standardized on OS/2 and Presentation Manager early in the GUI revolution—only to see sales of Windows and Window-based products take off.

Interoperability and portability are provided through adherence to standards. Portability means that software will run on other platforms without requiring modifications to application code. Although system-oriented code may have to be modified. Interoperability means that the software can work with software (both itself and other vendors' software) on other platforms.

However, even though standards exist at hardware, software, operating system, and network levels, they do not provide a complete solution. In some cases, there are multiple standards, in other cases, none at all.

4.3.2 Existing Standards

Currently, there are recognized standards for the server operating system environment and for network protocols.

UNIX

UNIX was developed (and the name trademarked) by UNIX System Laboratories (USL), then a division of AT&T, as an operating system for scientific, engineering, and technical applications. It is written in C and its source code is inexpensively licensed. It takes advantage of the power of the RISC technology and offers multitasking and multiuser support. It can deliver excellent price/performance characteristics. Vendors, such as IBM, Digital, and Microsoft, offer their own versions of UNIX—AIX, Ultrix, and XENIX, respectively.

The latest USL version, UNIX System V Release 4 (SVR4), provides a desktop-metaphor GUI on top of the traditional UNIX system. It has reduced memory and hard disk requirements so it can be used on client machines.

UNIX is discussed in detail in Chapter 10, Server Operating Systems.

POSIX

Portable Operating System Interface (POSIX) from IEEE is a UNIX-based specification that is viewed as a standard for server operating systems. It defines a uniform means for a C language application to request services from an operating system regardless of the underlying hardware architecture or operating environment. Programmers choose from a list of standard library functions and system header files that will work on any POSIX-compliant operating system.

TCP/IP

Transmission Control Protocol/Internet Protocol (TCP/IP) is a *de facto* standard for interconnecting otherwise incompatible computers. It is being used to connect LAN-based micros to corporate data on a (typically) UNIX host.

TCP/IP is a set of network and transport protocols that enable higher-level applications to communicate but lacks much of the functionality of a regular network operating system. TCP, which runs on top of IP, controls the packet's delivery. IP takes care of the interplatform and internetwork communications.

TCP/IP is discussed in detail in Section 13.2, Standard Architectures.

OSI

The Open Systems Interconnection (OSI) model was developed by the International Standards Organization (ISO) to provide a common basis for communication system standards. It adopted the best features of existing architectures and added features to support heterogeneous communications. OSI is discussed in detail in Section 13.2, Standard Architectures.

The OSI model provides a hierarchical layer structure, in which each layer performs a specific network function, services the next higher layer and accepts requests from the next lower layer. Nodes in the network communicate peer-to-peer with corresponding layers in other nodes.

The Government Open Systems Interconnection Profile (GOSIP) specification states that all government networking purchases must comply with or show long-term migration to OSI.

RDA and DRDA

Distributed data management, when the data and the DBMS are distributed among multiple systems, allows organizations to spread enterprise data over a network of computer systems. Distributed data management raises a variety of issues that are being addressed by ISO's Remote Data Access (RDA) architecture and IBM's Distributed Relational Database Architecture (DRDA). Both of these are discussed in detail in Section 12.1, Data Manager Features.

4.3.3 Open Systems

Open systems start with standard operating platforms and conform to a broad set of formal and *de facto* standards for distributed computing, networking, and application development. Open systems must support platforms from a variety of vendors.

Open systems, a methodology for integrating divergent technologies, creates a flexible environment for solving business problems using open (or non-proprietary) software and open hardware. Open systems can provide maximum availability across standard and scalable system platforms, interoperability between different vendors' systems, a greater choice in system procurement and optimized management of resources. All elements of the system can talk to one another. The focus is on solving problems for the entire organization, not one group (not even IS).

Open systems demands the strategic adoption of standards throughout the organization. To succeed, the open system standards must be acceptable to both the user community and system manufacturers and be adopted by all levels of the organization.

The current movement toward open systems makes client/server computing easier to accomplish. Openness allows many machines, software, and applications to be plugged together like components of a stereo system. New components can be plugged into existing systems at any time. Application program interfaces (APIs) can be used to link the different products.

Open systems can increase the productivity of IS professionals. With only one development environment, skills are immediately portable. Applications do not have to be re-engineered to be ported to another platform. The IS infrastructure is flexible and can quickly and easily adapt to changes in the business environment.

International Data Corporation (Framingham, Massachusetts) outlines three interdependent components that must be in place to create a true open systems environment. The components, summarized in Figure 4.2, are:

- Standards-based products and technology
- Open development infrastructure
- Management directives

4.4 Standards-Setting Organizations

Consortiums of vendors and developers are working on developing

Standards-based products and technology	Open systems technology provides portability and interoperability. Closed technologies will dead-end progress. While some proprietary technology is beneficial, the trick is to provide proprietary functionality within a structure of common APIs.
Open development infrastructure	Standards must ensure that current implementations of technology build on prior implementations and are able to support future implementations.
Management directives	These directives, established by consensus by those with a vested interest in the IS infrastructure, ensure that technology does not benefit one group at the expense of the organization.

Source: International Data Corp.

Figure 4.2 Components of an open systems environment

standards for information technology. Practically all hardware and software vendors belong to either Open Software Foundation (OSF), UNIX International (UI), or both. End users of the technology are beginning to join these consortiums to help develop the standards, work with early versions of the developed technology and receive compliant products ahead of commercial availability.

4.4.1 Open Software Foundation

The aim of the Open Software Foundation (OSF), a non-profit consortium of computer vendors, software developers, and chip suppliers based in Cambridge, Massachusetts, is to develop standards-based software that will become widely accepted technologies, as has been the case with its Motif GUI. Under the umbrella of its Application Environment Specification, OSF focused on developing a standard UNIX-based operating system, which, using microkernel technology, can be ported to many different hardware platforms. They have also announced specifications for related application environments, such as the Distributed Computer Environment and the Distributed Management Environment (see page 56), and user interface standards, such as Motif.

Some of the standards announced by OSF include:

- **GUI standards,** as implemented in OSF's Motif.
- **OSF/1.** This UNIX-based operating system for client/server platforms is a standards specification as well as a product. HP, IBM, and Digital had announced they would have compliant software but have opted for their own variants of UNIX until a production-quality OSF/1 is available. Currently, Digital is the only announced vendor that is actively using OSF/1 with its DEC/OSF/1. OSF/1.1 was commercially released in June 1992.
- **Distributed Computer Environment** (DCE). Announced in September 1991 and available as of September 1992, this set of products (and the standards they represent) provides the necessary services for distributing applications in heterogeneous hardware and software environments—all transparently to the user. Extensions to DCE, such as Transarc Corp.'s Encina products, support additional open functionality, including transaction management, two-phase commits, recovery and rollback.
- **Distributed Management Environment** (DME). These standards are evolving and are expected to be finalized by mid-1993 with products available in 1994. DME standards focus on the tools that are necessary to manage heterogeneous environments. DME is being designed for both UNIX and proprietary systems. It is based on DCE but does not require DCE for execution.

As discussed earlier, OSF originally focused on the development of an open operating system. Mid-1992, OSF announced its decision to base all further development on USL's UNIX System V Release 4, the UI standard operating system, instead of its own OSF/1. OSF also announced that it will focus on building distributed computing (DCE) and distributed management (DME) software and develop a new role as manager of *middleware* technologies developed by other companies. Middleware sits between the operating system and the application.

DCE is discussed in more detail in Section 9.3, Network Computing Environment; DME in Chapter 17, Managing the Production Environment; Motif in Section 6.1, GUI Environments.

4.4.2 UNIX International

The focus of an OSF rival (of late, friendly) consortium of computer vendors, software developers, and chip suppliers called UNIX International (UI) is the establishment of UNIX and related standards and direction of the development and licensing of UNIX products. UI's framework for open systems is called UI-Atlas.

UI does not develop products. It designates existing products as its standards. UI's standards include:

- OSF's DCE and SunSoft's Open Network Computing technologies as standards for an open computing environment
- Adherence to UNIX System V Release 4
- Adherence to OSI's network standards
- GUI standards, as implemented in OpenLook from USL

4.4.3 X/Open

The Transaction Processing Working Group of X/Open Ltd. Co., a London-based international open systems standards consortium, is working on the Distributed Transaction Processing (DTP) model, which provides vendors with industry standard APIs and architectures.

X/Open's XA protocol specifies the interface between a transaction manager and multiple, heterogeneous distributed DBMSs in an OLTP environment. XA supports two-phase commits, conversational transactions, and other advanced OLTP functions among multiple distributed XA-compliant heterogeneous databases. Its XA+ protocol allows communications managers and transaction managers to interface.

The X/Open Transport Interface, a POSIX-compliant transport API, provides reliable message transportation, regardless of the underlying network protocol.

The X/Open Portability Guide Issue 3 (XPG3) outlines X/Open's specifications for a Common Application Environment, which supports system interoperability and portability.

OSF and X/Open have announced a joint initiative to incorporate the OSF DCE into the X/Open Common Applications Environment.

4.4.4 Object Management Group

To focus on a framework and to develop standards for open systems, another standards-setting group, Object Management Group (OMG) of Framingham, Massachusetts, and a number of vendors, including Digital, NCR, HP, and Sun Microsystems, have defined the Common Object Request Broker Architecture (CORBA), a mechanism that allows objects (applications) to call each other over a mixed network. CORBA-compliance provides a high degree of portability.

The OMG, an international organization of system vendors, software developers, and users, advocates the deployment of object management technology in the development of software. By applying a common framework to all object-oriented applications, organizations will be able to operate heterogeneous environments.

Within CORBA, objects are identifiable entities which provide one or more services to clients. CORBA manages the identity and location of the objects, transports the request to the target object, and confirms that the request is carried out. CORBA is based on the service technology found in Digital's Application Control Architecture.

4.4.5 SQL Access Group

SQL Access Group is an industry consortium working on the definition and implementation of specifications for heterogeneous SQL data access using accepted international standards. (Currently, each vendor has its own, slightly different implementation of SQL.) SQL Access Group is supported by most DBMS developers except IBM. The focus of the group is to provide an environment where any client front-end can work with any compliant server database. SQL Access Group supports TCP/IP as well as OSI protocols.

The OpenSQL standards from SQL Access Group are based on ANSI SQL. Current specifications include SQL Access and a call-level interface. Compliance to these specifications allows relational DBMS (RDBMS) products from different vendors to access distributed databases without using special gateways. SQL Access Group is also working on a Persistent SQL Function, which uses a high-performance compiler to compile and stores an SQL statement, and a data type strategy for two-phase commits.

Microsoft's Open Database Connectivity (ODBC) is an extension of SQL Access Group's call-level interface (CLI) specification. The SQL Access available in Windows 3.x is CLI compliant, as is Borland's Object Component architecture. X/Open has announced its intent to use the SQL Access Group standards in its Portability Guide.

IBM does not back OpenSQL. Instead, IBM developed the Distributed Relational Database Architecture (DRDA), which third-party vendors can use to link to SAA relational DBMSs (DB2, SQL/DS, OS/2 Data Base Manager, and OS/400 Database). DRDA is discussed in more detail in Section 12.1, Data Manager Features.

By mid-1992, the continued existence of the four-year-old SQL Access Group was in question. Funding was drying up and development projects were halted. This leaves Microsoft's ODBC and IBM's DRDA as competing standards for distributed database access.

4.5 Factors for Success

There does not seem to be a consensus on what client/server means but there is agreement on the two critical success factors for the technology. Unless a client/server architecture can provide internetworking and interoperability, it is doomed.

It is important to identify the business motivation for the change to client/server computing. Whether it is reduced costs, increased productivity, or a competitive advantage, the implementation of the new technology must be carefully monitored to ensure that it does achieve the desired goal.

4.5.1 Internetworking

Internetworking deals with how separate platforms are linked. Some of the terms used when discussing internetworking are bridges, routers, gateways, and LANs. By adhering to a set of standards, such as TCP/IP and the OSI model, products to provide link capabilities can be developed.

An organization's internetwork—their internet—is the topology of the entire computer-based information structure. It includes the cabling and the connecting devices (bridges, routers, and gateways). The internet could be a simple LAN, connected LANs, a wide area network (WAN) or some combination. Each standalone network loop could be running a different network operating system, using a different protocol. For a client/server environment to be successful, these nodes must be accessible, even if they have different characteristics than the sending node.

It is also important that the internet support the way information really flows within the organization. If the internet does not support that flow, the organization must determine whether the flow itself is faulty and could change, or if the network needs modification and tuning to support the existing flow.

Client/server computing requires a well-designed network that can grow with the organization and deliver the expected return on investment made to capitalize on this type of computing environment. It must be able to evolve a regional LAN orientation into a single, corporate-wide network computing infrastructure that is required to take advantage of new client/server-based applications. The network computing platform must be both reliable and manageable to ensure that client/server applications can perform as designed in a real production environment.

4.5.2 Interoperability

All the pieces of a successful client/server application should have the ability to interact—interoperability. This is no small feat considering a client/server application has client machines, client software, a network, network software, a server, and server software. All six pieces have to be able to communicate reliably.

Users think of client/server applications as their workstation and (maybe) the software on their workstation and the server. They don't care about networks and protocols. They don't care about how (or where) data are stored and why it is difficult to access so many data architectures. They don't care that windowing interfaces have different underpinnings. Users care about getting their task completed.

To provide this interoperability, current client/server software products can transparently retrieve data from many different sources. APIs are being written to additional data sources.

Some of the client/server application development tools create GUI formats that can be re-compiled for another windowing environment. Conversion products can be used to translate a GUI format to another environment.

4.5.3 Compatible Environments

Whenever possible, avoid mixing architectures. The successful implementations of client/server technology replicated a proven architecture. It is not necessary that all the pieces be supplied by the same vendor. However, all the elements must work together and be treated as a single entity. They become the internal standards for the three components of client/server computing.

When new components are added to the environment, they must work as-is. Be wary of enhancements under development that will make the new component work with the existing environment. It is critical that the organization stick with its standards. The fewer the exceptions, the fewer the headaches.

4.5.4 Perceived Benefits

Managing expectations is an important part of any application that uses new technology. If the users or management expect more than they actually get, the success of the application is in question. More of what?—benefits, ease-of-use, cost savings, response time, functionality, accessible data, and the list goes on.

Many companies have started with host-based applications where only the client portion of the application is modified (to a GUI front-end). Much time, effort, and money was spent to convert 3270/5250-based screens into GUI-based screens. No changes were made to the network or the application running on the host. The primary benefit of this conversion is increased end-user productivity.

Users become accustomed to the GUI-based interface very quickly and start asking for access to more data using the new interface. IS ends up creating another backlog of requests. However, this is still a very low-risk entry into new technology with positive (but mostly intangible) benefits, which include:

- Users have adjusted to the new interface methods and are asking for applications.
- IS has gone through the learning curve of GUI development and knows the difference between a good GUI and a bad one, GUI-processing limitations, user likes and dislikes, and so on.
- Management should be positive about additional applications, since they represent less risk.

Other companies have started with client-based applications, providing access to existing data stored in the host RDBMS (relational DBMS) with all the application processing done on the client. This provides the users with more functionality while still using existing hardware. The GUI development and the linkage software to the RDBMS must be more robust. This architecture takes advantage of existing hardware and usually can be easily ported to a LAN/server environment.

Once an organization is comfortable with its client/server environment, the natural evolution is to move to concurrent updating transaction-oriented applications. Many organizations are starting at this end of the spectrum and report successful implementations, so it is doable. But there are many others that we don't hear about who are not at all successful.

The Client

The major functions of the client in a client/server environment are to perform the presentation functions and execute any business logic. Presentation logic handles user interactions with an application. It is the application layer whose input is the result of the business logic and server requests, and whose output is the user's actual interface.

Even though the server is the workhorse in a client/server environment, the client needs enough power to process the application and handle the presentation logic. The graphical user interfaces (GUIs) for client/server applications require a great deal of memory and processing power. The client operating system must be able to handle the presentation software, the application logic software, and network software. The resulting configuration has to give the user quick response times and be easy to use.

An organization has to decide what platforms to support. Converting from DOS and Microsoft Windows to OS/2 and Presentation Manager is not an easy task, although tools are available for converting the interfaces themselves.

Attention must be paid to the GUIs that are designed for the applications. An organization should develop their own guidelines and application standards for GUIs developed for their use.

In the initial implementation of client/server computing, an organization has many choices—the hardware for the client, server, and network; the software for the client, server, and network; development tools and management tools. None of these can be chosen in isolation. To the users, the most important decision may very well be the client platform (hardware and software) and their vote should weigh equally with IS's votes in the other areas.

Chapter

5

Client Hardware
and Software

Using client hardware and software, the user interacts with the
presentation logic. This, in turn, interacts with the application logic
and the network software on the client, which passes requests to the
server. Interfaces usually use graphics to facilitate ease of use.
Response times must be very quick to satisfy user expectations and to
support high productivity.

Since software does not run on all platforms, the rule-of-thumb for
host applications has been to select the software before selecting
hardware and operating environments. For client/server computing, the
reverse is true. Decide on the platform and operating system for the
clients first. Then select the development and application software. It
is important to determine the client side of the equation first in this
user-oriented technology.

5.1 Client Components

The components of the client side of the equation are fairly easy to
understand.

5.1.1 Client Hardware

The front-end client machine runs software that is responsible for the presentation and manipulation of data. The client software generates a data request and sends it to the server. The client machine must be powerful enough to run the required presentation software (often Microsoft Windows 3.x, which requires at least a 386 processor with 2 Mbytes of RAM and VGA color support). A server could also act as an agent, requesting data from another server.

To some, a client machine is a micro, to others a UNIX-based workstation. In this book, the term *client machine* refers to the desktop machine the worker uses, whether it is a Macintosh, a DOS- or OS/2-based micro, or a UNIX-based workstation.

All the classes of client/server applications discussed earlier (host-based, client-based, and cooperative) require similar client hardware. The most common client machine today has the power of a 386 processor running at 20 to 33 MHz with VGA color support.

The memory and storage required for an efficient client machine depends on the class of application and the application's complexity. Host-based processing client/server applications will typically require a lower level of power than the other classes of applications. They do little or no local processing outside of screen formation. The basic hardware requirements for the GUI platform (such as Windows 3.x) are usually sufficient.

Client-based processing applications and cooperative processing applications require enough memory to load and execute application logic. Higher processing speeds, a more powerful chip, and memory caching will improve response times. Storage requirements are based on the amount of data that is stored locally.

5.1.2 Client Software

All three classes of client/server applications use client software. How robust that software is depends on the application itself.

A client machine could be running as many as four software packages, as illustrated in Figure 5.1. At a minimum, a client machine runs an operating system and an interface environment, such as Windows 3.x, Presentation Manager, Motif, or OpenLook. It also runs a portion of the network software.

Application logic processed on the client machine requires a compiler or a runtime version of the client/server application development tool used to generate the application. The development machine compiles the application code, which is usually written in C, the *de facto* standard programming language for client/server computing. The compiled code is distributed to the client machines, where it is executed

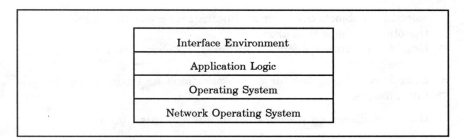

| Interface Environment |
| Application Logic |
| Operating System |
| Network Operating System |

Figure 5.1 Possible software on a client machine

by the runtime version of the development tool.

5.1.3 Interface Environments

The interface component of a client/server application does not know where the data is located. The interface is concerned with accepting data requests from the user, sending those requests to the server, receiving results data from the server, and manipulating and formatting those results according to stated requirements.

Graphical User Interfaces

Most client/server applications use a graphical user interface (GUI). Information is presented in areas called windows. Tasks are presented as small pictures, which are called icons. Tasks are chosen by clicking a mouse button when the mouse cursor is positioned over the icon for that task.

The major GUI environments are Windows from Microsoft, Presentation Manager from IBM, Motif from Open Software Foundation (OSF), and OpenLook from UNIX System Laboratories (USL). Each GUI environment has its own style guide—the rules for how the screen should look and react. To achieve the major benefit of GUIs— improved productivity from applications looking and acting the same—these rules must be followed.

Earlier GUI development software followed guidelines for IBM's Common User Access (CUA) methodology. IBM has developed a new set of guidelines—CUA '91—that specifically address GUI standards. CUA '91, also called WorkPlace Shell, was originally designed for IBM's office automation software Office Vision. These standards include:

■ **Drag and drop.** Best explained with an example—to change the color of an object, the color is chosen from a palette and *dragged* to the object, where it is *dropped*.

- **Control features**, such as container, notebook, spin button, slider and value set.
- **Standard dialogues** for such operations as Open, Save As, and font changes.

GUIs are discussed in more detail later in this chapter.

Other interfaces

A client/server environment does not have to confine itself to GUIs. GUIs present a static approach to accessing data. They do not reflect a user's vocabulary or allow them to follow their own train of thought. Natural languages are more appropriate than GUIs for some applications and user communities. They combine an understanding of English with knowledge about the database to understand the user's terminology and queries.

Languages such as Natural Language from Natural Language Inc. allow users to develop a query essentially free of syntax without having their thought processes proceduralized through menus and pop-up windows. The language processor parses the words in the query statement, asks for more information for unrecognizable words, generates the necessary SQL code, and sends the request to the server. The language processor then accepts the results of the query and formats it into the requested output form, graph, or report.

For example, to a college's alumni office, the phrase *students* refers to those students that have graduated. To the registrar's office, the phrase refers to those currently enrolled. If all past and present student records were in one database, each office would have to remember to include a WHERE clause when doing queries with SQL. A natural language can be programmed to include the appropriate WHERE clause based on the user-ID.

5.2 Client Operating Systems

The most popular operating systems used on client machines are:

- Microsoft's MS-DOS, IBM's PC-DOS, or a DOS clone such as DR DOS from Novell (DR DOS was formerly from Digital Research)
- IBM's OS/2

- A UNIX-based operating system, such as USL's UNIX System V Release 4, IBM's AIX, and HP's HP-UX

Most network operating systems can access DOS, OS/2, and UNIX clients.

In some cases the operating system for the client machine is selected after the user-interface environment has been chosen. Windows 3.x is DOS-based, Presentation Manager is OS/2-based, and Motif and OpenLook are UNIX-based.

It is also important to understand that the user-interface software sometimes includes enhancements to the operating system itself. For IBM's offerings, things are pretty clear. OS/2 is the operating system and Presentation Manager, the GUI, is considered a part of OS/2.

With Microsoft's products, things are not so clear. MS-DOS is the operating system and Windows is the GUI, but sometimes Windows is also the operating system. Microsoft had to include some operating system-like input/output functions and some systems functions in Windows because they were not available in DOS.

Many organizations use Windows 3.x for its memory management and ability to manage desktop applications. To them, the friendly GUI is a secondary consideration.

5.2.1 DOS with Windows 3.x

One of the disadvantages of DOS, a 16-bit operating system, has been the memory ceiling of 640 kbytes. Any memory over this limit is used for caching. The latest version of Microsoft DOS, MS-DOS 5.0, has improved memory management, data protection, and online help.

To free up memory for application use, MS-DOS 5.0 is automatically loaded into extended memory on 286 or higher machines. Also, in 386 or higher machines, device drivers, terminate-and-stay-resident (TSR) software, and network software can be loaded into upper memory.

Windows 3.x augments the capabilities of DOS with its own memory management routines, simulates multitasking operations, and provides queued input messages that permit event-driven interaction. TSR software can be run in virtual machines and accessed via a hot-key. The recommended minimum configuration is 4 Mbytes of memory and a 40-Mbyte hard drive.

Windows 3.x also includes three technologies that boosts its applicability as a client software tool. They are:

- **Dynamic link libraries**. DLLs allow routines to be coded as modules and linked by applications, as needed.

■ **Dynamic Data Exchange**. DDE is used to exchange data between Windows-supported applications.

■ **Object Linking and Embedding**. OLE is used to create a compound document, which is a collection of objects with links to the software tool that created it. (Windows 3.1 only.)

Microsoft is developing a new operating system, Windows New Technology (Windows NT), which is designed for high-end workstations and is expected to compete with OS/2 2.0 and UNIX. Microsoft maintains that Windows NT is not an updated Windows GUI or an enhanced MS-DOS. It is a completely new operating environment.

Windows 3.x is discussed in more detail in Chapter 6, Client Software Products. Windows NT is discussed in Chapter 10, Server Operating Systems.

5.2.2 OS/2

OS/2 2.0, a 32-bit operating system from IBM, is supported on most IBM-compatible 386SX micros and above, provides true multitasking support and recognizes and uses all available memory—there is no 640 kbyte limitation. An application can use up to 48 Mbytes. The recommended minimum configuration is 6 Mbytes of memory and an 80-Mbyte hard drive.

Its new icon-driven interface called WorkPlace Shell (WPS) replaces the Group Manager interface used by OS/2 1.x. Desktop functions are represented as a menu with icons for frequently-used applications. Icons are also used to represent objects, such as files, folders, and devices.

OS/2 2.0 can simultaneously run DOS, Windows (currently not Window 3.1, however), and OS/2 applications in separate windows on the same screen. Users can launch the Windows programs directly from the Presentation Manager WPS or launch the Windows Program Manager and run their applications from that interface. Cut-and-paste and DDE are also supported.

Because OS/2 2.0 is a multitasking operating system, it supports multiple threads of execution. DOS supports one thread. This allows TSRs to run as virtual clients. Another major feature of OS/2 2.0 is its use of named pipes, which allow processes to pass information to each other and are not hardware or software dependent.

By loading only the parts of a program that are needed at that moment into memory, OS/2 turns real memory into seemingly endless amounts of virtual memory. OS/2 applications can access up to 16 Mbytes of physical memory and 1 Gbyte of virtual memory.

The OS/2 High Performance File System (HPFS) reads, writes, and caches intelligently so HPFS knows whether data is on disk—and, therefore, must be retrieved—or is already in RAM. Contiguous sector allocation reduces head movement. These two features speed up the read/write process.

IBM plans to split OS/2 2.0 into two versions. The client version will support enhanced multimedia and pen- and voice-based applications. The server version will be the workhorse, providing multiprocessing and distributed computing capabilities across platforms running OS/2 and UNIX. The versions will share system-management functions. Most industry analysts maintain that OS/2 2.0 competes more evenly with UNIX and Microsoft's Windows NT; that comparing Windows NT to MS-DOS is like comparing a Rolls Royce to a Volkswagon.

OS/2 2.0 is discussed in more detail in Chapter 10, Server Operating Systems.

5.2.3 UNIX-Based

UNIX-based operating systems are, in many cases, overkill as client operating systems. UNIX was designed to operate in a multitasking, multiuser environment and, as such, is more likely to be installed on a workstation than a micro. OS/2, which also provides multitasking, was designed to provide such support to a single user *or* multiple users, making it a cost-effective candidate for client machines.

UNIX, more typically used as a server operating system, is discussed in more detail in Chapter 10, Server Operating Systems.

5.3 What Is a GUI?

A graphical user interface (GUI) presents its users with information in windows, which are rectangular areas on a screen. Tasks displayed on a window are chosen by pressing (clicking) a mouse button when the cursor is on an icon, a small picture that is an illustration of the task. For example, some *de facto* standard icons are a file cabinet for storage and a trash can for discard.

A GUI entity is any area on the screen that is "clickable." Clicking in that area will result in an action.

5.3.1 Screen Characteristics

The user can change the color, size, and position of a window and can open a new window (task) almost at will. Windows can overlap or can be placed side by side. A window can be miniaturized to become an icon. The user can restore the iconized window by clicking on it with the mouse pointer.

Each window has a label bar along the top that indicates what task it contains. The corners of the label bar are used to size or close the window. Other features, such as sliders (sometimes called elevators) for scrolling and buttons for choices, reduce the need for keyboard use, and allow users to control the interface and interact with the application. A sample screen is illustrated in Figure 5.2.

5.3.2 Event Driven

To the IS professional, the real difference in GUI use is that the user is always in control. For example, the user can start another application at any time.

Whereas conventional interfaces are data-driven, GUIs are event-driven. Common events for GUI interactions include the following:

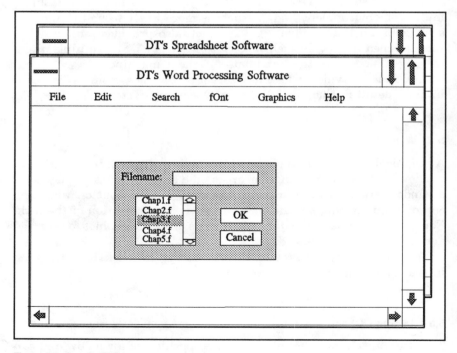

Figure 5.2 Sample GUI screen

- **Mouse events.** The mouse is moved in or out of an entity or a mouse button is clicked.
- **Keyboard events.** The user has pressed and released a key on the keyboard.
- **Window update events.** An overlaid window must be redrawn to its original version.
- **Resizing events.** The user changes the size of the window.
- **Active/Deactive events.** The user picks a new current (active) window.
- **Menu events.** The user chooses from a menu.
- **Start/Stop events.** An application executes setup or clean-up logic when a GUI entity is created or destroyed.

The processing for user-driven events is distributed among the GUI itself, the API for that GUI, and the application logic, if any exists. There are several models for distributing this processing:

- **Event loop.** Shown in Figure 5.3, the event loop, which consists of an event-handling routine and a dispatcher, calls a specific library routine that checks for pending events. If there are any, the application dispatches an event-handling routine before control is returned to the event loop.
- **Event callback.** An application registers an event-handling function for each GUI entity that it creates. When an event is detected, the GUI calls the appropriate event routine for that entity, as shown in Figure 5.4. The event routine is called once for each event.
- **Hybrid.** This model combines an event loop model and an event callback model. For example, the Microsoft Windows model requires an application to contain an event loop for calling library routines but also registers functions for created entities.

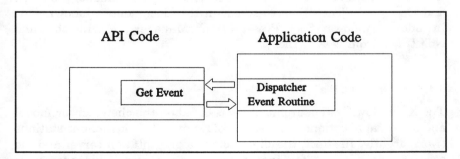

Figure 5.3 Event loop

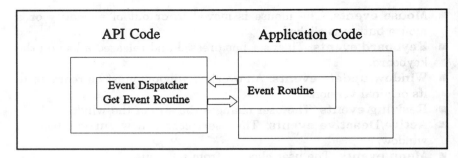

Figure 5.4 Event callback

5.3.3 Native API

Every GUI environment has its own application programming interface (API). An API consists of a set of programming routines that are used to provide services and link different types of software. For example, a GUI API would consist of function calls such as CreateWindow and CloseWindow. APIs can also be used to access database servers and network services.

Coding an interface using a native API is similar to coding CICS screens with macros. GUI screens can be developed using APIs to the Windowed environment of choice or by using one of the many available tools, such as Flashpoint and Accesspoint from KnowledgeWare (formerly from Viewpoint), PowerBuilder from Powersoft, and EASEL Workbench and ENFIN from Easel. Such tools make the process easier, just as screen painters make CICS screen development easier.

5.4 X Window vs. Windowing

Currently there are two GUI camps. One, called X Window, runs on UNIX-based systems. The two major X Window environments are Motif and OpenLook. The other is called, in this document, windowing. It includes Windows 3.x, Presentation Manager, Macintosh, and NeXTStep from NeXT, Inc.

5.4.1 X Window GUIs

The X Window System architecture is based on the client/server model and allows applications to access displays on networked client stations transparently. In effect, the client acts as a presentation server and the server runs a client for that presentation server. This process is illustrated in Figure 5.5.

An X Server program controls the display and provides an interface between itself and X Clients, which are usually application programs. The X Clients and X Server may be running on the same or different network nodes and communicate by exchanging messages using the X protocol. To communicate with an X Server, an X Client builds X protocol requests using a library of C routines. To augment these routines, toolkits provide high-level graphics functionality, including menus and special window objects called widgets, which are data objects such as scroll bars and buttons. An X Client is constructed using widgets from the Widget Library. The user can change the size or contents of the widget but its appearance is determined by the native GUI functions supported by the toolkit. The Widget Library uses an Intrinsics Library for managing widgets (creating, deleting, etc.) and event message handling.

A Window Manager is used to move, resize, and iconize windows. An X Window Manager acts as an X Client. It interacts with the client applications through the X Server, controls the positioning and size of the client's windows, and determines the way input is directed to client applications. The Window Manager determines the look-and-feel of the GUI. The popular X Window GUIs, Motif and OpenLook, behave and

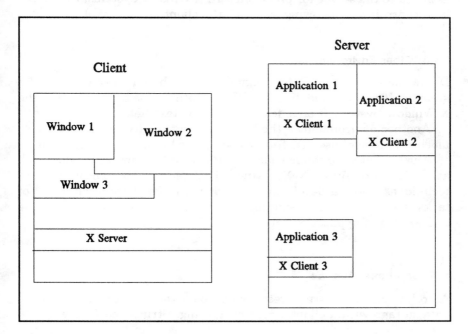

Figure 5.5 X Window System architecture

look differently because they use different window managers.

UNIX is, by design, a multiuser operating system. Access has typically been character-based and therefore not very user-friendly, based on today's expectations. X Window provides graphical, networkable access and allows users to share the processing power of UNIX-based machines.

5.4.2 Windowing GUIs

In the windowing environment, each interface has its own look-and-feel and there are some commonly available functions in each environment. Both Windows 3.x and Presentation Manager adhere to IBM's Common User Access (CUA) standards—Windows to the '89 standards, Presentation Manager to the '91 standards. Motif's style is closer to CUA guidelines than OpenLook's style.

In contrast to the X Window System environment, windowing GUIs provide the application's logic processing as well as the application's presentation logic. The server is a data repository and data manager for the application. Any processing it might do is data related, such as integrity checks and validation, or is application logic that has been assigned to the server for processing. In X Window Systems, the server is in control; in windowing systems, the client is in control.

5.4.3 Other Environments

DECwindows is a GUI for Digital's UNIX-based Ultrix and VMS systems. It is the foundation for OSF's Motif and is built on top of the X Window System. It adds features such as text fields and scrolling.

Another environment is the Macintosh. A primary benefit of Apple's machines, ease of use, has finally been ported to non-Apple machines.

The Macintosh interface has been the basis for new GUI styles, such as NeXTStep from NeXT, Inc. The NeXTStep object-oriented techniques allow a developer to work with visual representation of tasks and their corresponding code and add consistency to the appearance of application screens.

5.5 Database Access

As relational data structures have become the *de facto* standard for data storage within client/server computing, Structured Query

Language (SQL) has become the *de facto* standard data access language. SQL queries are generated by the client and executed on the server. Some SQL queries may be stored on the server as stored procedures and called by a client application for execution on the server.

5.5.1 SQL Interface

How the user accesses the data on the server depends on the tool used to generate the interface. Ideally, the user should not have to know SQL to build an SQL query. Some interfaces use graphics to lead the user through every step of the building process. For example, two scrollable boxes would appear on the screen. One box lists the names of the tables that the user can access. As the user scrolls through the list, the other box displays the data fields in the highlighted table. As the user clicks on choices from the fields lists, that table is automatically selected for the FROM clause. If more than one table is chosen, the interface lists the fields from two tables at a time and asks the user to indicate how they should be joined. The interface then prompts the user for criteria for the selection.

Intelligent SQL interfaces can determine join patterns when multiple tables are selected and can optimize the retrieval process when criteria is given.

5.5.2 Extended SQL

Most vendors of relational database products have their own version of SQL, which extends ANSI SQL to include some proprietary extensions. While extensions may make their products more attractive, extensions reduce the openness of that particular RDBMS. If an SQL query includes extensions and must access another version of SQL to complete the query, one of two things will happen. Either the query will not be accepted by the other version of SQL or the results could be faulty.

If an organization is striving for openness and portability, generated SQL queries must be as close to ANSI standards as possible. One way to ensure this is to use a development and production tool that can generate the appropriate SQL code for the target data source. These products from third-party vendors include Forest & Trees from Channel Computing, PowerBuilder from Powersoft, and Ellipse from Cooperative Solutions.

5.6 Application Logic

Some client/server applications simply use the front-end interface to access data. There is no application logic running on the client. Other applications, such as those downsized from larger platforms, do quite a bit of processing on the client. Application logic is either generated through the use of a development tool or customized.

5.6.1 Generated Application Logic

The application development environment products discussed in Chapter 16, Application Development Tools, generate application code automatically. They also generate the presentation logic for menus and forms. The generated code is bug-free, although testing is still required to ensure that there are no business-related errors.

Some products generate C code, others SQL (or their version of SQL) code. Some application logic is stored on the server in the form of stored procedures, which are compiled versions of SQL statements. Stored procedures are called by client applications and can be called by multiple applications. Stored procedures are discussed in more detail in Section 11.5.

5.6.2 Customized Application Logic

Generated code can be customized by a developer or new code can be written. Customized code requires a skilled programmer/developer. Altered or enhanced code could possibly impact the workings of the generated code. Thorough testing is required.

Customizing code also reduces the portability of the application. If the application is to be deployed as a runtime version, portability may not become an issue.

Chapter

6

Client
Software Products

Tools used to build GUIs differ in capabilities. Those that are C
language shells only build resource files and resource-definition files.
The resource files contain details concerning the icons, cursor movement, and strings used in the screens. The resource-definition files
contain statements that describe dynamically loadable resources.

Client/server development tools and the tools discussed below build
GUIs using rules for the target environment, thereby making optimal
use of that environment's strengths. The GUI's native style guide
should be used in the development of GUIs. Developers must agree on
and adhere to any internal style guide rules so that every application
will have the same look-and-feel.

There are currently three classes of software that build client GUI
interfaces. The classes differ on their approach to client/server
applications, as follows:

- One class converts existing character-based interfaces into GUI
  interfaces.
- One class provides a GUI-based interface to data on a host/server.
- One class builds GUI interfaces as a component of an application.
  This third class of client software is discussed in Chapter 16,
  Application Development Tools.

6.1 GUI Environments

Each of the popular GUI environments draws on the strengths of its base operating system, and, in some cases, builds on it.

6.1.1 Windows 3.x

Two of the strengths of Microsoft's Windows operating environment are its powerful memory management and its Dynamic Data Exchange (DDE) protocol, which supports hot links between programs.

Windows uses two memory pools. The local pool is specific to the application. The global pool can be accessed by any program in the system. Local memory is faster and more efficient but limited to chunks of 64 kbytes, a DOS limitation.

Windows 3.x relies on DOS as its base operating system and inherits some of its limitations, such as the 64-kbyte segments. Applications that require a great deal of systems resources (in Windows terms), such as text-intensive or data-entry applications, are limited to storing these system resources in 64-kbyte areas. The amount of physical memory on the machine has no bearing on this limitation. Companies that have designed systems to overcome this technical obstacle admit that it is doable but not easy.

Dynamic Link Libraries

Dynamic link libraries (DLLs) allow coded routines to be modularized and improve the execution performance and maintainability of an application. Code can be packaged according to functionality and performance considerations. However, poor packaging decisions will result in poor performance.

A change in any module requires relinking the libraries of which it was a part. DLLs can be loaded with the application or as needed. Both Windows and OS/2 Presentation Manager support DLLs.

Dynamic Data Exchange

Dynamic Data Exchange (DDE) provides automatic information exchange between applications. DDE can be used to link a group of cells between two programs, such as Microsoft's Excel and Word for Windows. If part of the spreadsheet or a graph of the spreadsheet data is loaded into a document and the spreadsheet numbers change, the corresponding area of the document is automatically updated.

The Windows 3.1 alternatives to DDE that Microsoft is promoting are OLE and DDEML. DDEML (DDE Management Library) is a DLL that provides a higher-level interface than the bare bones DDE specification. Instead of setting up a dummy window to receive DDE messages, with DDEML a callback procedure is registered and used by the library. Instead of sending or posting messages directly during a conversation, calls to DDEML functions are made. DDEML makes some aspects of managing a DDE conversation easier, although an API with 26 functions can hardly be called uncomplicated.

Probably the best motivation for switching to DDEML is future compatibility. The documentation hints that DDEML may, in the future, take advantage of better interprocess communication methods available in Windows NT.

Object Linking and Embedding

Microsoft's Object Linking and Embedding (OLE) technology allows users to build compound documents and focus on their data (words, numbers, and graphics) rather than their application. A document is treated as a collection of objects, rather than a file. Each object retains a link to the tool that was used to create it. Double clicking on the object starts up the originating application software, allowing the user to modify the object.

Figure 6.1 illustrates the differences between DDE and OLE. When data is linked using OLE, Windows only stores a pointer to the data. The view of the linked data is automatically refreshed when the original data is modified. However, if the linking application is offline from the source application, the data cannot be accessed by the linking application. When data is embedded, Windows stores a copy of the data in the application. The data is not refreshed until the user double clicks on the data to start up the originating application.

Windows APIs

The foundation of Windows network interaction is the Winnet driver, a set of APIs that bridge the Windows front-end with the network operating system. By using Winnet, which is part of the Windows Device Driver Kit, a developer can write network-aware applications that are not specific to a particular network operating system. Most vendors add their own touches. Novell has Windows-aware utilities. LAN Manager uses Winnet APIs to browse network servers.

Banyan's StreetTalk, its proprietary distributed database, provides

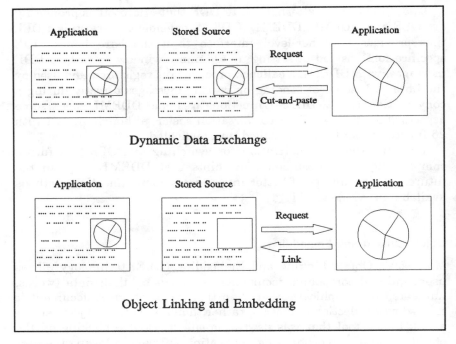

Figure 6.1 Comparison of DDE and OLE

seamless access to Windows 3.x, which is a big selling point for the VINES network operating system. VINES also permits the installation of one copy of a site-licensed Windows 3.x on the server and permits each user to develop an individual configuration from the central version, thus eliminating the requirement to install Windows on each client machine.

Windows Upgrades

Microsoft has announced an object-oriented version of Windows, code-named Cairo, due to be released in 1994. Current plans are to ship a software-development kit mid-1993 and begin Beta testing the operating system by the end of 1993.

Cairo uses an Object File System that stores data and application components as objects and tracks links between objects. Unlike today's file managers, Cairo uses a data-retrieval front-end that lets users search for information using attributes such as topic and author. Cairo includes a new object model, directory services and distributed security.

Although versions of Cairo had originally been planned for both DOS and Windows NT, Microsoft decided to ship the system entirely on Windows NT. Responding to software developers' objections, Microsoft is now trying to determine how much of Cairo can be delivered in Windows for DOS. The DOS-based version of Cairo will include at least the new object-based user interface and programming model but will lack the distributed security system. Whether it will include the Object File System and other core components of Cairo has not been announced.

A 32-bit version of Windows for DOS, code-named Chicago, will be an upgrade to Windows 3.1 for 386 and higher CPUs, due in the second half of 1993. It will include a superset of the Win32's API, but not the entire Win32 API of Windows NT. It will include multithreading but not advanced Win32 graphics functions.

Windows New Technology

Currently due for release mid-1993, Microsoft's Windows NT 32-bit operating system will eliminate the DOS limitations. However, Microsoft claims Windows NT is not designed to replace Windows on desktop machines; it is designed as an operating system for servers and high-end workstations. Windows NT is not an updated Windows GUI or an enhanced DOS. Windows NT is discussed in more detail in Section 10.2.

6.1.2 Presentation Manager

IBM's OS/2 and Presentation Manager (PM) are usually considered a package deal. As a part of OS/2, PM has built-in support for OS/2 features, such as multitasking, dynamic link libraries, and named pipes.

Contrary to popular belief (wishful thinking?), effective PM applications cannot be based on DOS, Windows, or Macintosh code. The idea of multithreading must be built into the applications.

To run under PM, applications are registered and assigned an anchor block handle, which is used to link classes of windows to the application. PM classes and objects relate to windows and their types, not necessarily object-oriented classes and objects. Each class of windows is given an identifying name. Next, the message queue for the application and the necessary windows for the application are built.

Because OS/2 2.0 is multithreaded, each application has a primary thread and can have additional secondary threads. The system message queue gets input (keyboard or mouse interaction) from the users and directs the message to the primary engine of the relevant application. PM translates the input into PM messages, which are stacked in the queue and processed one at a time by the input router, which is part of the OS/2 PM environment.

The input router directs messages to the appropriate application's message queue. Any subsequent handling and routing of the messages is done by the application. Since the system message queue is usually feeding multiple applications at the same time, individual applications cannot tie up input or output devices.

When a quit message is received by an application, it cleans up after itself by destroying the message queue and terminating the anchor block handle, thus notifying PM that the application is no longer active for that session.

Secondary threads are started by the primary thread of the application and have a message-based loop identical to the program's main window procedure. For example, an application can be designed to process all messages in the primary thread or can reroute messages to a secondary (or background) thread for processing. The primary thread should route the most time-consuming tasks to the background threads. The background threads process the tasks while the primary thread goes on to accept other messages. This handshaking algorithm brings a new layer of complexity to applications, but its speed makes it worth using.

While secondary threads are not a requirement for PM applications, they should be used for their performance and design ramifications. Multithreading is one of the prime features of OS/2 and represents an important difference from Windows.

As mentioned earlier, OS/2 2.0 supports dynamic link libraries for modular code. Because PM runs under OS/2, it also supports the concept of named pipes, which are redirected pipes that allow processes to communicate from machine to machine.

Comparisons

In the battle between Windows 3.x and Presentation Manager for first place in the user interface market, the following criticism is usually voiced. At present, a Windows application can destroy an entire multiapplication session due to unrecoverable application errors (UAEs), which are errors detected by Intel 80x86 exception traps. The most common causes of UAEs are reading or writing to a block of memory that is not assigned to the application, exceeding segment bounds (the 64-kbyte DOS-imposed limit), executing invalid instructions, or trying to divide by zero.

Microsoft maintains that these are not Windows bugs—they are errors within applications that have some incompatibilities with Windows. Whatever the reason, the situation is not acceptable. Recognizing this, Microsoft has built monitors into Windows 3.1 to provide software protection and prevent these errors. The trade-off is that software monitors can slow network performance.

These types of errors are less likely to occur with OS/2 PM, which uses a hardware solution that provides more speed rather than the software solution used in Windows 3.1. However, OS/2 PM requires more memory and more horsepower.

6.1.3 Motif

OSF's Motif GUI is implemented using a single API for all supported platforms. Based on the DECwindows technology, Motif was enhanced to support Presentation Manager-style behavior (and therefore has some CUA-compliance). Motif is based on OSF standards and is considered an enabling technology—it is open. The resource definition is stored separately from the application code, which simplifies enhancements. Motif contains few, if any, operating system and network protocol dependencies.

Motif's development environment includes the following tools:

- **User Interface X Toolkit**. This toolkit contains the graphical objects (widgets and gadgets) used by Motif.
- **User Interface Language**. This language is used to describe the visual aspects of the Motif GUI for an application, such as menus, forms, labels, and push buttons. Developers create a text file that contains a description of each object and its associated functions. The text file is compiled by the user interface language into a resource file, which is loaded at runtime.
- **Window Manager**. Motif Window Manager allows windows to be moved, resized, and reduced into icons. It supplies Motif's three-dimensional appearance.

Motif supports X/Open's XPG3 standards for native language support and is supported by most hardware and software vendors that provide a version of UNIX.

6.1.4 OpenLook

OpenLook was developed by Sun Microsystems and AT&T and is very popular on their systems. OpenLook Window Manager is required for interclient communications. The look-and-feel of OpenLook differs significantly from CUA-based interfaces, such as Windows 3.x, Presentation Manager, and Motif. It also contains few (if any) operating system and network protocol dependencies.

One of the following three APIs can be used to develop OpenLook-compliant applications:

- Sun's **NeWS Development Environment** API for Sun's platforms is an emulated PostScript interpreter modified to support a windowing system. It consists of client and server portions interacting to produce the OpenLook GUI.
- AT&T's **Xt+** API for AT&T platforms contains the graphical objects used by OpenLook.
- Sun's **XView** API for SUN SPARC and Digital VAX systems, Intel 80386, and Motorola 680x0 architectures implements the OpenLook API on top of the Xlib level of the X-Window System. (In comparison, Motif implements its API in the X toolkit built on the X-Window System X11 Intrinsics level, which is a higher level than Xlib.)

6.2 Converting 3270/5250 Screens

There are a few products that are designed to add value to existing host applications by building graphical front-ends to existing applications. These tools are sometimes called frontware or screen scrapers. Their chief advantage is that they capture 3270/5250 data streams and provide routines for developers to use to convert them to CUA-compliant graphical presentations. No changes are required to the host application code.

Some of the common capabilities for the products mentioned are:

- Multiple host screens can be combined on one display panel.
- Support for the Windows DDE interface allows data from Windows programs, such as Microsoft Excel or Lotus 1-2-3 for Windows, to be placed into windows on the display panel or data to be downloaded to Windows programs.
- Supported GUI objects include file folders, fields, tables, icons, action bars, drop-down menus, radio buttons, dialog boxes, and check boxes.
- GUI objects have predefined characteristics that can be customized.

EASEL from Easel Corp. was the first product to capture 3270/5250 screens and convert them into a windowing environment, which allowed companies to build intuitive interfaces that required less application training and improved user productivity. This product has evolved into EASEL Workbench, which uses the EASEL language and standard programming facilities. EASEL Workbench was designed to support the building of client/server applications for DOS, Windows, and OS/2 environments with access to Microsoft SQL Server and OS/2 Data Base Manager. EASEL Workbench is discussed in more detail later in Chapter 16, Application Development Tools. The focus here is on the ability of EASEL, the first generation product, to convert 3270/5250 screens into graphical interfaces.

The screens are captured from the 3270/5250 screen buffer. Field attribute information is read from the buffer and the fields mapped onto a display panel. The EASEL-based interfaces sit on top of a 3270/5250 local application module, which translates action requests to either HLLAPI function calls or direct hardware function calls, depending on the emulation board used. HLLAPI is IBM's High Level Language Application Programming Interface, which allows micro applications to communicate with mainframe applications. Supported communication interfaces include 3270, 5250, APPC, VT100, CICS OS/2, and Asynchronous.

Flashpoint was developed by Viewpoint Systems, which was purchased by KnowledgeWare. Flashpoint permits developers to add a front-end to existing 3270/5250 screens and perform data validation. Data can be accessed from IMS, DB2, IDMS, ADABAS, and flat files. Independent software vendors are using the product to revamp the interfaces to their mainframe products. Flashpoint supports Windows as a development platform and as a target platform.

Flashpoint consists of a developer tool for creating the GUI and a runtime component that manages the desktop interface and supports the communication function. The software is based on graphical, object-oriented development techniques. All displayed objects can be selected from menus.

Flashpoint converts 3270/5250 screens by accessing their data streams and parsing the screens. Fields are mapped from their position on the host screen to their position on the display panel and a direct link is established between the two. Modifications to a display field do not break the link with the host screen field. Flashpoint does not capture CICS .BMS and IMS .MFS files directly.

Flashpoint has a *tagging* feature that allows host screen images to be partially defined to Flashpoint. Every transmitted screen image is checked to see if it matches a stored panel definition. Screens that match are displayed as a panel. Those that do not match are translated, using graphical defaults, into a CUA-compliant graphical representation of the host screen, ensuring that unexpected screens from the host do not hang up the system.

Flashpoint offers a point-and-click interface for scripting actions. EASEL (and Mozart, which is discussed below) provide languages for defining actions.

Flashpoint allows the network configuration to be specified at runtime. It is not hardcoded into the application. Pull-down menus enable the developer to select the 3270/5250 emulation software and LAN operating environments for the target system.

Mozart from Mozart Systems Corporation provides screen emulation for 3270/5250 host screens and has built-in routines for performing data entry validation. Mozart supports DOS or Windows as the development environment and DOS, Windows, or OS/2 as the target environment. Its object-oriented approach renders portability across DOS, Windows, and OS/2 environments.

Unlike Flashpoint, Mozart can access host-generated CICS .BMS and IMS .MFS files, which are coded *snapshots* of host application screens and are used by the host to generate the 3270/5250 data streams. Developers work with these files on the micro to create the new graphical front-ends. Direct access to these files assures the consistent use of variables on both the host and the micro.

6.3 Database Access Tools

These tools are provided by third-party vendors or DBMS suppliers. In general, each DBMS supplier's tool works best with its own DBMS although most tools can connect to any DBMS that supports SQL. Third-party tools offer access to a wide variety of data sources.

Accesspoint from KnowledgeWare (formerly from Viewpoint Systems) is a Windows-based product for accessing data residing on LAN-based SQL servers and host databases. The initial release supports Microsoft SQL Server and DB2. Future releases are expected to support SYBASE SQL Server, Gupta SQLBase Server, ORACLE SQL Server, OS/2 Data Base Manager, and VSAM.

Database queries are generated using point-and-click functions. The corresponding SQL code is automatically generated. Accesspoint does not include an intelligent SQL interface to hide the details of SQL database access from the user.

SQL code can also be generated directly. A built-in macro facility can be used to script activities for reuse. The Windows interfaces—DDE, DLL, and OLE—are all supported.

Builder Xcessory 2.0 from Integrated Computer Solutions is a building, prototyping, and testing tool for X-Window and Motif interfaces. It includes X-based widgets and a tree structure for the widget hierarchy. It provides a paint program for painting menus.

Developers use Builder Xcessory to access Centerline Software's CodeCenter to develop, debug, test, and maintain code. Builder Xcessory has a drag-and-drop feature, which lets users incorporate any X-based widget by using the standard OSF Widget Meta-Language, and, when used to handle complicated tasks, can accelerate the development process.

Integrated Computer Solutions is also marketing a library of the most commonly used Motif widgets on CD ROM. The Widget Databook includes generic widgets, such as icon editors, and industry-specific widgets. The widgets will work with any GUI builder that supports X Window and Motif.

Data Workbench, a subset of SYBASE SQL Toolset, provides a query tool, interactive SQL support, a report writer, a data-entry tool, and a data dictionary facility. Data Workbench can access data in SQL Server and non-Sybase data structures such as ORACLE, INGRES, DB2, INFORMIX, and Rdb using SYBASE gateways.

Visual Query Language allows users to develop and execute complex SQL statements without knowing the details of SQL. This intelligent SQL interface can determine the appropriate joins if two or more tables are involved, eliminate the complexities of multiple selection criteria, sort orders and aggregation, and display the corresponding SQL statement on the screen as a learning tool.

Interactive SQL is used by the SQL-proficient user to generate and execute SQL queries and build stored procedures, triggers, and integrity rules using Transact-SQL, Sybase's extensions to ANSI-standard SQL.

Report Workbench uses defaults; handles control breaks, totals, and subtotals; and provides tools to move, delete, or modify text or the location of data. Specifications can be saved for later execution. A runtime version, Report Execute, can be used for deployment of reports.

The other tools in Data Workbench include:

- **Data Entry,** default screens for data entry.
- **Utilities,** a list of previously executed queries, a clipboard scratch-pad and specification of user-specific defaults and options.
- **Data Dictionary,** information about the databases and their objects (tables, views, stored procedures, triggers, rules, defaults, indexes, and datatypes). It is stored as a series of database tables, which are accessible via an easy-to-use interface.

■ **SQR** (Structured Query Report Writer), a combination of SQL and a procedural programming language, which can be used to develop reports within environments such as SYBASE, ORACLE, INGRES, Rdb, and INFORMIX. A runtime version is also available.

Forest & Trees (2.0) from Channel Computing, is a query-only tool that allows a Windows user to access data from a wide range of data sources, such as DB2, ORACLE, SQL Server, SQLBase, NetWare SQL, Lotus 1-2-3, Xbase, Paradox, and Excel. Standard SQL is used for all data access, even to non-relational data sources. AS/400 connectivity is also available.

The user interface uses views (windows) to display data in the form of a value, list or graph. Views can be grouped together into a folder and iconized on the main window, referred to as the *view file*. Data in a view can be the result of a query or the result of calculations using data from other views.

The Query Assist feature hides the SQL generation from the user. It also provides context-sensitive help based on where the user is in the development of a query. For example, the first click on Query Assist results in a prompt for a SELECT statement and a view of the table and column names available. The next click on Query Assist results in a prompt for a WHERE clause.

Forest & Trees also includes a timed-query and alarm feature, which allows developers to set queries and views to calculate automatically at determined intervals and trigger a visual or audio alarm if the results are outside a defined range. Forest & Trees includes a "What you see is what you get (WYSIWYG)" report writer and adequate graphic capabilities. The product also includes the ability to *drill down* from one view to a related view, a feature used in EIS applications.

Impromptu from Cognos Inc. is a Windows-based SQL query tool. Users can develop and execute SQL queries using a point-and-click interface without knowing SQL, relational data structures, or network navigation. Queries can access multiple databases on different nodes in the network. Data can be exported into 1-2-3 and Excel formats. The product can access data stored in Cognos's Starbase, ORACLE 6.0, Borland's InterBase, Digital's Rdb 4.0, and HP's ALLBASE/SQL. Impromptu can run on VAX, HP-UX, and HP MPE/Ix platforms. It requires a network or serial connection to Cognos QueryServer software.

Impromptu includes a utility that allows the results of queries against a corporate database to be pulled down to the user's micro and stored for immediate or later processing. This reduces server and network requirements by accessing the data only once.

Customized prompts can be built to provide user-specific shortcuts to the query process. For example, sales managers who often request data for particular regions within a sales territory can set up a custom prompt for a specific region every time they click on the icon for sales data.

Quest, a member of the Gupta SQL System family of products, is a graphical data access tool for accessing SQL databases, without requiring knowledge of SQL. Quest runs under Windows and supports DDE, which allows Quest data to be shared with other Windows programs such as Microsoft Excel.

Quest acts as the data control center for bringing data stored in DB2, ORACLE, SQLBase Server, SQL Server, and other SQL databases on a mainframe, midrange, or server into a Windows environment. Quest requires Gupta's SQLBase Server or SQLNetwork connectivity software on the data source. Each copy of Quest includes a single-user SQLBase Server database engine.

The Quest environment consists of a workspace and the Quest Activity bar, which contains the following four activities:

- The **Table** activity allows the user to create, browse, and edit SQL tables. New tables can be created from dBASE files, Quest queries, and existing tables.
- The **Query** activity gives users the ability to build, save, and execute queries against data stored in SQL databases. Tables can be linked for query purposes. The results of a Quest query can be printed or copied to the clipboard for use in a spreadsheet. Once a query has been defined, it can be saved and reused. Users can review the SQL that is built behind the scenes at any time.
- The **Report** activity is used to generate custom reports based on data from Quest with a WYSIWYG screen designer. Reports can range from simple three-across label templates to complex reports with multiple nested break groups. Reports generated from open queries are created with a click on the Activity bar and use default values for initial formatting. Developers can lay out new fields, boxes or lines, and change fonts and styles. Quest reports are compatible with the Gupta SQLWindows.
- The **Catalog** activity manages the data definitions in the database and is used to review definitions.

SequeLink from TECHGnOsIs, Inc. provides direct, transparent access to data and services from a variety of client applications. TECHGnOsIs describes SequeLink as middleware because it optimizes the use of host resources with security, data consistency, and network efficiency, as well as GUI development tools.

SequeLink consists of core modules on both the client and server platforms with interfaces to specific network protocols and applications, as illustrated in Figure 6.2. The highly-optimized memory-resident core modules are available to applications as virtual extensions to the operating system and contain a support module to interface to the network protocol and one or more other modules to interface with specific client applications or the host DBMS.

The Application Links allow the applications to transparently access DBMS data as if it resided locally on a desktop computer. Currently supported applications include Microsoft's Excel and Visual Basic, Lotus's 1-2-3, Informix's Wingz, Apple's Hypercard, and Asymetrix Corp.'s Toolbook.

The SequeLink Client Core modules are tailored to take full advantage of each unique environment. Modules are available for Windows, OS/2, and Macintosh.

The Client Network Links and the Server Network Links are specific for the platform's protocols. They can support a combination of network architectures, which may include Novell's NetWare, Microsoft's LAN Manager, DECnet, AppleTalk, NetBIOS, TCP/IP, and IBM's APPC/LU6.2.

The SequeLink Server Core is specific to the server operating

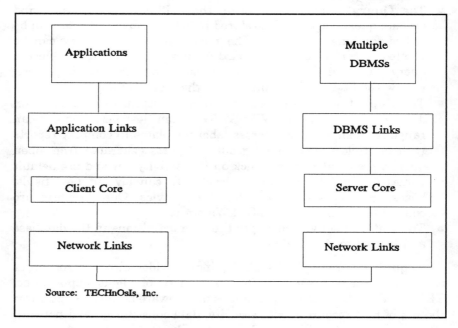

Figure 6.2 Architecture of SequeLink

system, which may be OS/2 or UNIX-based. The Server Core and the DBMS Links process the data.

The SequeLink DBMS Links manage security and SQL calls to the host DBMS with minimal demand on the host processor. Server DBMS choices include ORACLE, Rdb, INGRES, SQL Server, DB2, SQL/400, OS/2 Data Base Manager, and INFORMIX. When a statement is passed to the DBMS, a database cursor is created on both the client and server side. (A database cursor is a structure that contains information about the record that is being referenced.) If the statement is executed a second time for another variable, only the changes in the cursor have to be transmitted.

Client Requirements

To the user, the client is the system. It is imparative that the interface be error free, flexible, and reflect the working style of the user. Only then can optimal productivity gains be realized.

7.1 GUI Design Standards

Most GUI development tools assume that its users know how to build effective GUI applications. But a GUI-based application does not automatically guarantee an increase in productivity. There is such a thing as a bad GUI design!

GUI development tools must begin to incorporate some intelligence for building tasks, such as screen design. In addition, each organization should develop standards and preferences for GUIs so that all GUIs developed for the organization will look alike and act alike. Even if it is something as simple as *All OK buttons will be green* and *All Cancel buttons will be red.*

When evaluating interface software, it is important to remember that the software provides an environment, not just an interface building package. An application's interfaces should look the same regardless of what operating system controls the network, the client machine or the server.

There are also two groups of users of GUI software to consider when planning the implementation of a client/server application. The first is the obvious one—the end users. Since the GUI is developed for their use, users should find the GUI easy to learn and use. The other group of users consists of the developers of the GUI-based interfaces for a particular application. These people will have to be trained. All major GUI development product vendors offer training classes in their offices or on-site. A learning curve must be anticipated. Some people will be better suited for GUI development than others. GUI developers must understand and feel comfortable with GUIs. In some cases, they must get comfortable with the platform itself.

Developers have to put themselves in the user's chair and think like a user. It is critical that a GUI be designed to support the way users work, not the way the developer thinks they work. Developers have to get used to the idea that the user is in control, not the application. A well-designed GUI will eliminate the need for documentation, to which the user probably wouldn't refer anyway. Applications and other menu choices should be referred to by function rather than by name. A user should be able to look at the icon for an application and instantly know what the application is. Menus with lots of submenus are better than one menu with lots of choices. Applications should be forgiving and provide aids for error correction. A user should not have to switch between keyboard and mouse very often.

Just because it is a graphical interface, a GUI is not necessarily easy to use. A well-designed GUI is easy to use. A poorly designed GUI can lead to an unsuccessful system. Each GUI environment has built-in strengths that should be uniformly used in the development of interfaces for that environment.

Some basic principles for effective GUI design are explained in Figure 7.1.

7.2 Open GUI Standards

Consistent interfaces are key to the success of open systems and client/server computing. Each new interface requires retraining and modifications to applications. Many GUIs are not portable to other GUI environments (although there are products that will do the necessary translations, as discussed later).

After an organization has invested in developing GUI guidelines for their current platform, they do not want to lose that look-and-feel when they move the application to another platform.

Ideally there should be a standard GUI that would have the same look-and-feel on every platform but such a standard is unlikely. Consensus on how a screen will look among all vendors and user

Know the users. Developers must understand the users' orientation and work profile. How comfortable are they with computers? Do they prefer a keyboard or a mouse or both? What terminology do they use for the functions in the application?

Simplify often-used tasks. These tasks should be on a tool bar for quick access or reflected in the order of items on a menu. Accelerator keys allow users to use the keyboard to quickly go through a menu series. Users should be allowed to turn off tasks, which removes them from the tool bar, if they don't expect to use them.

Provide feedback to the user. The cursor should be changed to an hourglass to signify a short wait while the system is processing. A long wait (more than 10 seconds) should be indicated by a message box with a progress indicator. Beeps should be used only for actions that require immediate attention. Error message boxes should explain the error (in user-ese) and offer suggestions for correcting the error.

Be consistent. Don't let developers stretch their creative juices too far. Consistency guidelines should include grammar, syntax, icons, and color. If users are happy with the products from a major vendor, copy the look of their products. Consistency is necessary if users are expected to go quickly from one application to another.

Test early and often. In addition to the users of the application, GUIs should be tested by other developers and users of other applications.

Figure 7.1 Basic principles of effective GUI design

communities is doubtful. Even the two major UNIX-based GUIs do not look or behave the same. OpenLook uses two-dimensional boxes, Motif uses three-dimensional boxes.

7.3 Interface Independence

Portable applications is one of the most discussed benefits of client/ server computing. However, if the GUI is not portable, the application is not portable. For a GUI to be truly portable, the GUI interfaces should be able to be moved, for example from Motif to Windows 3.x, with no application changes and no impact on its fundamental look-and-feel of the interface. This reduces application development time and allows an application to be written for multiple target GUI platforms. However, to be truly portable, most tools cannot take advantage of the native GUI toolkit. When the native GUI toolkits are used, the development tool supports portability for only those functions

Application Logic					
API Code	API Code	API Code	API Code	API Code	API Code
Motif					
X Window	OpenLook	Macintosh	MS-Windows	OS/2 PM	Terminal

Figure 7.2 API libraries for each GUI environment

that are common to the supported GUI environments.

Tools that allow development on one platform and deployment on another promote this portability. Developers and users should be able to learn and use one GUI environment and, if they begin to use a new application, specify the GUI environment of their choice.

However, today's GUIs each have their own libraries of APIs, as illustrated in Figure 7.2. Runtime portability is not possible unless third-party tools are used such as ALEX from Alex Technologies, Neuron Data Open Interface from Neuron Data Inc., XVT from XVT Software Inc., PC-XView from Spectragraphics Corp., and ORACLE Toolkit from Oracle.

Alex Technologies' **ALEX** software converts character-based interfaces into interfaces for the X-Window System, thus providing a migration path to the Motif and OpenLook GUIs. With ALEX, GUIs are programmed without actually using the native toolkit. Using ALEX's C-like script language, a translation module is created, which contains a GUI front-end and the logic for communicating with existing character-based applications. Although ALEX does not actually use the native toolkit, programming with ALEX requires a knowledge of widgets, resources, and callbacks. The ALEX technology has been licensed by Sybase and is being used to develop its APT-GUI graphical extensions.

Neuron Data Open Interface from Neuron Data is a toolkit for building GUIs that are instantly portable and support the active look-and-feel of the five major windowing environments—Windows, Presentation Manager, Motif, OpenLook, and the Macintosh. It provides an object-oriented, extensible development toolkit with a superset of all the widgets and functionality of the native toolkits. The object-oriented features, such as encapsulation and inheritance, improve development time.

Open Interface is CUA '89 compliant. Neuron Data has not given a release date for an OS/2 32-bit CUA '91 compliant version.

Figure 7.3 illlustrates the architecture of Open Interface. The developer is shielded from the nuances of the underlying windowing and operating systems. Open Interface does not use the native toolkits for supported GUI environments. Instead, it simulates the look-and-feel characteristics of each environment through the Virtual Graphics Machine and a superset of all the native functionality and widgets of the supported windowing systems. Widgets can be built that are portable to all environments.

The Virtual Graphics Machine, the foundation of Open Interface, provides a complete set of routines for drawing lines, text, and colors which behave identically on every platform; and maps the events from the native windowing systems into a common representation across all platforms.

A set of libraries provides object-oriented services to developers beyond creating GUIs. These services include pre-built services, for example, pre-constructed libraries provided by Neuron Data; and custom services, which are provided by developers for their applications. The two main categories of services are:

- **Portable GUI services.** The pre-built services include generic windows and widgets such as tables, spreadsheets, and browsers. Each widget comes with its own text editor. The custom service allows a developer to create custom widgets or classes of widgets that are completely portable and can become pre-built services within the organization.

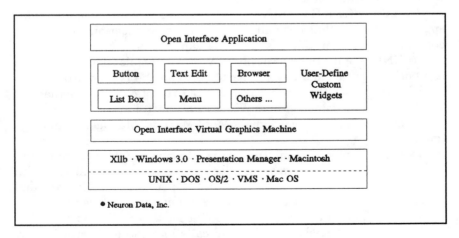

Figure 7.3 Open Interface architecture

- **Portable application services.** The pre-built services include standard C libraries for such functions as memory and window management, file I/O, and data structures for storing elements of widgets. The architecture of Open Interface supports the integration of additional custom services.

The developer builds the application interface once on any supported platform and then generates in ANSI C code, a makefile (a resource file that describes the interface) and a C template that describes the behavior of each widget on the screen. The developer then customizes the C code to link in the application functionality. The makefile is then compiled and linked to the platform-specific Open Interface libraries. An environment variable is set to indicate the windowing environment of the completed application. To port to a different platform, the code is recompiled onto the target platform and linked to the Open Interface libraries for that platform. The developer then sets the environment variable to the new platform.

ORACLE Toolkit uses a layered architecture to provide a common API for Windows, X Window, Motif, Macintosh, and character and block terminals. The bottom layer consists of a driver for the native user interface. These drivers are then layered with the Adaptable User Interface Kit, which gives all native user interfaces a common interface to which multimedia extensions can be added.

The layered architecture allows users to develop portable applications that automatically adapt to the look-and-feel of any supported GUI environment. The layering also allows Oracle to deliver tools as part of an integrated development environment for multiple GUIs without rewriting the tool-specific code.

PC-XView from Spectragraphics Corp. lets X Window applications appear on micros that normally run Windows applications and allows both to appear simultaneously on the same screen. Micro users can access UNIX applications as easily as Windows applications. Users can run both programs and cut and paste between the two environments.

PC-XView uses the concept of local and remote window managers. The local window manager uses Windows to control window placement. The remote window manager uses Motif Window Manager to manage the screen.

XVT (Extensible Virtual Toolkit) is a library of GUI programming tools that allow developers to develop source code that will run with Presentation Manager, Windows, Motif, OpenLook, Macintosh, and character-based interfaces. It comprises an additional layer on top of the native GUI and uses the native toolkit for that GUI environment.

The libraries translate application calls into the form required by the underlying GUI toolkit. For example, a Motif application developed using XVT uses the Motif widgets and intrinsics.

XVT generates C source code. Its interfaces to the windowing platforms are implemented in a virtual toolkit that includes a resource compiler.

To provide this level of portability, XVT supports a subset of basic GUI functions that are common across all supported environments. It does not provide portability for custom GUI widgets or support widgets that are unique to any one environment. XVT has been chosen by the National Institute for Standards and Technology and IEEE as their standard GUI portability tool.

7.4 Testing Interfaces

Testing character-based screens is easy—do a screen capture and compare screens. If they match, success; if not, the detective work begins.

Windowed interfaces are not tested that easily. A user can customize a window by changing its color, size, and position. As applications are accessed, windows overlay windows or are reduced to icons. Objects do not appear the same on a VGA monitor and a Super VGA monitor. In fact, it is rare that screens would match, but a mismatch might not represent a software error.

Recently released products aid developers in testing windowed interfaces. Some client/server application development products, such as Ellipse from Cooperative Solutions, include testing routines in their environments.

Automatic Testing Facility (ATF) from Softbridge, Inc. supports unattended testing of single or multiuser applications running OS/2 or Windows. The performance analysis software includes two components: The Controller and The Executive. The ATF architecture is illustrated in Figure 7.4.

The environment-specific (DOS, OS/2 or Windows 3.x) Controller software is installed on each target test workstation in the network. Its capture/playback capability records user interaction (keyboard and mouse) with the application being tested and stores a snapshot of a full screen or a window as a file, called a tape file. Tape files can be stored in any data file or SQL format and replayed on any machine to simulate the user's session. Scripted tests can be run under control of the Executive or can be run as a satellite by the Controller, and the tape files can be uploaded to the Executive at a later point.

ATF also provides Executive software as a central point for

controlling a distributed system. This OS/2 program provides a language for scripting test cases, which has a Presentation Manager interface. The Executive supports bitmap viewing and comparisons. Scripts run tests on remote machines and the results are sent back to the Executive. If a test fails, ATF reports the precise point of failure and tape files can be replayed to that point for debugging purposes.

ATF can test dynamic link libraries and can store and compare results of multiple test cycles. ATF currently only runs over NetBIOS LANs.

SQA:Manager and **SQA:Robot for Windows** from Software Quality Automation help proceduralize testing of Windows software. SQA:Robot for Windows is a capture/playback/comparison tool that captures windows instead of screens. It requires Visual Basic, which can be used to provide a range of options for running and managing scripts. Other events from the message queue, including screen images, can also be captured. Robot Image Comparator is used to view failures alongside file images. Comparison tests are window specific, not screen-specific. Portions of an image can be masked to avoid triggering a comparison failure.

SQA:Manager serves as a project management tool for software testing. It helps developers plan, design, and organize resources; track problems; apply measurements; and generate reports. The package creates databases in Paradox format. In addition to the actual manager, administrative tools are provided to set up the database relations and

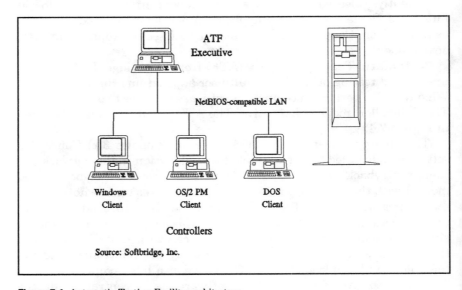

Figure 7.4 Automatic Testing Facility architecture

assign users and products to the system. Templates used by SQA:Manager can be customized. A tutorial is included that shows how incoming bug reports are catalogued, reports generated, and forecasts made.

Using SQA:Robot for Windows with SQA:Manager integrates test design, procedure, and report processes.

Microsoft's **Test for Windows** has been used for years as an internal tool at Microsoft. It was used to test Windows 3.1. Microsoft Test can be used to examine applications and automate test scripts for Windows programs. Developers can also use the program after an application is fully operational to create a system endurance test.

Microsoft Test is designed to address the ways in which applications for Windows differ from character-based applications. For example, it can simulate keyboard and mouse strokes, compare actual and expected screen results despite variation in window size and location, and accommodate unexpected events that usually terminate other test suites. Microsoft Test works with any Windows application, regardless of its size or the tools used to create it. Any hardware capable of running Microsoft Windows can run Microsoft Test.

The product can run unattended and log results can be analyzed later. Screens can be compared against saved screens to determine the areas in which they differ. Microsoft Test can also be used to determine approximate equality, which allows tests to be designed to run on different video systems. For example, a button in a dialog box may not look the same on VGA and Super VGA. The "fuzzy match" feature of Dialog facility can confirm that they are indeed the same.

Microsoft Test is capable of trapping serious errors, such as the dreaded Windows UAEs (unrecoverable application errors), missing files, division by zero, and dynamic link libraries failing to load. Upon trapping errors, Microsoft Test can take pre-specified actions, such as logging conditions of the event or starting another test.

Microsoft Test provides two programming languages, which are versions of BASIC. TestBasic is a full-featured programming language that supports complex data structures and loops. FastTest is a subset of the Microsoft TestBasic that uses defaults and high-level English-like functions to make it easy to start writing test scripts with no BASIC experience. The Record mode can be used to record a test script in the FastTest language, by recording user actions such as keystrokes or mouse movements.

Other integrated utilities offer users testing flexibility. These include:

- **Test Dialogs** capture and compare Windows controls such as menus, buttons, and dialog boxes.

- **Test Screen** captures and compares screen bitmaps.
- **Test Event** and **Test Control** are DLLs that simulate any combination of mouse or keyboard input. Users can control the timing of events and identify and change the availability and state of any individual control by name. They can also be called from any programming language that supports DLL access, such as C, Pascal, or Visual Basic.
- **Test Driver** includes an enhanced version of the Basic language, a recorder and a debugger with single stepping and breakpoints.

7.5 Development Aids

Products that allow developers to focus more on the business problem and less on the programming details will improve productivity. This is usually accomplished through built-in interface intelligence. There are three areas in which an interface can have built-in intelligence. They are:

- GUI
- Data-access (SQL access and data dictionaries)
- OLTP

7.5.1 Smart GUI Interfaces

Some GUI development products use object technology to facilitate the building of GUIs. Items that can be displayed on the screen—icons, file folders, action bars, radio buttons, menus, dialog boxes, and tables, to name a few—are treated as objects. As objects, they have predefined attributes and behaviors, which can be customized by the developer. As soon as an object is placed on a screen, it assumes these predefined characteristics. These smart interfaces also support object inheritance, which allows a new object to inherit attributes and behaviors from existing objects. Products currently using smart display objects include Flashpoint from KnowledgeWare, Mozart from Mozart Systems Corporation, ENFIN from Easel Corporation, Gupta's SQL System products, and Ellipse from Cooperative Solutions.

7.5.2 Smart SQL Interfaces

One of the goals of client/server computing is to provide transparent access to corporate data, no matter where it is located. However, one obstacle to this goal is that the users have to know what data is available and, more importantly, the structure of the data with which they are working. Just giving them a list of data tables and access to SQL is not enough. Users have to understand the concept of *join* and how tables should be joined when the field names in the tables do not correspond.

There are currently two methods for shielding users from this requirement and allowing them to focus on the business problem (not on the details of how to get the data). One is the use of an intelligent SQL interface, which allows the user to work with SQL databases with no knowledge of SQL commands, using point-and-click interfaces to make their choices.

A smart SQL interface determines the appropriate joins if more than one table is involved in a query. It will analyze multiple WHERE clauses and simplify them (for efficiency). The resulting SQL code would be displayed as a learning tool for the user.

7.5.3 Data Dictionaries and Repositories

The other method is using data dictionaries or repositories. Data dictionaries contain all the business data available through the IS-infrastructure, whether it is from CASE tools or from database catalogs. Because the dictionary is centralized, users have a single reference point for determining the location and structure of data and IS can easily control and secure the access to that data. One thing to bear in mind about dictionaries is that in order for them to provide consistency, the consistency must be in place to begin with. The corporate data sources must be reviewed for redundant data, inconsistent naming conventions, and incomplete business models. Integrated CASE tools generate dictionaries which are stored in the repository of the CASE software.

A repository is a very robust data dictionary. It offers a central place to store information about data (called metadata), a place to store CASE models, and some capability to generate program code that specifies information about the data. This code, often termed database definition or program specification block, helps standardize the portions of systems that deal with data.

IBM's **Repository Manager/MVS**, the cornerstone of AD/Cycle, has not been a success in the marketplace. It was intended to serve as a central storage place and directory to better develop and reuse code throughout an organization. IBM is redirecting its AD/Cycle strategy from a mainframe-centered plan, based on Repository Manager/MVS, to a modified plan oriented toward workgroup-based application development on UNIX- and OS/2-based LANs. Organizations looking for repositories are evaluating third-party products, such as DB Excel from Reltech Products, InfoSpan from IBM business partner InfoSpan Corp., and DataDictionary/Solution from BrownStone Solutions, Inc.

DataDictionary/Solution (DD/S) is a DB2-based data dictionary workbench that provides an extensible, entity-relationship (E-R) model dictionary hub. Referring to the visual E-R model displayed on the screen, users point-and-click on the data they are interested in. The object-oriented scripting facility allows events to be fired up to DDE or some other interprocess capability on the client machine.

DD/S includes a bi-directional CASE interface, DB2 catalog imports, IMS bridge, a scanning facility for program source code, automatic dictionary population with reusability strategies and reporting, and collision monitoring. Because it is extensible, users can use DD/S to integrate applications as well.

Reltech's **DB Excel** and Brownstone Solutions' DD/S are competing products with excellent reputations in the repository marketplace. They both feature menus, dialogues, and customizable online help; are fully extensible; and support DB2, IMS, and a range of CASE tools.

DB Excel allows customization of objects, screen maps, and system messages. A user's access can be limited to a given field or group of objects. Multiple screen maps for the same element can be constructed, allowing different users to see the data in different ways. DB Excel has a query builder to assist in building SQL queries to filter the retrieved objects. There are 80 built-in reports and any standard DB2 reporting tool (hooks are provided for directly accessing QMF) can produce additional *ad hoc* reports.

The Path Report reporting option can be used to trace the objects in the models in the defined path. The Navigator is a macro language, which can be used to guide the user through a predefined series of steps when filling in data.

InfoSpan runs in an open systems mode (under OS/2 and UNIX) on top of relational databases, such as INFORMIX from Informix, ORACLE from Oracle, and IBM's OS/2 Data Base Manager. Using an E-R paradigm, access to data is through GUIs. The dictionary is the controlling point.

7.5.4 Smart OLTP Interfaces

While there is indeed a great deal of complexity in building online transaction processing systems, they can usually be broken down into fairly standard finite steps. For example, to update a customer's address record, a developer would have to code the following steps:

- Verify user authorization to update database
- Ask for the customer number
- Verify it is valid
- Retrieve the record and populate the screen
- Position the cursor on the address
- Accept user input
- Verify input against any rules
- Ask for user feedback on correctness
- Rewrite the record

To the user and developer, it should be as easy as "Update a customer's address record." The system should be concerned with the numerous steps it takes to accomplish the task. Smart OLTP interfaces will take care of the detailed transaction management steps. In client/server architectures, smart OLTP interfaces handle distributed transaction management (initiation, completion, and backout on error), session management, and service-request management.

Currently, the only client/server development tool available with a smart OLTP interface is Ellipse from Cooperative Solutions.

The Server

Ten years ago choosing a computer was easier. Mainframes processed corporate data, midrange computers handled the needs of departments and small businesses. Midrange vendors were trying to sell into the mainframe's installed base and the micro was not even considered a business computer. The lines between the machines were very distinct.

Today the distinctions are fading fast. Organizations have to decide among high-end micro-based servers, workstations, traditional midrange machines, multiprocessing systems, and mainframes. Which will meet their application server needs with the best combination of price and performance?

Server is a broad term for any computer that provides a service to other machines on a network—be it file sharing, network bridging, or applications processing. In most corporate settings, a server is usually a machine that provides multiuser access to shared files.

The server is very often thought of simply as a manager of data. In fact, the server is also the hub for most of the software needed to keep the client/server infrastructure healthy. Managing the data is in itself a full-time job but the server also has to worry about network issues, applications version control, execution of a portion of the application logic, requesting data from other machines, and responding to requests for data from other machines. In spite of its important role, users are not usually aware of all it does—such a critical but thankless job.

There are different types of servers: database, data, compute, communications, application-specific, and organization-wide. They come in all sizes and a wide range of components: 4 Mbytes to 256 Mbytes of RAM, 80 Mbytes to 32 Gbytes of storage. Servers are optimized to perform specific functions, but it is often difficult to decide what server, or combination of servers, best meets the needs of the organization.

IS has always taken many of the mainframe features for granted, like security, backup and recovery, monitoring software, and reliability. Most of these features are just now finding their way into server offerings, some as built-ins, some as options.

Server Hardware

In the client/server architecture, the back-end server manages the data resource: it stores, retrieves, and protects data. The server reviews the data requests and, if necessary, generates and sends data requests for other servers. A server also handles other data management tasks such as file and record locking, rollback, and audit trails. Depending on the application, the server could also be used to do data manipulation that requires a great deal of resources, such as a sort, regression, or consolidation.

A server could be a business-specific server, such as a departmental server, as illustrated in Figure 8.1, or a cross-business server, such as a server for an entire organization, as illustrated in Figure 8.2. The server machine could be a simple server (such as a device server or a file server), a superserver, a micro/server, or a database server machine.

8.1 Benchmarks

Benchmarks are often used to compare server hardware. Transaction Processing Counsel (TPC), a consortium of major hardware and software companies worldwide, was founded in 1988 to define database and transaction processing benchmarks. Vendors perform the benchmark tests using TPC-provided guidelines for administering the tests and reporting the results. Its three major benchmark tests are:

- **TPC-A** uses a single, update-intensive transaction to load the test system and measures how many transactions per second the system can perform when driven from multiple terminals. Although its workload is intended to simulate an OLTP application, TPC-A does not reflect the multiple transaction types of varying complexity that characterize current OLTP requirements.
- **TPC-B** is considered a database engine test. It measures the batch-oriented transaction processing performance.
- **TPC-C**, a new benchmark modeled on an order-entry workload, is designed to test processing capabilities in client/server environments and focuses on using a variety of system components associated with OLTP environments. This benchmark simulates the processing requirements of clients on the server rather than actually testing connected clients. TPC-C also incorporates online and batch execution modes, high contention levels on data access and update, requirements for full I/O screen formatting, and a complex database structure. Business throughput is recorded according to the number of orders processed per minute.

These benchmark tests approximate transaction processing capabilities. How well the machine performs in an organization's environment depends on how well balanced the system is and what the traffic mix is. The fastest element in any network server system is the processor, but it can only process data as fast as the I/O channels and buses move data in. Benchmarking a system with the number of expected users in the environment will not accurately represent traffic

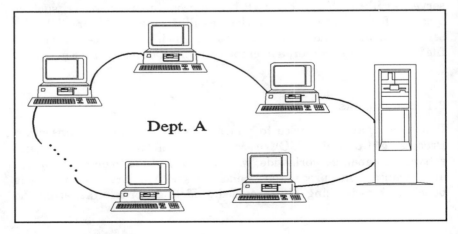

Figure 8.1 Business-specific server

mix, unless the benchmark users are performing the same tasks as the users in the proposed environment.

8.2 Categories of Servers

The concept of a server developed as organizations needed to share expensive peripherals, such as laser printers, CD ROM readers, and

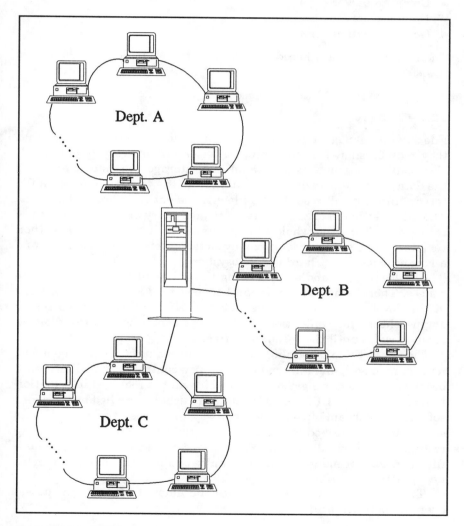

Figure 8.2 Cross-business server

FAX machines. Our discussion of servers will, however, relate to servers that promote the sharing of data as opposed to the sharing of peripherals.

The six types of servers are:

- File server
- Application server
- Data server
- Compute server
- Database server
- Communication server

Their differences are based on where data is handled and how it is transferred.

8.2.1 File Server

File servers manage a work group's applications and data files, so that they may be shared by the group. File servers are very I/O oriented. They pull large amounts of data off their storage subsystems and pass the data over the network. When data from the file is requested, a file server transmits all records of a file and the entire index to the client. The client either selects records (based on query criteria) as they are received or loads the whole file and its index into memory and then reviews it. File servers require many slots for network connections and a large-capacity, fast hard disk subsystem.

File locking is handled by locking the entire file or by locking byte ranges. There is no differentiation between read locks and write locks at this level. When multiple users access shared files, the file server engine checks for contention. If it detects contention at the file-lock level, it waits until the resource is free.

There can be no scheduling of multiple users, no cache management, no lock manager, and minimal concurrency control in the DBMS sense because there is no single engine to which all the required information is available. These DBMS-like features are usually handled by the client software which anticipates the best way to process the data. Unless each data file is locked for exclusive use and some client-side indexing technique is used, all data must be moved across the network before filtering, sort, or merge operations can be applied. This situation forces heavy network traffic.

Two techniques used to minimize the amount of data that passes over the network are:

- Organizing data so that the data needed by a particular application

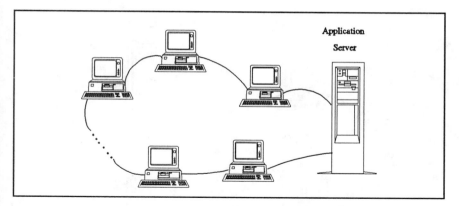

Figure 8.3 Application server

request is stored in a single contiguous block.
■ Storing copies of data accessed by more than one user to help with concurrency problems.

Of course, these techniques require developers to build integrity and synchronization handling into the processing of the application.

8.2.2 Application Server

An application server is a machine that serves as a host replacement (and in some cases actually is a host). When applications are downsized from a host, one option is to install the applications on a smaller machine that runs the same software and to hook all the users to the new box. This process requires no modifications to the host-based application software. For client/server applications that are classified as host-based, the host is the server to the GUI-based clients, as illustrated in Figure 8.3.

8.2.3 Data Server

A data server is data-oriented and used only for data storage and management, as illustrated in Figure 8.4. A data server is used in conjunction with a compute server and may be used by more than one compute server. A data server does not perform any application logic processing. The processing done on a data server is rule-based procedures, such as data validation, required as part of the data management function.

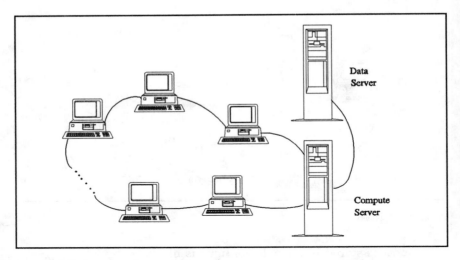

Figure 8.4 Data server and compute server

Data servers perform multiple searches through large amounts of data and frequently update massive tables. These tasks require fast processors, large amounts of memory, and substantial hard disk capacity. However, for the most part, these computers send relatively small amounts of data across the network.

8.2.4 Compute Server

A compute server passes client requests for data to a data server and forwards the results of those requests to clients (see Figure 8.4). Compute servers may perform application logic on the results of the data requests before forwarding data to the client.

Compute servers require processors with high performance capabilities and large amounts of memory but relatively low disk-subsystem capacity and throughput.

By separating the data from the computation processing, an organization can optimize its processing capabilities. Since a data server can serve more than one compute server, compute-intensive applications can be spread among multiple servers.

8.2.5 Database Server

This is the most typical use of server technology in client/server applications. Most, if not all, of the application is run on the client. The database server accepts requests for data, retrieves the data from its database (or makes a request for the data from another node), and passes the results of the request back to the client. Compute servers working with data servers provide the same functionality.

Using a database server or a combination of data and compute servers, the data management function is on the server and the client program consists of application-specific code as well as presentation logic. Because the database engine is separate from the client, the disadvantages of file servers disappear. Database servers can have a lock manager, multiuser cache management, and scheduling, and thus have no need for redundant data.

Database and data/compute servers improve request handling by processing a SQL client request and sending back to the client only the data that satisfies the request. This is much more efficient in terms of network load than a file server architecture, where the complete file is often sent from the server to the client.

Because SQL allows records to be processed in sets, an application can, with a single SQL statement, retrieve or modify a set of server database records. Older database systems have to issue separate sequential requests for each desired record of each of the base tables. Because SQL can create a results table that combines, filters, and transforms data from base tables, considerable savings in data communication are realized even for data retrieval.

The requirements for these servers are a function of the size of the database, the speed with which the database must be updated, the number of users, and the type of network used.

8.2.6 Communication Server

Communication servers provide gateways to other LANs, networks, midrange computers, and mainframes. They have relatively modest system requirements, with perhaps the greatest demands being those for multiple slots and fast processors to translate networking protocols.

8.3 Features of Server Machines

Many features first introduced as superserver features are finding their way down to the micro/server platform. These include support for:

- Multiprocessing
- Multithreading
- Disk arrays

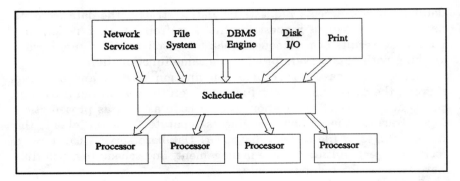

Figure 8.5 Symmetric multiprocessing

- Memory subsystems
- Redundant components

8.3.1 Multiprocessing

Vendors are including multiple processors in their hardware to increase processing speed or productivity. Multiple processors permit servers to do either symmetric or functional multiprocessing.

Symmetric multiprocessing allows a task to be dynamically assigned to any processor, as illustrated in Figure 8.5. Processing resources are maximized. A processor does not sit idle if there is work to be done. However, this capability has to be supported by either the network operating system or the server operating system. The application software must be able to support multiprocessing as well.

Among the major LAN operating systems, Banyan's VINES SMP and the Santa Cruz Operation's SCO MPX currently support symmetric multiprocessing. Microsoft claims that Windows New Technology will support symmetric multiprocessing.

Functional multiprocessing permanently assigns a set of tasks to a processor, as illustrated in Figure 8.6. Consequently, one processor

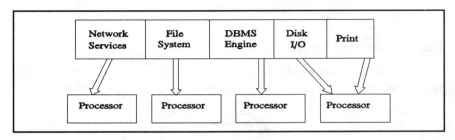

Figure 8.6 Functional multiprocessing

(usually the I/O processor) may sit idle while another is overloaded. Using LAN Manager as an example, one processor is dedicated to the OS/2 API set, which includes APIs for logon and client/server APIs such as named pipes. The other processor is dedicated to network I/O, including the Network Interface Card drivers, printing subsystem, OS/2's High Performance File System (HPFS), and other file-related code.

Superservers with Extended Industry Standard Architecture (EISA) buses support bus mastering, a form of functional multiprocessing. Under bus mastering, each LAN card does some of the low-level network I/O, thus freeing up the processing resources for other tasks.

Processors are either tightly coupled or loosely coupled. In loosely coupled systems, each processor has its own memory. In tightly coupled systems, the most popular today, the processors share the same memory. The processors interact with memory over a special memory bus. Each processor typically has its own RAM cache, which reduces the traffic on the memory bus. This requires routines to ensure that all copies of a given memory location in different processor caches are consistent.

Multiprocessing supports *multithreading*, the concurrent execution of multiple tasks. However, applications—as well as operating systems and network operating systems—must be written to be multithreaded, to allow parts of the application to run as different tasks on different processors.

8.3.2 Multithreading

A thread is the smallest unit of execution that the system can schedule to run; a path of execution through a process. Each thread consists of a stack, an instruction pointer, a priority, the CPU state, and an entry in the system's scheduler list. A thread may be blocked, scheduled to execute, or executing.

Threads communicate by sending messages to each other and they compete for ownership of various *semaphores*, which govern the allocation of computing resources between the individual threads. The threads ask the system for an instruction to carry out. If no instruction is ready, the thread is suspended until it has something to do. If an instruction is ready, the thread performs the task and makes another request to the system for work.

Older operating systems achieve multitasking by creating multiple processes, which creates a great deal of overhead. In a multithreaded environment, a process is broken into independent executable tasks (threads). These threads then collectively perform all the work that a single program could execute, allowing applications to perform many tasks simultaneously. The separate threads complete their tasks in the background and allow continued operation of the primary assignment. The challenge is to break the application up into discrete tasks that can become threads.

An ice cream parlor is an example of a multithreaded process. As demand increases, more counter help is added. Each additional person shares the floor space and the equipment (the ice cream, the cones and dishes, the scoops, the cash register). In an environment that is not multithreaded, each additional person would have their own equipment and floor space. At some point, even though shared resources are being used, it may make sense to add a whole new environment to service the additional demand. Hence, a new ice cream parlor opens up one mile away. In IS terms, a larger server machine is added to the environment.

Tightly coupled processes that execute concurrently require programmers to push problem abstraction further than they have in the past. A *thread of execution* is a new conceptual unit that performs the work in the system by moving from one instruction or statement (thread) to the next, executing each in turn.

The greatest adjustment to multitasking may be in users' work habits. Users are accustomed to taking a break or staring at the screen after issuing a command. Under multithreading, users need to adjust to the idea that they don't have to wait after issuing a command—they can switch to another task.

8.3.3 Disk Arrays

Fault-tolerant disk arrays, which are referred to as redundant arrays of inexpensive disks (RAID), are standard on superservers and optional on other platforms. Disk arrays usually include a 486 file server and software that controls access to the individual drivers. Multiple drivers are treated as a single logical drive by the server operating system.

Redundant disk arrays can transparently recover from the failure of any single drive and allow a failed drive to be replaced while the server is online. As illustrated in Figure 8.7, data is actually broken into chunks and simultaneously written to multiple disks, a process called striping. If a disk fails, the data can be reconstructed by reviewing the remaining pieces of data. Server performance is degraded while the reconstruction process is going on, but the self-healing process is otherwise transparent to the user.

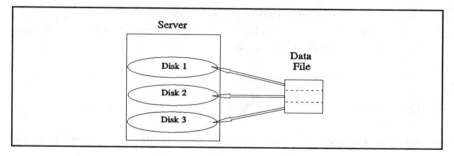

Figure 8.7 Redundant arrays of inexpensive disks (RAID)

RAID currently has five levels of data protection and error correction. A proposed sixth level would include the ability to recover from multiple concurrent disk failures.

The levels are not aggregate levels, they are five different methods of implementation. The levels of RAID are:

- **RAID-1** uses mirrored disks to provide complete data redundancy on a one-to-one basis. Each disk has a twin that contains the same data as the primary disk. This is the most common method used today.
- **RAID-2** provides for multiple parity drives with a slightly lower cost per megabyte because less than 50 percent of the total available storage is used to maintain data integrity. Although prevalent in the supercomputer and mainframe worlds, products that support Level 2 are not currently available for the micro market.
- **RAID-3**, also called disk guarding, provides for a minimum of two (although four are usually used) data drives plus a dedicated parity drive, which is used to maintain the error-correction code (ECC) information necessary to rebuild a failed data drive. The data is striped across all the available data drives. Performance is improved over that of Level 2, and the cost per megabyte drops even further because there is only one parity drive.
- **RAID-4** also uses dedicated ECC drives to provide data integrity and stripes files in blocks rather than in bytes (as is done in Levels 2 and 3), eliminating the need for synchronization. Level 4 also provides the ability to perform multiple simultaneous reads, which can significantly improve system throughput.
- **RAID-5**, also called distributed data guarding, eliminates the need for a dedicated ECC drive by striping data and ECC information across all available drives. It extends the ability of Level 4 to perform simultaneous reads by allowing multiple simultaneous

writes. The greatest advantage of Level 5 is its ability to perform reads and writes in parallel. RAID-5 can provide the lowest cost per megabyte in a redundant data-protection storage scheme.

There are two versions of RAID-1. They are:

- **Disk mirroring**, which uses two drives attached to the same disk controller
- **Disk duplexing**, which uses individual controllers for each drive

These configurations provide 100 percent data redundancy at a 100 percent (or greater) increase in cost per megabyte.

The other RAID levels use the following techniques to keep the penalty for reliability to a minimum with little or no impact on performance:

- **Parity checking** improves reliability. An extra bit is added to ensure that the information is transmitted accurately. Parity checking allows information to be restored in the event that a hard disk crashes.
- **Data striping** improves I/O performance. Data are spread by bytes or sectors across many disks using an algorithm.

Most systems provide error checking and data protection at the RAID-3 level.

8.3.4 Memory Subsystems

Error-correction code (ECC) memory and parity checking (often includes automatic recovery) is used to prevent corruption of data traveling within the server. ECC memory is a memory subsystem design that automatically corrects single-bit errors and detects multiple-bit errors.

Each time data is written to the disk array, an ECC is written to an extra disk in the array or to a primary storage disk. The actual code for the ECC is calculated by applying an error-correction formula to the data written to the other drives. If one drive fails, the lost data is reconstructed from the ECC, the intact data on the remaining drives, and the formula.

Many physical faults can be tolerated by a system memory that is designed with ECC. However, the physical faults must be within the error correcting capability of the ECC. The ECC method uses the conventional one-bit-per-chip design and stores each bit of a codeword in a different chip. Failures can thus only corrupt one bit of codeword.

8.3.5 Redundant Components

Redundant server components, such as disk drives, power supplies, fans, and automatic recovery features, are options on micro/servers and standard on superservers. Some superservers offer mirrored processors and include remote alarms that immediately warn of network trouble.

8.4 Classes of Server Machines

A host-based processing application usually does not require additional server hardware because the host running the application is acting as the server. Depending on the reliability required, the amount of data involved, the complexity of the application, and the number of users, applications that fall into the other classes of client/server applications will require either a micro/server, a superserver, a database server machine, a midrange computer, or a fault-tolerant machine.

8.4.1 Micro/Server

A micro/server, an upright (vertical) micro that can fit under a desk, has been optimized for server functionality. Micro/servers use Intel 486 chips, run at 33 MHz or higher (and may also use a speed doubler processor to achieve even higher speeds), and have expanded memory capabilities (usually in the 16-Mbyte range with expansion up to 128 Mbytes). Internal hard drives offer capacities ranging from 80 Mbytes to 500 Mbytes. Intelligent disk subsystems (disk arrays) can provide access to several gigabytes of data.

Multiprocessing is a non-issue for the vast majority of LANs because Novell's NetWare, the most widely installed LAN operating system, does not support multiprocessing. Microsoft's LAN Manager supports functional multiprocessing. Banyan's VINES and The Santa Cruz Operation's SCO UNIX support symmetric multiprocessing.

Compaq introduced the COMPAQ SystemPro/LT family of micro-based servers designed for midsized workgroups. System/Pro LT uses the Intelligent Drive Array disk technology used by its big brother, Compaq's SystemPro. However, memory capacity of the SystemPro/LT is limited to 64 Mbytes and it lacks dual-processing capabilities.

8.4.2 Superservers

Superservers, developed specifically for the client/server architecture, are an important option for server hardware. Superservers should not be confused with UNIX-based servers that provide hardware features such as multiple processors, large amounts of memory, and massive high-speed disk arrays and were built for specialized applications, such as technical or scientific applications. Historically, when UNIX-based machines have been used as servers for NetWare or LAN Manager LANs with DOS workstations, they have not matched the performance of superservers running a LAN operating system in native mode.

Available since 1989, superservers are micros that have been optimized for server functions by including multiple processors, increased memory, disk capacity, and speed. When superservers were first announced by NetFrame Systems Inc. and Tricord Systems Inc., the least expensive models were in the $25,000 range. Today, a NetFrame NF100ES superserver with 16 Mbytes of memory, 380 Mbytes of disk storage, and a Token Ring or Ethernet I/O processor costs about $13,000. Tricord's PowerFrame 30L comes with 8 Mbytes of memory and 418 Mbytes of disk storage for about $15,000. The SystemPro from Compaq comes with 4 Mbytes of memory and 840 Mbytes of disk storage and costs about $18,000.

The early models of superservers almost exclusively used proprietary buses. Even though standard buses, such as Extended Industry Standard Architecture (EISA) and Micro Channel Architecture (MCA), are used by recent entries, such as Compaq, Advanced Logic Research (ALR), and Parallan, there is still very little standardization in superservers. Once a superserver vendor is chosen, an organization is locked into that vendor.

A superserver has the following advantages over a micro/server:

- **Increased processing power**, using multiple processors
- **Increased I/O capabilities**, using multiple buses or I/O processor modules for I/O support
- **Increased disk capacity**, using arrays of inexpensive disks, which are treated as a single logical drive
- **Improved memory management**, using faster memory chips, better memory architectures, and optimal use of large amounts of memory and memory caches
- **Improved reliability**, using redundant components and ECC memory
- **Improved maintainability**, using built-in routines for remote troubleshooting and management, they are easier to configure and maintain

The capabilities of micro/servers and superservers are compared in Figure 8.8.

The power of a superserver allows it to do multiprocessing, increase network support, and boost disk I/O capabilities. The I/O capabilities vary among the superservers. Some machines are designed to support a maximum of two processors, such as ALR's PowerPro Array and Compaq's SystemPro. These systems use one EISA bus for network and disk I/O and another EISA bus for processor and memory I/O. If more processors were added without increasing I/O capacity, the processors would be waiting for data most of the time with a resulting throughput roughly the same as a EISA-based 33 MHz micro.

Multiple (proprietary or standard) I/O buses can be used to improve I/O but how much is limited by the capabilities of the network software. Instead of using LAN cards, which go into a bus slot, NetFrame sells I/O processor modules with their own processor and proprietary 12.5 Mbps I/O bus. By increasing the processing power and I/O capacity at the same time, this system can support larger numbers of I/O processors (up to eight in the NetFrame NF400).

Applications with large amounts of data, substantial processing needs, and a great deal of network traffic can justify the cost of a

	Micro/servers		Superserver	
	Low	High	Low	High
Users	2-16	16-64	64-128	128-1000
Price	$5,000	$15,000	$25,000-50,000	$60,000-300,000
Chip	386	2 x 386-486	Mips, Intel, Sparc	Mips, Intel, Sparc, RS/6000
RAM	8-16 Mbytes	16-64 Mbytes	32-128 Mbytes	64-256 Mbytes
Disk	80-180 Mbytes	180-840 Mbytes	640 Mbytes - 2 Gbytes	1 - 32 Gbytes
OS	DOS, OS/2, NetWare	OS/2, UNIX, NetWare	UNIX, SCO UNIX	UNIX, SCO UNIX

Source: Computer Associates International Inc.

Figure 8.8 Comparison of micro/servers and superservers

superserver. However, today's typical client/server applications, even with a lot of network traffic, are just beginning to stretch a basic micro/server (a 33 MHz 486, which costs about $4,000) to its limit. If more power is needed, the 486 can be replaced with a 586 and the retired server can be used as a single-user workstation. A superserver is a superserver (or host) for its entire life.

The acceptance hurdle for superservers has been cost. To make their products more attractive, superserver vendors are making their machines more modular, which reduces initial outlays for organizations while still supporting expandability. For example, when an upgrade is necessary, a second processor can be added to a single-processor.

Two popular superservers are IBM Server 295, which is based on the Parallan Server 290 Series, and Compaq's SystemPro.

IBM Server 295

IBM purchased a minority stake in Parallan Computer, Inc. in June 1992. Under the agreement, Parallan, no longer selling its Series 290 servers, assumes the role of an IBM development laboratory focusing on a product that combines its Series 290 multiprocessor architecture with IBM's PS/2 Model 95. The product, IBM Server 295, was released late 1992. To understand the capabilities of the new product, a review of the Server 290 Series is necessary.

The Parallan Server 290 Series uses Intel 50 MHz 486 chips, has redundant, hot-swappable (a component can be replaced without bringing the system offline) RAID-5 disk arrays, and includes a minimum of 128 Mbytes of main memory. The Server 290 Series has two processors, each with its own MCA bus. One bus manages peripherals (monitors, printers, and so on) and its processor runs OS/2 and applications. The other bus and processor handle the network. This bus is used for the network adapter cards and the processor handles network protocol and OS/2 HPFS processing. Since disk I/O is handled by the high-speed internal system bus, there is no disk traffic on the MCA buses.

The Parallan Server 290 Series can be maintained by remote or local administrators. In addition, a combination of hardware and software, called the Maximum Availability and Support Subsystem (MASS), provides monitoring and control features, such as viewing activity on the system, keeping records, providing alerts, and reconfiguring and restarting the system in the event of a failure.

The IBM Server 295 Series uses a 33 or 50 MHz 486 processor with 32 Mbytes of ECC memory running OS/2 1.3. It supports hot disk swapping and provides redundant elements, such as dual power supplies. The new MASS/2, which incorporates a new GUI interface, allows administrators to monitor, tune, configure, and control the Server 295 locally or remotely. The Server 295 Series supports only Microsoft's LAN Manager and IBM's version of that network operating system, OS/2 LAN Server.

COMPAQ SystemPro

The COMPAQ SystemPro 486 Series, first introduced in 1990, has Intel 486 processors running at 33 MHz or higher, an EISA I/O bus that can accommodate multiple I/O bus masters, and Compaq's Intelligent Drive Array (IDA) controller. The SystemPro 486 Series can support 256 Mbytes of memory.

The COMPAQ SystemPro uses symmetric and functional processing. It uses symmetric processing to allow two or more main processors to run applications simultaneously. These processors share a common memory bank and have equal access to systems resources. SystemPro's IDA controller uses a dedicated Intel processor to move data to the disk (functional processing).

At the core of Compaq's ability to deliver reliable and predictable performance is its IDA controller, which ensures a high degree of data reliability and I/O performance. The IDA controller can stripe data across hard disks and mirror or guard the data—all in its hardware. A second IDA can be added to duplex the data.

Compaq's new Intelligent Drive Array Controller-2 (IDA-2) is a Compaq-designed bus master device, which eliminates bottlenecks by using a faster processor and the 4-Mbyte Array Accelerator Write Cache, which allows the system to temporarily store data in the Array Accelerator, rather than directly to the disk. Later, during less write-intensive activities, the stored data is written to disk. This improves performance for write-intensive environments, such as database or fault tolerant configurations, or any environment where performance is critical. The IDA-2 can perform RAID-1, RAID-3, and RAID-5 functions.

The Array Accelerator includes on-board batteries which allow data to be held for 8 to 10 days in the event of a power loss. In addition, the memory of the Array Accelerator is mirrored, keeping a clean copy of the data in the event of a parity error.

The tools designed into Compaq's servers to provide performance, security, configuration, and fault management capabilities include:

- The **COMPAQ INSIGHT Manager,** a Windows-based server

management application, delivers greater network control of servers running NetWare. The INSIGHT Manager displays a sketch of the server and its internal components in adjoining icons. The sketch is compiled by the software's auto-discovery feature, which lists the server's components upon configuration.

- The **COMPAQ Server Manager** (previously called the COMPAQ System Manager board) provides advanced remote monitoring and control capability for micro/servers and superservers. This product is integrated with Novell's NetWare Management System API. The Server Manager is viewable through INSIGHT Manager or Novell's NetWare Services Manager.

In addition to the server management tools and services, the INSIGHT strategy provides support for leading network operating systems and complies with network standards. The strategy will be extended to include built-in fault tolerance using disk arrays, error-correcting memory, and dynamic-sector repairing of hard disk drives.

Compaq also offers an optional administrator notification system that can call a preset number in case the system malfunctions.

8.4.3 Database Machines

Using specialized hardware and software, database machines can run as high-speed database servers or as application servers. Because they usually support parallel processing, data searches are performed at high speeds. Large database machines can have hundreds of processors.

The Teradata DBC/1012 Data Base Computer, a parallel processing database server from Teradata (now a part of NCR Corp.), includes a RDBMS optimized for their equipment. DBC/1012 can support databases in excess of 1 Gbyte.

Teradata allows users to connect multiple, heterogeneous computers to the DBC/1012 using its Client Server and Shared Information Architecture. Standard SQL commands are issued to the database machine, which interprets them using Teradata interface processors. The software breaks down the SQL command and can assign multiple Intel processors to work on the command in parallel.

The new Teradata DBC/1012 Model 4 Communications Processor can support as many as 120 sessions using a new TCP/IP Ethernet adapter, and allows users to access data in the DBC/1012 directly from a micro or workstation using a variety of GUIs.

The next release of DBC/1012 (due mid-1993) is expected to support other parallel databases and add an Applications Processor with general purpose UNIX processing capabilities. Disk arrays will also be offered as an option starting with the following release.

8.4.4 Fault-Tolerant Machines

As mainframe data is moved to servers, it becomes critical that server machines remain operational. Businesses are looking to fault-tolerant computers to keep these applications available to end users. *Fault tolerance* is the ability of a component to withstand a fatal failure without corrupting data or disrupting service. Fully fault-tolerant machines have duplicated the significant hardware, including the processor, memory system, disk storage, communication links, and backup power supplies.

Some degree of fault tolerance is now available in servers of all sizes with mirrored-disk subsystems and built-in monitoring capabilities. These servers, called high-availability servers, offer a price/performance compromise between fully fault-tolerant servers and disk-level fault tolerance. Unlike fully fault-tolerant servers, these servers provide recovery from the failure of critical components such as disk drives but may shut down for other errors. The key is to minimize downtime. Many of the high-end servers have high fault tolerance and high availability built into the hardware rather than providing redundant components.

A fully fault-tolerant machine uses a dual-redundant hardware architecture with two complete processing systems in one enclosure to ensure no single point of failure. Each system bus, together with its corresponding CPU, memory, EISA module, and attached peripherals, comprises a system.

The two systems operate simultaneously, one shadowing the other. Maintaining constant inter-computer communications, the systems monitor each other and provide the synchronization and coordination needed for fault-tolerant operation. In case of failure in either system, the functional system continues to operate. The failed system can then be repaired while the functional system is on-line, thus providing continuous operation.

Fault-tolerant computers provide continuous operation and online recovery. They have long been noted for their reliability, data integrity methods, expandability, and user-transparent data distribution. They achieve these high standards by making every component redundant. If a primary component malfunctions, its redundant component begins operating without bringing the system to a halt, although performance may be impacted while the recovery occurs.

Fully fault-tolerant servers use modular plug-in boards for

processors, as well as disk and I/O controllers. In the event of a failure that has been isolated to a faulty component, the system manager can replace or repair the failed component while the server is running.

While these recovery capabilities are necessary for fully fault-tolerant servers, they are expensive. Fault-tolerant machines used to be marketed only to financial companies, such as banks, stock markets, and stockbrokers. They are now becoming an important (although expensive) piece of the client/server computing puzzle. They are especially important as cross-business servers, where the entire organization relies on the server.

The two major vendors of fault-tolerant machines are Stratus Computer, Inc. and Tandem Computers, Inc. These two companies have aimed their machines at telecommunications, banking, and other computing-intensive businesses that keep their critical applications online and find downtime unacceptable. The other major vendors in this market are IBM and Digital.

There are some new players in the market as well. Everex Systems, Inc. offers its Step Multi-Processing Fault-Tolerant (MPFT) 2001 server for Novell's forthcoming System Fault Tolerance Level III (SFT III) software. The machine contains two servers in a single chassis connected by a 25 Mbps internal bus and mirrors each network transaction on both servers. Step MPFT has additional NetWare Loadable Modules (NLMs) that work in conjunction with SFT III and allow Step MPFT and the NLMs to monitor one another's software and hardware, synchronizing data and detecting failures.

Hewlett-Packard's presence in the fault-tolerant computer market includes products that span the low-end to high-end performance categories. Their product line, which includes the HP 9000 Models 1210, 1240, and 1245, uses hardware-fault detection with software-based recovery. The operating system also achieves a high degree of resiliency against software faults.

Texas Microsystems, another newcomer to the fault-tolerant market, offers its micro-based Fault-Tolerant System Architecture (FTSA). Because it lacks a redundant CPU, it is vulnerable to a catastrophic CPU failure, but it goes further than any other machine in its price range (below $10,000) to ensure both system availability and data integrity.

The FTSA provides clean power, with complete insulation from secondary damage due to power irregularities. By integrating an intelligent power monitor with a redundant, modular hardware design, the FTSA ensures data integrity and protects itself against surges, sags, spikes, brownouts, and other power anomalies.

The FTSA also promises hard disk subsystem availability, with data integrity and effective data recovery in the event of catastrophic failure or data corruption due to single-point hardware failure, software glitches, or user errors. The system also anticipates and diagnoses hardware failures, generates prompts for preventive maintenance, and recovers quickly from maintenance actions. The vendor claims these components of FTSA are available 99.9 percent of the time.

The foundation for FTSA's fault tolerance is its enhanced BIOS, a set of programs that coordinates data transfer and controls instructions among the FTSA central processor, various peripherals, and the machine's custom co-processors. Operating as a multitasking operating system, the enhanced BIOS functions one layer below DOS and asynchronously controls the interaction of the system processor, multiple diagnostic co-processors, and peripherals.

Hewlett-Packard, IBM, Pyramid, and Digital are working on fault-tolerant workstations for a 1993 delivery.

Server Environment

While the user might view the client machine and its software as the system, the server is the critical component. It manages the network, provides access to data residing on its storage devices, generates data requests for data residing on other nodes, and transmits those requests to the appropriate nodes. The client machine makes a request and the server does all the coordination necessary to fulfill that request.

9.1 Eight Layers of Software

There could be as many as eight categories of software working on a server, as illustrated in Figure 9.1:

- Network management environment
- Network computing environment and extensions
- Network operating system
- Server operating system
- Loadable modules
- Database manager
- Database gateways
- Application

The application develops requests for data that are sent via the network operating system to database gateways, database managers, or

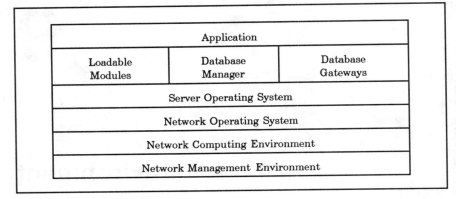

Figure 9.1 Eight categories of server software

a loadable module. They translate the request into machine code and pass it on to the server operating system. The server operating system is guided by the network computing environment software, which handles the services required to support distributed applications in heterogeneous environments. The entire networked enterprise is guided by the network management environment software.

9.2 Network Management Environment

As IS works towards a distributed computing environment, the management of networked systems, regardless of their hardware and software platforms, becomes a necessity. Networks and systems should be viewed as a single entity and their management handled as one process, not two.

Standards-setting organizations and vendors are developing frameworks to manage the interconnected information technologies. Currently, these products are primarily in the specification stage, although components may currently be available. The products discussed below (DME, OMA, and UI-Atlas) are reviewed in more detail in Chapter 17, Managing the Production Environment.

9.2.1 Distributed Management Environment

As discussed earlier, the Open Software Foundation (OSF) is focusing on building distributed computing and management software and developing a new role as manager of middleware technologies developed by outside companies. Middleware sits between the operating system and the application. One of its open software technologies is Distributed Management Environment (DME).

OSF's DME provides a framework for a vendor-neutral, object-oriented, cost-effective environment that can be used by hardware and software vendors to develop products. DME provides:

- An **object-oriented application interface** for administration and management of multivendor objects, such as network devices, systems, applications, files, and databases.
- A **standard API** to manage a wide range of networked systems via either OSI's Common Management Information Protocol (CMIP) or Simple Network Management Protocol (SNMP).
- A **common GUI** across different network management applications and services.

DME is designed to cover network management as well as systems management. By integrating systems and networks, IS can handle the management of their interconnected information technologies as a single process, not multiple processes. Applications written to DME specifications will run on any DME-compliant network management system.

Some of the DME pieces are available from contributing vendors. The integration of the pieces into the DME platform is not slated until at least the second quarter of 1993. DME-compliant software will not be available until 1994. As parts of the DME specification are complete, OSF is releasing snapshot versions to its members.

Although DME is designed to manage DCE-compliant systems, DCE is not a requirement for DME.

9.2.2 Object Management Architecture

Object Management Group's Object Management Architecture (OMA) combines distributed processing with object-oriented computing. It provides a standard method for creating, preserving, locating, and communicating objects, which can be anything from entire applications to pieces of applications such as graphical screens or complex number-crunching algorithms. Using this mechanism, cooperative-processing applications can be supported within a heterogeneous, distributed, networked environment.

The OMA performs as a layer above existing operating systems and communication transports that support standard RPCs such as SunSoft's Open Network Computing (ONC). The OMA consists of four main components:

- **Object Request Broker** (ORB), the interface that must be used and the information that must be presented for an object to communicate with another object.
- **Object services**, utility-like objects that can be called on to help perform basic object-oriented housekeeping chores and provide for consistency, integrity, and security of objects and the messages that pass between objects.
- **Common facilities**, functions commonly used by applications such as printing and spooling or error reporting.
- **Application objects**, applications or components of applications, which are created by independent software vendors or in-house software developers.

To link to the other OMA components, the Object Request Broker uses its Interface Definition Language (IDL), an OMG-developed language with its roots in C++. Mappings between the IDL and common programming languages such as C (currently the only mapping specified) or COBOL are provided which allow developers to write to the ORB interfaces.

The ORB also specifies features for managing the interobject messages. These features include name services (similar to an object directory) and exception handling. ORB allows objects to communicate dynamically or via a set of faster, preprogrammed static facilities.

ORB is the foundation for OMG's Common Object Request Broker Architecture (CORBA) discussed in Chapter 4, Understanding Client/ Server Computing.

OSF has not endorsed the OMA and has specified its Management Request Broker and Interface Definition Language, both of which are part of the OSF's DME.

9.2.3 UI-Atlas

UI-Atlas, the open systems solution from UNIX International Inc. (UI), specifies how to create an open systems architecture using hardware, software, networking, and other standards-based components.

UI-Atlas includes:

- The OSI seven-layer network services model
- A GUI that uses one API to support both Motif and OpenLook
- An expanded version of Sun's Network File System that operates over wide area networks and supports file replications
- A global naming support system

- A system management framework
- A distributed object management model that complies with OMG specifications

UI-Atlas is expected to base much of its distributed applications and management environment around the ORB and the OMA. The version of UI-Atlas expected to be released in the second quarter of 1993 will focus on system management applications for object management. UNIX International will then layer the ORB and OMA services on top of UNIX System V Release 4 with a graphical user interface on the desktop.

9.3 Network Computing Environment

Network computing environments allow applications to be distributed among heterogeneous platforms and software. OSF's standard to support this architecture is Distributed Computing Environment (DCE). UNIX International's standard for open computing environments is SunSoft's Open Network Computing (ONC), which is similar to DCE except in the area of RPCs.

9.3.1 Distributed Computing Environment

DCE, illustrated in Figure 9.2, provides a framework of services for

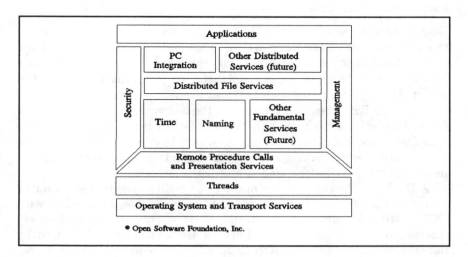

Figure 9.2 Distributed Computing Environment model

distributing applications in heterogeneous hardware and software environments. The details of the basic services are hidden from end users. DCE is an open system that can run on any platform or operating system. It is not restricted to UNIX.

The DCE model provides an integrated approach to distributed processing. Its layered architecture provides flexibility to include future technologies. Each layer provides its own security and management.

DCE supports OSI standards and protocols and Internet standards, such as TCP/IP transport and network protocols, the Domain Name System, and Network Time Protocol; and uses standard interfaces, such as POSIX and X/Open. DCE can be ported to OSF/1, UNIX System V, AIX, Ultrix, HP-UX, and SunOS and adapted to VMS and OS/2.

DCE provides two sets of services:

- **Basic distributed services** allow developers to build applications.
- **Data-sharing services**, which require no programming by the end users, include a distributed file system, diskless system support, and micro integration.

The tools provided by DCE as basic distributed services are:

- Remote procedure calls
- Distributed Directory Service
- Threads Service
- Time Service
- Security Service

Remote Procedure Calls

DCE's remote procedure calls (RPCs) allow an application's programs to execute on more than one server in the network, regardless of the other machines' architectures or physical locations. Because information transfer is transparent between different platforms, the use of RPCs allows heterogeneous operation.

The DCE RPC standard is based on the Network Computing System from Hewlett-Packard and Interface Definition Language (IDL) compiler-generated C-program files, which handle the interfacing of clients and servers. Its specifications include special semantics for network transport independence and transparency.

A DCE RPC can specify communication with a specific file server or with any file server offering a required service. The integration with DCE's Threads Service component allows clients to simultaneously interact with multiple servers. Servers are identified and located by name. Developers use the IDL to specify server-to-client operations.

Integration with DCE's Security Service provides communication privacy and integrity for distributed applications.

Because DCE's RPCs support connectionless and connection-oriented transports, an application does not have to be rewritten to use different transport services. DCE's RPCs can also efficiently handle bulk data for large data-processing applications.

The RPC syntax, semantics, and presentation services represent the major differences between OSF's DCE and SunSoft's Open Network Computing (ONC) architecture. These differences are discussed in the ONC section later in this chapter. Remote procedure calls are discussed in more detail in Section 11.3.1.

Distributed Directory Service

This service provides a single naming model throughout the distributed network. Users locate and access servers, files or print queues by name, not their physical location. Users use the same name even if the network address changes. The Directory Service uses a local cell directory service and a global directory service. Global names can reside in the X.500 standard directory service or Internet Domain Name System name space.

The Directory Service can accommodate large and small networks and is easily modified to incorporate expansion. Using transport-independent RPC, DCE's Directory Service can operate in both LAN and WAN environments.

The Directory Service is integrated with other DCE components, such as the Security Service and the Distributed File System.

Time Service

This software-based service synchronizes system clocks among host computers in both LAN and WAN environments. It provides an accurate timestamp for application development files that must be stored in sequence. The Time Service also supports time values from external services used for distributed sites using the Network Time Protocol. The Time Service is integrated with other DCE components such as RPC, Directory, and Security services.

Threads Service

DCE requires threads for operation. The Threads Service allows multiple threads of execution in a single process and synchronizes the global data access. One thread can be executing an RPC, while another processes user input. Applications do not need to know whether threads are executing on one or several processors.

The Thread Service is used by RPCs; Security, Directory, and Time Services; and Distributed File System. The Thread Service conforms to Draft 4 of the emerging POSIX standard for multithreaded programs.

Security Service

Data integrity and privacy are provided by three facilities:

- **Authentication** is based on the Kerberos Version 5 standard from MIT. It verifies a user through a third server.
- Once users are authenticated, the **authorization** facility decides if they should have access to the requested resources.
- A **user registry** facilitates the management of user information. The registry ensures that user names are unique across the network. It also maintains a log of user and login activity.

Distributed File System

Distributed file systems (DFS) allow users to access data on another system via the network. In DCE's DFS terms, the user's system is the client and the system where the data is stored is the server.

When data is accessed, a copy of it is cached (stored) on the client system, where the client can read and modify it. Modified data is written back to the server. DCE's DFS uses tokens to keep track of cached information. Tokens (read or write) are assigned by the server when data is cached. To modify data, a client requests a write token. When a write token is assigned, the server informs other clients that a write token for that data has been assigned. If other clients cached the same data with a read token, the server notifies them that the data is no longer current and voids their tokens.

DCE's DFS, based on the Andrews File System from Transarc Corp., provides the following advanced distributed file systems features:

- **Access Security and Protection.** Security is enforced through user authentication and an access control list.
- **Data Reliability.** To ensure a client's ability to process, DCE's DFS supports replication of all network services. If one of the servers fails, the system automatically switches a client to one of the replicated servers.

- **Data Availability.** Routine maintenance of the server, such as backup, can be done in real time.

DCE's DFS works with Sun's Network File System (NFS), the current *de facto* standard, but differs in the following areas:

- DFS has **integrated support** for LAN and WAN networks. NFS only supports LAN networks.
- DFS uses a **global file space**, where all network users see the same paths to accessible files. Global names are used to ensure uniform file access from any network node via a uniform name space. In NFS, each network node has a different view of the file space.

DCE's DFS supports diskless workstations with general-purpose protocols. The DFS cache manager can cache files in the diskless client memory instead of on a local disk. This gives organizations options. They can purchase less expensive diskless micros to be used as client machines or specify that micros use server disk space instead of more expensive local disk space.

Desktop Support

DCE supports the distribution of network processing power among a large number of computers and allows interconnected clients to work with other DCE-compliant systems and to access files and peripherals.

DCE RPCs allow low-end systems to work with other architectures and share applications with other systems in the network. They can use Directory Service to access information and compute resources anywhere in the enterprise network. Micros and Macintosh computers can view and copy files to and from systems running UNIX-based and proprietary operating systems.

DCE Client/Server Model

DCE is more than just a server software package. As illustrated in Figure 9.3, DCE components are placed between applications and networking services on both the client and the server. The interaction between the layers is transparent to end users.

9.3.2 Open Network Computing

Although, DCE and SunSoft's Open Network Computing architectures are similar, their major differences are:

- Data translation
- Location transparency
- Transport independence
- Multithreading
- Security

Data Translation

Open Network Computing (ONC) uses a standard known as the External Data Representation (XDR), or canonical data representation, for messages passed between systems. Using XDR, the client and server translate all outgoing RPC messages into XDR form, and then translate all incoming messages from XDR to the native format. This conversion always occurs, adding unnecessary overhead if both client and server use the same data representation.

DCE RPC tags all calls with a description of the calling system's internal data representation and the called system translates the data only when it is necessary to do so. Direct data conversion complicates the translation code used, because it has to be prepared to handle more data formats. But since required data only is translated, it will usually be more efficient.

Location Transparency

Both DCE and ONC RPC methods provide location transparency through directory services. This allows the client application to use a symbolic name for a resource, rather than a hard-coded network

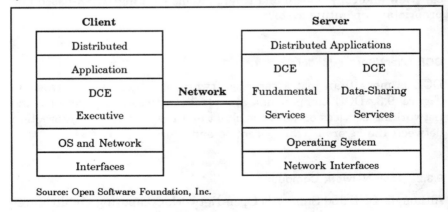

Source: Open Software Foundation, Inc.

Figure 9.3 DCE integration of applications and network services

address. Because all network names are resolved by the name server before the RPC is created, a served resource can be moved without requiring client application changes.

To provide location transparency, ONC uses the Sun Microsystems's Network Information System, formerly known as the Yellow Pages service, to manage the domain name space. DCE uses its hybrid of Digital's domain name service and X.500 to handle name resolution.

Transport Independence

Some applications, such as transaction processing, require a reliable message transport to guarantee that client requests are handled in the proper order and that transactions are not missed or duplicated. DCE and newer versions of the ONC RPC use a transport interface API to isolate client requests from the underlying message transport and to reliably support a wide variety of networks.

Older implementations of the ONC RPC are protocol-dependent and support only the connection-oriented TCP/IP transport or the User Datagram Protocol (UDP), which does not guarantee delivery or the proper sequencing of messages. RPCs behaved differently depending on the chosen protocol. The older versions cannot support OSI or proprietary network transport like DECnet.

ONC's RPC are transport independent, using the UNIX SVR4 Transport Layer Interface (TLI), which provides its own connection-oriented virtual circuits for reliable message transport, regardless of the underlying network protocol. The RPC can provide equivalent service with TCP, UDP, or OSI protocols. DCE's RPC uses the X/Open Transport Interface, which is the POSIX transport API, to achieve approximately the same result.

Multithreading

DCE is based on the multithreaded Mach kernel used by the OSF/1 operating system. Multithreading allows a server process to handle multiple RPC requests. Other UNIX variants, including SunOS, are single-threaded and must complete one client request before proceeding to the next one. ONC RPC servers have to run multiple agents for each service if they wish to process multiple requests in parallel.

Security

The two RPC offerings also differ in how they handle security. ONC uses its own blend of UNIX access control, RPC message encryption, and key passing to authorize and authenticate RPC clients. DCE uses Kerberos authentication, which requires a dedicated security server and enhanced variants of UNIX access control lists.

Other Comparisons

Some of the other major differences between DCE and ONC are:

- DCE is independent of any operating system; ONC relies on UNIX SVR4.
- DCE supports some OSI standards and is evolving toward greater OSI compliance. ONC was not designed to be an open standard and is not as OSI compliant.

ONC's RPC exists and works, perhaps with a few bugs as OSF is more than happy to point out. However, DCE exists largely in specifications and partial products. It's too early to tell which RPC will emerge as the winning standard.

An interesting side note: DCE has been unable to convince the large and apparently happy installed base of Sun's Network File System (NFS) users to convert to its Andrew File System. OSF was forced to support enough of ONC's RPCs to handle those NFS clients.

9.4 Extensions

Currently, the most important DCE extension is the ability to manage online transactions across distributed open systems. Online transaction processing (OLTP) monitors (or transaction processing monitors) are a set of interfaces and procedures which manage the allocation of systems resources and provide scheduling, queue management, fault resilience, security, and recovery of aborted transactions.

A basic unit of work, a transaction, may consist of several SQL statements that retrieve or update data stored on a server. For distributed environments, an update transaction is more complex because the data could span multiple machines and LANs. To ensure data consistency, data management software uses two-phase commits and server-to-server communications.

Using an OLTP monitor, up to 10 times as many terminals can be supported, transaction rates are faster, failure rates decrease, and application maintenance and development costs are reduced. Open OLTP monitors include Tuxedo/T from AT&T, TOP END from NCR, and Encina from Transarc. These OLTP monitors are discussed in more detail in Chapter 17, Managing the Production Environment.

Tuxedo/T was chosen by UNIX International as the reference model for its transaction API. It is based on a request/response architecture and provides communications between the processes through a name server. Because Tuxedo requires all participating applications and resource managers to adhere to standard interfaces, Tuxedo can provide service location transparency, transparent data format conversion, context-sensitive routing, and network independence.

The product is nearly 10 years old and is supported by vendors such as Hewlett-Packard, Digitial, Unisys, Sequent, Pyramid, and Tandem.

TOP END simplifies transaction processing by dividing it into service-requester processes and service-providing processes. This fairly new product differs from Tuxedo in the following areas:

- Administration
- Security
- Communications
- Timer services
- Load leveling

TOP END uses the X/Open Distributed Transaction Processing (DTP) model as a base and the X/Open Resource Manager interface (XA) to communicate with leading databases such as those from Informix, Oracle, Sybase, and Teradata.

Since the merger of AT&T and NCR, industry observers speculate that one of these products will be phased out and predict that TOP END may eventually replace Tuxedo as the OLTP monitor of choice.

The **Transarc Encina** product line consists of two tiers of layered and horizontally integrated software modules. The lower tier provides distributed transaction processing toolkits. The upper tier offers modules that provide high-level TP application functionality, such as two-phase commits over multiple processors and network nodes. The product is based on DCE technology, supports nested transactions, and provides interaction to the mainframe via LU6.2. Transarc has support from such vendors as Hewlett-Packard, Digital, IBM, and Stratus.

9.5 Network Operating System

A network operating system manages the services of the server. It shields application programs from direct communication with the hardware. GUIs are an overlay to the network operating system. Originally offered as tools that supported the concept of a server, network operating systems have evolved into enablers of other software packages and network management tools.

Networks and network operating systems are discussed in Part 4, The Network.

9.6 Loadable Modules

Loadable modules are software modules that are loaded onto the server to improve the functionality of the server's operating system. Most loadable modules used in client/server computing are NetWare Loadable Modules (NLMs). NLMs, which require Novell's NetWare, are used to provide support for various transport protocols, database managers, and network management software.

NLMs can be loaded and unloaded as needed without taking the server offline. Unloading an NLM frees up the memory and other resources used by the NLM. The other attraction is performance; since they run in native 32-bit mode, NLM applications tend to run faster. Data manager NLMs can also improve speed by using NetWare's Direct File System to speed database I/O activity.

There is some controversy surrounding the use of NLMs. When the operating system is juggling two or more tasks, there is the possibility that one task could modify either the data or the executable code of another task, including the operating system. A well-designed operating system works with the underlying hardware to prevent this.

Novell's NetWare is a combined operating system and network operating system. It runs in Ring 0 (or privilege mode), the execution mode associated with Intel 80286 and higher microprocessors. Small ring numbers usually mean more privileges and less protection than higher ring numbers. Since NLM code is physically linked to NetWare code during the linking process, NLMs also run at Ring 0. Since there is no distinction between an NLM application and the operating system, there is no way for the true operating system to stand back and reclaim control from an errant NLM.

This concern is discussed in more detail in Chapter 14, LAN Hardware and Software.

Novell provides an NLM for its NetWare SQL data management product. Many database vendors provide an NLM to their products. These products include Gupta's SQLBase Server, Progress Corp.'s PROGRESS, Oracle Corp.'s ORACLE Server for NetWare 386, and Informix's INFORMIX. Sybase and Microsoft released an NLM version for SQL Server in 1992. Borland is reportedly working on an NLM for InterBase. Cooperative Solutions is working on an NLM for their client/server development product Ellipse.

10

Server
Operating Systems

The server operating system manages the resources of the server. It interacts with the network operating system and the data handling software to receive and respond to user requests for services. While there are many choices for the server operating system, currently the most popular are OS/2 and UNIX-based operating systems. There is also a great deal of interest in Microsoft's yet-to-be-released Windows New Technology.

These 32-bit operating systems support multithreading and multi-tasking. A 32-bit processor, such as an Intel 386 or 486, has more address space, a wider physical bus, and larger instruction operand and register sizes than a 16-bit processor like the 80x6 or 80286.

A 32-bit processor's most important benefit comes from the processor's larger address space—up to 4 Gbytes, compared with a 16-bit processor's 16-Mbyte limit. But a 32-bit operating system is needed to reap this benefit. Software written for DOS or for the segmented architecture of Intel 808x or 80286 chips must manage data and programs in 64-kbyte segments. That requires a lot of overhead. A true 32-bit operating system's large memory address space eliminates that overhead, so programs are faster and more efficient.

OS/2 2.0 and Windows NT provide preemptive multitasking, which means programs that perform time-critical tasks can get control of the processor when they need it. This allows terminal emulation, LAN connectivity, and asynchronous communications programs to run more reliably. For example, when the processor receives an interrupt from a LAN adapter or a modem, the operating system can preempt the program presently running to give the communication software control.

Windows 3.x provides cooperative, not preemptive, multitasking. Once the programs get control of the processor, the operating system cannot intervene when another task requires the processor.

10.1 OS/2 2.0

OS/2 2.0 from IBM is supported on most IBM-compatible 386SX micros and above. It has true concurrent multitasking support with data integrity protection. OS/2 2.0 recognizes and uses all available memory, eliminating the DOS-imposed 640-kbyte limitation.

Its new icon-driven interface called WorkPlace Shell is more object-oriented than Windows and is based on IBM's CUA '91 specifications for windowing applications. It replaces the Group Manager interface used by OS/2 1.x. All desktop functions are represented in a menu with icons for frequently used applications. Icons are also used to represent objects, such as files, folders, and devices.

OS/2 2.0 can run DOS, Windows (currently not Windows 3.1, however), and OS/2 applications in separate windows. Windows programs can be launched directly from the Presentation Manager WorkPlace Shell. Users also have the option to launch the Windows Program Manager and run their applications from that interface. Cut-and-paste and DDE are supported. The interfaces and applications that OS/2 2.0 can support are summarized in Figure 10.1.

OS/2 2.0 is a layered architecture as illlustrated in Figure 10.2. The hardware and transport layer communicates with the device drivers that manage the system's interaction with hardware devices such as a mouse or a keyboard. The kernel communicates with the session manager, such as LAN Manager, which in turn communicates with the parent and child processes such as NETADMIN. HPFS, Named Pipes,

Interfaces	Text Characters	Presentation Manager Windowing		WorkPlace Shell Objects
Applications	DOS 16-bit	Windows 3.0 16-bit	OS/2 16-bit	OS/2 32-bit

Figure 10.1 OS/2 2.0 supported interfaces and applications

Mail Slots, and System messages can be used by any layer.

To support multithreading, OS/2 uses:

- **Semaphores** (program signals about availability of resources), which prevent one process from writing to a memory location actively used by another process.
- **Pipes,** which allow processes to pass information to each other and can be temporary or permanent. Pipes operate at the presentation layer of the network architecture and are not hardware or software dependent. Interprocess pipes operate within a single machine. Redirected pipes operate between machines.

OS/2 Named Pipes uses a programming interface to permit bidirectional communication between two programs, running on the same or different systems. When an OS/2 Named Pipe is created, it is assigned various characteristics, such as the number of instances (concurrent requesters) it will allow.

OS/2 also uses demand loading to maximize memory utilization. Only the parts of a program that are needed at that moment are loaded into memory. This turns real memory into seemingly endless amounts of virtual memory. OS/2 applications can access up to 16 Mbytes of physical memory and 1 Gbyte of virtual memory.

In the OS/2 protected mode, access is partitioned to the lower levels of hardware managed by the operating system. This area, called Ring 0, is the most protected from damage by other software. The OS/2 memory protection assigns each active application absolute boundaries, beyond which it cannot access. This prevents one application from accessing memory that is in use by another application. So if one program should crash, it will not affect the operation of the rest of the system. Since most system crashes are caused by memory conflicts, this adds considerable stability to the environment.

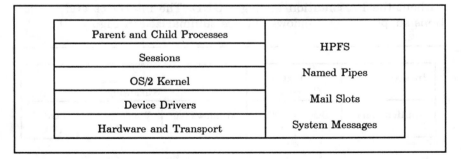

Figure 10.2 OS/2 2.0 layered architecture

The memory protection increases system reliability to the point where many users never have to reboot. If a program crashes, it can be restarted without impacting the rest of the system. It is virtually impossible for the behavior of one application program to impact the performance of another.

The OS/2 High Performance File System (HPFS) reads, writes, and caches intelligently and uses contiguous sector allocation to reduce head movement. This means that HPFS knows whether data is on disk—and must be retrieved—or already in RAM. This speeds up the read/write process.

Where OS/2 2.0 is headed is hard to predict. Apple (through Taligent) is working on Pink, an object-oriented operating system it will share with IBM. Little is known about this system, except that it is due around 1994 and robust enough for IBM to have publicly stated that OS/2 2.0 is merely transitional.

Amid speculation that OS/2 3.0 would be based on the Windows NT kernel, IBM announced that the Mach kernel is likely to be the foundation of the next generation multiprocessor OS/2.

10.2 Windows New Technology

Microsoft's Windows New Technology (Windows NT) is based on the Mach variation of the UNIX kernel. The microkernel architecture ensures its compatibility with applications not written specifically for Windows NT or future supported operating systems. (Since Windows NT is in beta test and therefore does exist, we will refer to it in the present tense and assume that Microsoft's capability claims are true.)

The Windows NT Executive kernel provides basic operating system functions and supports additional subsystems layered above it. In its initial release, Windows NT supports five subsystems: 32-bit Windows, 16-bit Windows, DOS, POSIX, and OS/2 (but only in character-mode, without the Presentation Manager GUI). The interfaces and applications supported by Windows NT are summarized in Figure 10.3.

Interfaces	Text Characters		Windows 3.1 Windowing		
Applications	DOS 16-bit	OS/2 16-bit	Windows 3.0 16-bit	Windows 3.1 32-bit	POSIX

Figure 10.3 Windows NT supported interfaces and applications

Windows NT can be used on a client and on a server in networked environments and can perform redirecting services for LAN Manager, NetWare, and LAN Server. Windows NT runs on the Intel 386 and 486, the Mips R3000, and R4000 RISC and the Digital Alpha chips.

Windows NT supports multiprocessor systems. Each application thread—even the Windows NT kernel itself—can run on any processor in a multiprocessor box. IBM has announced plans to introduce multiprocessing capabilities into OS/2 in the future, but as yet with no specific time frame.

As true 32-bit operating systems, both OS/2 and Windows NT overcome the unidentified application errors often encountered in Windows-based applications by taking advantage of the protected-mode architecture of 80386 and 80486 microprocessors. Under a 32-bit addressing scheme, each application is limited to a predefined section of memory with a separate address space and cannot move outside of that space.

Multithreading supports multiple threads of execution, which can operate simultaneously to complete a task. Windows NT desynchronizes the user interface so that a locked-up application cannot in turn lock up the system, even if it has not been optimized for Windows NT. The OS/2 user interface, on the other hand, is synchronous. As a result, an application can freeze out user input unless the application has been written to support threading.

Windows NT incorporates several fault-tolerant features to further enhance stability. These include a built-in, fully-recoverable file system, which incorporates features such as disk mirroring, duplexing, and striping to minimize file damage from power outages and hardware failures. In addition, Windows NT includes exception handling routines to catch program anomalies and impose strict quotas on each process in order to protect system resources. At present, OS/2 does not have comparable fault-tolerant features.

OS/2 and Windows NT will run each other's 16-bit applications but it is expected that, at least initially, neither Windows NT nor OS/2 2.0 will run 32-bit applications written for the other operating system.

Microsoft's intention to port Windows NT to 64-bit RISC processors provides organizations with many options. The RISC processors offer the additional capacity required for applications that combine workflow and imaging, such as insurance claims processing, and that require simultaneous communications sessions for large-scale data transfers, such as airline reservations. OS/2 also supports simultaneous communications sessions but, since it is written largely in Assembler, porting it to RISC technology requires rewriting the code to each new platform's specifications. This may have been a motivating factor for IBM's decision to use the Mach kernel in future versions of OS/2.

In addition, since Windows NT runs on a variety of platforms, an application running on the 64-bit server at corporate headquarters could be scaled down to run on a laptop in the field.

Windows NT also includes features for network administration. The Windows NT Configuration Registry lets network administrators configure and monitor networks via the Windows Control Panel.

In addition to DOS's File Allocation Tables (FAT) and the OS/2 HPFS file systems, Windows NT includes a new file system called NT File System (NTFS), which is a recoverable transaction-based system that retains a log of every change to the disk. This can be used to reconstruct a disk in seconds if system failure occurs. NTFS also supports striping, which spreads data across multiple disks to improve performance, and spanning, which lets one large file cover multiple disks.

Because Windows NT offers plug-in support for any number of API subsystems or installable file systems, it can be extended to include other operating environments which, when installed, become a part of Windows NT. Theoretically, Microsoft only has to write an API to add support for other operating systems, such as the Macintosh.

In contrast, OS/2 2.0 can host multiple DOS, Windows, and OS/2 applications simultaneously because it was designed to support those particular operating systems. To add support for other operating systems (adding APIs) would require a major rewrite of the operating system.

Both Windows NT and OS/2 provide methods for networking disparate systems along with support for distributed processing. OS/2 currently relies on third-party solutions such as Microsoft's LAN Manager and Novell's NetWare, which provide LAN-based access to SAA (Systems Application Architecture) through the OS/2 Communications Manager and Database Manager.

Windows NT incorporates basic networking services and APIs for file and print management, messaging, and security directly into the operating system. In addition, Windows NT supports local protocols, such as Novell's IPX/SPX, and enterprise transports, such as TCP/IP, DECnet, OSI, AppleTalk, and Banyan's VINES. OS/2 support for these transports has to come through third parties.

Both Windows NT and OS/2 support IBM's Advanced Peer-to-Peer Networking and Digital's Network Application Support, which enable distributed applications to operate in multiplatform environments. Both operating systems also supply facilities for the OSF's DCE-compliant RPCs, which expedite calls for distributed processing.

To facilitate application porting, Windows NT isolates the Executive kernel from system hardware through its Hardware Abstraction Layer, which acts as an interface between the operating system and the specific hardware on which it runs, making Windows NT applications portable at the source code level.

Windows NT also provides National Computer Security Center C2-level security features—the operating system is secure on both file and thread levels. Access can be restricted to resources and objects alike. Through the use of domain names, an enterprise-wide network can be constructed to allow access to components on a group or individual basis. IBM has also committed to C2-level security for OS/2, but has not announced a release date.

When Windows NT ships, Microsoft intends to introduce a version of LAN Manager for NT, which will include directory-like functions, multiple domain services for the enterprise, advanced administration and security tools, support for NetView alert services, and other advanced enterprise networking services. IBM also plans to support NetView through its System Network Architecture.

Many of the LAN Manager for Windows NT features will be integrated into Windows NT as the operating system. This integration will simplify network management and performance tuning. The tight coupling of networking services with the core operating system should enhance stability and robustness and improve network performance.

Companies will be able to buy one copy of Windows NT and attach an unlimited number of DOS, Windows 3.x, and Apple Macintosh computers using redirectors that Microsoft will provide. Support for attaching Windows NT clients for existing NetWare and Banyan networks will also be available when Windows NT ships.

Microsoft has announced that, after the release of Windows NT, it plans to implement most of the functionality of Windows NT into MS-DOS and Windows for MS-DOS to complete the client side of the equation. Microsoft has also committed to releasing a subsystem for Windows NT shortly after its initial release, which would allow it to run OS/2 Presentation Manager applications.

There are, however, three points to keep in mind. The scheduled release date for Windows NT has already been delayed from late 1992 to mid-1993 and the product isn't expected to be on the shelves until six months after its release. Secondly, there is only Microsoft's word (no pun intended) concerning all the fantastic features Windows NT will include—OS/2 is here today.

The last point is that if Windows NT does live up to its promises, it will afford more opportunities for multiplatform growth than OS/2, which perpetuates a closed shop. Because it supports portability and openness, Windows NT should be able to support future hardware, particularly RISC-based processors and multiprocessors.

10.3 UNIX-Based Operating Systems

In the 1970s, when the company was rewriting UNIX in C at Bell Laboratories, AT&T was forbidden by law from competing in the computer business. Having no commercial interest in UNIX, the company licensed it liberally, first to educational institutions and then to commercial computer vendors. Over the years, third parties have made substantial revisions to the code received from AT&T for a variety of reasons, which include:

- To add lacking functionality
- To adapt the software to new hardware and new technologies
- To improve on the supplied code
- To add proprietary features

By the early 1980s, a multitude of UNIX versions existed, all of which were incompatible to some degree. Constrained from competing in the computer industry and having little to gain or lose from the situation, AT&T took no action. However, once AT&T was freed from its legal bonds, the company quickly recognized there would be a significant business opportunity in making UNIX an industry standard, and that the existing fragmentation would have to end if UNIX was to emerge as a standard.

10.3.1 UNIX System V Release 4

In 1988, UNIX System Laboratories (USL), then a division of AT&T and now a susidiary of Novell, recruited Sun Microsystems as its development partner. Sun, whose UNIX operating system is based on a Berkeley Software Distribution version, was to work with USL in merging Berkeley and UNIX System V, using Sun's SPARC as the reference platform. The new version was refered to as UNIX System V Release 4 (SVR4). AT&T, in turn, made an equity investment in Sun.

There were a number of other vendors, including IBM, Digital, Hewlett-Packard, Siemens, Bull, and Hitachi, that were uncomfortable with the idea of Sun, their biggest UNIX competitor, playing such a central role in the development of SVR4. Another concern was the requirement that UNIX licensees would, as a condition of their license, have to certify that their products would pass the System V Verification Suite, meaning that licensees had to follow USL's lead in UNIX development. This prompted the formation of the Open Software Foundation and the vision of a single unified version of UNIX was lost, for the time being.

USL's plan was to merge the major UNIX variants into a single release, SVR4, with three major components:

- A superset of its most popular version, System V Release 3.2
- The best technology from Sun Microsystems' SunOS (including selected facilities from the Berkeley version of UNIX)
- Integration with Microsoft's XENIX, a 16-bit version of UNIX for micros

The potential for SVR4 is obvious. A single version of UNIX would incorporate the best technology from the most popular versions of UNIX and offer compatibility, portability, and interoperability. It was just what the market needed to implement open systems.

To support the old versions of UNIX while migrating to the new, SVR4 was restructured to allow new components to be added while maintaining older facilities. This maintained compatibility for applications written for earlier versions of UNIX System V, SunOS, and XENIX. Improved modularity would also make it easier for other vendors to create device drivers to match the hardware components of their systems.

SVR4 is divided into three distinct components. Figure 10.4 shows how these are organized in layers. The layered approach allows licensees and third parties to add value on top of the operating system in a variety of ways, from the inclusion of different file systems to the use of different user interfaces.

The kernel schedules processes and controls their execution, manages memory, and handles I/O. It also provides access to system resources via a set of system calls. Ultimately, it is these system calls that define SVR4.

On top of the kernel are the C language libraries which provide access to the system calls and, in addition, contain a number of

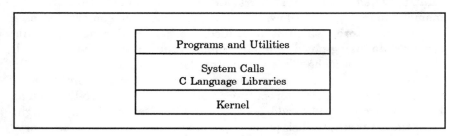

Figure 10.4 Components of UNIX System V Release 4

frequently required services such as string manipulation routines. However, the raw system call interface is not very programmer friendly.

On top of the interface provided by the system calls and the C libraries are the programs and utilities which have made UNIX a rich environment for software developers. Unlike most other operating systems, these shells have no special privileges and are in fact just ordinary programs.

There are three shells in popular use. The Bourne shell has a syntax not dissimilar to Algol-60. The C shell, the oldest of the three, has a syntax like C. The Korn shell incorporates the best features of the Bourne shell and the C shell.

To move quickly in this competitive environment, USL brought in partners to accelerate the implementation of new functionality. Security extensions have been implemented in conjunction with Amdahl and Motorola. USL licensed software from Veritas to add disk-mirroring and fault tolerance to SVR4. Sequent, which has experience implementing multiprocessing UNIX system kernels, has been working closely with USL developers in that area. By using these developments in various combinations, USL has released a robust set of operating system options and has accomplished the XENIX-Berkeley-SunOS-System V merger.

SVR4 is a much better operating system than its predecessors. Function and design issues have been addressed both in the base operating system and in additional SVR4 versions that support multiprocessing and enhanced security. These issues include the modularity of the kernel, the functionality and organization of the file system, and other capabilities lacking in other versions of UNIX System V.

Some of SVR4 improvements are included as kernel components, such as the shells and commands, handling of virtual memory, file systems, basic communication and networking, and administration.

SVR4 has borrowed the virtual memory management system from SunOS, which includes support for memory-mapped files. SVR4's memory mapping also allows physical memory to be constructed as a single-level store, which is a unified mechanism for accessing file system data, using physical memory more economically by treating all user memory as cache. This eliminates the use of buffer cache for file I/O, reducing overhead and making operations more efficient.

In contrast, programs executing in other versions of UNIX, such as Berkeley, are mapped to address space and then automatically brought from the system into disk page by page, requiring repeated, memory-intensive I/O calls. Traditionally, it has been difficult to fine tune the use of memory because of the split between memory used for I/O and memory used for programs.

Shared memory is enhanced by dynamic linking, which provides flexibility at runtime and in the program development cycles—compile, debug, and recompile. Dynamic linking is especially important for low-end systems because it allows users to automatically shift pages in and out of memory. It also plays a critical role in implementing object-oriented concepts, where objects need to have a dynamic linking mechanism at runtime.

The file system has always been a key weakness of the UNIX operating system. The native UNIX System V file system was not modular and treated all files equally. A long-standing irritation has been the difficulty involved in changing file system size. To change the size of a local volume, the user had to dump the files to tape and rebuild them. These problems have all been addressed in SVR4.

Because USL has to contend with the past as well as look to the future, a Virtual File System (VFS) is offered, allowing users to switch between file system options. As users move to more advanced file systems such as the DCE's Andrew File System, they have an easier migration with VFS, which is a merger of the traditional UNIX System V File System Switch and the SunOS VFS mechanism.

Important improvements to UNIX System V are in the area of file system reliability. SVR4 now handles bad blocks dynamically and by including a deferred-write scheme for modified files. In the initial design, SVR4 included a write-through option but not disk mirroring. The Veritas technology adds a disk-mirroring option. However, rollback and recovery features are not yet included.

Another significant improvement is in the area of file locking. The key enhancements include advisory and mandatory file and record locking, synchronous write mode, and XENIX file- and record-locking compatibility. However, as SVR4 moves ahead into areas such as multiprocessing and parallel processing, even more granular locking will be required.

STREAMS is a framework for character I/O that allows standard interfaces to be placed within it, making an interface between each device driver and the kernel unnecessary. The most important benefit for distributed computing is that STREAMS hides the network protocol and media and enables a program to link to resources across the network transparently. An application's use of the X.25 protocol or TCP/IP is hidden from the developer since either can be run over any STREAM.

Since its introduction as part of UNIX System Release 3, STREAMS has been a major improvement over traditional UNIX I/O mechanisms.

Prior to the development of STREAMS, new kernel software had to be written any time a new device driver was developed in order to interface to that device—in effect, rebuilding the UNIX kernel.

Another important facility in SVR4 is Transport Level Interface (TLI), which provides for protocol and media independence. Any network conforming to the Transport Provider Interface specification can be accessed by a program using TLI.

USL is developing a desktop version of its SVR4, called Destiny, which will feature a GUI environment and desktop metaphor allowing users to manipulate icons to create customized environments. Destiny will support the OpenLook and Motif GUIs and XENIX (from Microsoft) and SCO UNIX (from Santa Cruz Operation Inc.) operating systems. USL is also working on an object-based distributed system management framework that will be compliant with OSF's DME.

While all this work was progressing on SVR4, OSF was developing its own version of a better UNIX. OSF/1 offers many of the features of SVR4. USL has stated that it will support DCE within SVR4. OSF has indicated that it will modify OSF/1 to work with SVR4 and base its software extensions on SVR4 rather than its own OSF/1. The better-UNIX war has come to an end. Facilities such as DCE make the differences among core operating systems less important.

10.3.2 Solaris 2.0

Solaris 2.0 from SunSoft provides a graphical interface, responsive performance from a multithread design, and enhanced productivity from integrated end-user tools for SPARC-based workstations.

As illustrated in Figure 10.5, Solaris comes bundled with SunOS 5.0, OpenWindows 3.0, DeskSet 3.0, ONC ToolTalk, and OpenLook. A mid-1993 release is planned for Solaris for Intel architectures.

The OpenWindows GUI is built around three windowing systems:

■ SunWindows
■ X Window System

DeskSet 3.0	ONC ToolTalk
OpenWindows 3.0	OpenLook
SunOS 5.0	

Figure 10.5 Components of Solaris from SunSoft

■ Network Extensible Window System

These choices give developers the freedom to create new software without outdating older software. Solaris includes object-oriented toolkits to create applications designed to support OpenLook.

Point-and-click and drag-and-drop are the basic techniques of OpenWindows, which can be customized so that certain tools appear automatically. The environment provides great flexibility in both screen appearance and behavior. For instance, you can arrange to activate a window by clicking on one or by merely moving the cursor into it.

DeskSet, a unifying desktop manager, includes applications to enhance productivity. Some of the most useful are the Calendar Manager, File Manager, and Print Tool. Two other built-in applications are electronic mail and network file management. Solaris's new mail system, Multimedia Mail, enables users to attach graphics, sound, and video to their E-mail documents.

Unlike most GUIs, OpenWindows and DeskSet are designed to exploit the resources of a network—not just the power of a single system. Users may never know that the DeskSet applications they're working with may actually be running on systems scattered across a building.

SunOS 5.0, a 32-bit operating system, runs both on SPARCstations and 80x86 systems, supports SVR4, and adds multiprocessing and multithreading support.

Solaris 2.0 strong points include its networking capacities—SunSoft invented the Network File System. The first step in this direction is Sun's Distributed Objects Everywhere (DOE), which is built around SunSoft's ToolTalk, which, in turn, is built upon SunSoft's Distributed Object Management Facility.

ToolTalk is SunSoft's network-capable mechanism for exchanging services between applications. Rather than requiring one application to request services specifically from another, ToolTalk lets an application receive servicing messages by registering its message pattern with the ToolTalk server. Many different applications may receive a single message, though only one will respond. To users, the details of ToolTalk are invisible—they see a convenient drag-and-drop interface.

Although ToolTalk itself is not object-based, it does support transparent data exchange, including objects. As a result, in its first iteration, DOE will be a step towards true application interoperability where programs and data can work together across the network. The final steps will come in later versions of Solaris.

Solaris meets varying enterprise computing needs with a modular kernel, through which systems can be dynamically configured to provide only the services required for an application. This minimizes memory demands without the excessive message handling that occurs in some "micro kernel" designs.

Non-desktop environments often require real-time performance, which has not been a traditional asset of UNIX-based operating systems. Solaris 2.0 has addressed this area with a multithreaded, symmetric multiprocessing kernel in the system's foundation layer, Solaris SunOS 5.0. This lets even low-level functions distribute themselves across multiple processors.

Mechanisms, such as priority inheritance, speed the completion of a low-priority process to free resources for use by a high-priority task. This design also provides preemptive task scheduling within the operating-system kernel, permitting prompt handling of new high-priority tasks.

Applications can move between SPARCstations and 80x86 platforms with only a recompilation, permitting common code development for the highest-volume processor lines in RISC and CISC architectures.

Interactive UNIX from SunSoft is a 32-bit operating system for 386 and 486 computers and is based on UNIX System V Release 3.2. The product offers multitasking and multiuser support and can run UNIX and XENIX applications and most DOS applications. Its windows technology offers pop-up menus with context-sensitive hypertext help. The product is available in a number of bundling options: a stand-alone single operating system with a windowing system or as a software developer kit. The product offers a migration path to Solaris 2.0.

10.3.3 Other Variants

AIX

IBM's AIX (Advanced Interactive Executive) runs on IBM's RS/6000 POWER architecture and represents a collection of interfaces, conventions, and protocols that include UNIX, industry standards, and IBM extensions, all supported across a range of IBM computer environments. AIX with the RS/6000 creates a powerful UNIX system which, with its promise of compatibility and interoperability, should expand the role of UNIX workstations to include many traditional business environments.

To compete with USL's Destiny, IBM has announced that it will divide AIX into client and server versions that will share as much of the AIX infrastructure as possible.

A/UX

Apple's A/UX 3.0 UNIX operating system for the Macintosh includes many powerful new features, such as X Window support and System 7 compatibility. It offers a multiuser, multitasking environment with reliable, secure file sharing. Powerful shell scripting languages are included. A/UX provides transparent access to the Macintosh operating system and the wealth of applications available for the Macintosh. A/UX 3.0 includes better support for Apple and third-party peripherals, a working UNIX-to-UNIX Copy Program and bundled versions of MacX and the X Window System. Macintosh applications must be completely 32-bit compliant to run under A/UX, but most up-to-date programs work seamlessly. Integration between the Macintosh and UNIX takes place in the background and is largely transparent. A/UX 3.0 is a full-fledged UNIX implementation, allowing A/UX 3.0 users to run POSIX applications and System 7-compatible programs simultaneously. The product supports other standard windowing systems including Motif and X Window.

PowerOpen

PowerOpen, the joint Apple and IBM operating system, is based on IBM's AIX and Apple's A/UX and built around the OSF/1 kernel. The aim of PowerOpen is to make Macintosh productivity applications and AIX technical applications accessible to clients.

IBM/Apple Pink

The Pink operating system being jointly developed by IBM and Apple may prove influential in the mid-1990s. It currently appears that Pink's object-oriented environment might be running on top of PowerOpen.

ACE Efforts

Microsoft, Digital, Santa Cruz Operations (SCO) and their compatriots in the Advanced Computer Environment (ACE) are working on a UNIX backbone to their multipronged operating system plans. If the alliance lasts, 1994 might see an operating system with a Windows-like front-end and a UNIX-like back-end.

Server Requirements

Pioneers in server technology maintain that server database software is the critical piece of software in the client/server environment. It handles all the data management (storage, retrieval, updating, and deletion) and should support online transaction processing, referential integrity, and recovery procedures.

It is important to understand the characteristics of an OLTP environment. These include:

- Many users
- Many relatively short interactions
- Large shared databases

To maintain vendor independence and provide a flexible migration path for future decisions regarding data sources, it is better to provide such functionality at a higher level than database management software and, ideally, independent of the database vendor. Currently, products that provide this level of middleware include Ellipse from Cooperative Solutions, Encina from Transarc, Tuxedo from AT&T, and TOP END from NCR.

11.1 Platform Independence

Platform independence (hardware and software) is a major benefit of client/server computing. Upgrading hardware should be almost as simple as backing up the data and restoring it on a more powerful machine (micro, midrange, or mainframe) running the same server database software. The same should be true for downward migration.

Software should be compatible between platforms. Data, programs, and front-end software should need only system-related modifications.

11.2 Transaction Processing

Transaction processing forces additional requirements on the server database software. Transactions are generated at the client and sent to the server for processing. Very often these transactions affect two or more data tables that could reside on different machines. When the system crashes (and it will!), the server database software must be able to roll back the transactions that were in process (and therefore not committed) and roll forward those transactions that were committed before the crash but not reflected in the last backup of the database.

A transaction is one or more operations that are performed together to complete a task. A postal address change is a simple transaction. A slightly more complex transaction is a banking transaction that debits one account and credits another.

For a transaction to be considered successful, ALL operations must be performed. If ANY operation of a transaction cannot be completed, the operations that have taken effect must be undone, a process called *commit and rollback*. While executing the steps of a transaction, the system keeps a log of the work, including before and after images of the data. When the transaction is successfully completed, the system commits all the changes permanently. If the transaction is not successfully completed, the system uses the log to restore (rollback) the database to its state prior to execution. This function is mandatory for transaction processing systems to keep the database in a consistent state between transactions.

Commit and rollback facilities are aimed at recovering from data errors or software malfunctions. Safeguards for hardware malfunctions, such as power outages or hardware failure, should also be considered. Some typical safeguards are an uninterruptible power supply and disk mirroring, which copies data to separate disks so if one disk fails the other can be accessed.

In distributed transaction processing, transactions have the following traits (known as the ACID test):

- **Atomicity**. The entire transaction must be either completed or aborted. It cannot be partially completed.

- **Consistency.** The system and its resources go from one steady state to another.
- **Isolation.** The effect of a transaction is not evident to other transactions until the transaction is committed. But any data that a transaction in progress needs is locked to prevent other transactions from changing it.
- **Durability.** The effects of a transaction are permanent and should not be affected by system failures.

To understand the process, consider a banking transaction. A customer transfers $500 from a savings account to a checking account. The transaction has two operations: debit the savings account $500 and credit the checking account $500. For this transaction to be complete, both operations MUST occur. If the debit is handled first and the credit doesn't occur, the savings account will reflect the $500 withdrawal but the checking account will not reflect the deposit. The table for this transaction may be on the same server or different ones.

11.2.1 Two-Phase Commits

A two-phase commit ensures data consistency and completeness for transaction processing when a transaction uses more than one table. The client application designates one server as the commit server (the record keeper) to decide to commit or roll back a transaction.

The two-phase commit process is illustrated in Figure 11.1. In the first phase, each server involved in the update process performs its portion of the transaction and informs the commit server that it is ready to commit its work. In the second phase, the commit server broadcasts a commit message to the other servers and records the transaction. Once this happens, the transaction is committed regardless of subsequent failures. If any server fails during the second phase, the commit server cancels the entire transaction and instructs the participating servers to roll back their work.

IBM's Customer Information Control System (CICS) is an example of a mainframe-based transaction processing monitor that supports distributed transaction processing. Using a master/slave tree approach, the initial request starts the front-end transaction (the master of the tree), which initiates a communications session, and specifies the remote system and then initiates a back-end transaction.

The front-end transaction allocates a conversation with another remote transaction (its slave), which then initiates its slave, and so on. The tree master coordinates the following tasks:

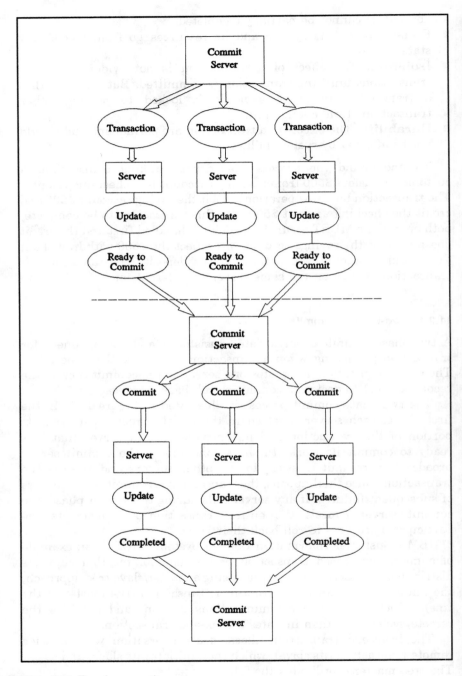

Figure 11.1 Two-phase commit

- Identifies all participants involved in the transaction
- Sends prepare-to-commit (PTC) requests to all participants
- Ensures that all participants acknowledge the PTC request
- Logs the fact that all participants are prepared
- Sends the commit request to all participants
- Ensures that all participants acknowledge the commit request
- Logs the fact that all participants have committed

If any participant does not commit, the master sends an abend to every other transaction in the tree and all transactions are backed out.

Some vendors of the new middleware products are building two-phase commit capabilities into their software. Products, such as Ellipse from Cooperative Solutions and Encina from Transarc, internally handle the integrity of transactions. This important feature allows the software to handle transactions that span multiple data sources as well as multiple machines.

Products such as Encina and TOP END are also including local two-phase commit procedures for transactions that are executing in multiple tables on a single node. Novell's NetWare 3.11 has a similar feature called Transaction Tracking System that handles transactions affecting a single database.

11.2.2 Locking Schemes

Transaction processing applications also require the use of locking schemes to ensure that the database record a user is accessing is protected while in use. When a transaction locks a record, that record can not be updated until the lock is released.

Data transmissions handle data in blocks. To allow a client to update the transmitted data, the server must prevent an update by another application after sending the data to the client. To maintain this concurrency control, the server locks the result data.

Figure 11.2 summarizes the locking rules used by most DBMS

	Current Lock		
Asking for	Unlocked	Shared Lock	Exclusive Lock
Unlocked	OK	OK	OK
Shared Lock	OK	OK	NO
Exclusive Lock	OK	NO	NO

Figure 11.2 Locking rules

products. A shared lock allows more than one transaction to read the same data. An exclusive lock is granted when a transaction wants to update data. When an exclusive lock has been granted, other transactions cannot obtain any type of lock on the data and, therefore, cannot access the data at all. An exclusive lock can be obtained by a transaction only if no other transaction currently has a lock on the data.

If blocking is used, the block can be entirely locked (all rows/records) or the block can be locked one row at a time as data are fetched by the client application. If blocking is not used, a row could be locked as it was sent across the network. Data would be transmitted one row at a time.

Another alternative is to use optimistic concurrency control. This method, based on the premise that records are usually only updated by one application at a time, checks for update collisions at commit time. If the record has been read by other applications, they are notified of the impending update.

11.2.3 Transaction Logs

These files are used when a database needs to be restored after a failure, such as a system crash.

A well-designed transaction processing environment should include a history log that records committed transactions. The loss from a brief power outage can be restored using the transaction log and a simple redo procedure.

To recover from a hardware failure, transactions must be re-created from an archive so that the database can roll forward. Some DBMSs, such as SYBASE SQL Server and ORACLE Release 7, provide such functionality. If failure recovery is not built into the DBMS, it must be coded into the application. CSTP applications development products, such as Ellipse from Cooperative Solutions, include this functionality as part of the generated application code.

11.3 Connectivity

Server software must provide access to a variety of data sources and not be restricted to vendor-supplied sources. The software gateways discussed in Chapter 12, Server Data Management and Access Tools, provide such links. This connectivity is in part due to vendors' "opening" up access to their data structures via APIs.

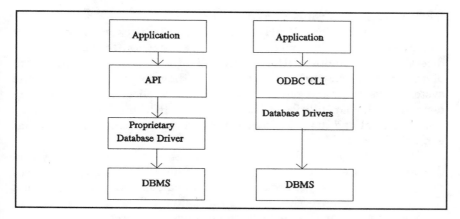

Figure 11.3 Comparison of Microsoft's ODBC and proprietary database access

Database gateways provide access to external databases. Most database gateways use SQL as the access language. With a simple pass-through database gateway, the vendor provides software only on the requestor side. The SQL request has to be acceptable to the target database. Intelligent database gateways have software on both the sending and receiving nodes. This allows the software to optimize the query and supports portability but does not allow the use of any special features that might be in the SQL of the target database. Database gateways are discussed in Section 12.3.

Microsoft's Open Database Connectivity (ODBC) API permits applications to communicate with relational and non-relational data sources. ODBC, compared to proprietary DBMS access in Figure 11.3, is based on the call-level interface (CLI) developed by the SQL Access Group. ODBC drivers allow developers to write Windows-based applications that transparently access the data sources supported by the drivers. Announced ODBC drivers include links to SQL Server, ORACLE, and EDA/SQL from Information Builders, Inc.

11.3.1 Remote Procedure Calls

Designing client/server applications is fundamentally different than building traditional mainframe or macro-based micro applications. Programmers should be isolated from network intricacies and given easy access to network functions. Remote procedure calls (RPCs) and message queuing systems provide this service. RPCs are currently more widely used than message queuing systems. A simplified version of how

RPCs work is illustrated in Figure 11.4.

RPCs, which are APIs layered on top of a network interprocess communication (IPC) mechanism, allow servers to communicate directly with each other. They allow individual processing components of an application to run on other nodes in the network. Distributed file systems, system management, security, and application programming depend on the capabilities of the underlying RPC mechanisms. Server access control and the use of a directory service are common needs that can be met with RPCs.

RPCs also manage the network interface and handle security and directory services. The paradigm of using high-level languages to call procedures is not new. A remote procedure call should look and act just like a local procedure call to the programmer. The idea is to spread work and data over the network to optimize resources.

Although RPC implementations are roughly the same, RPCs from different vendors are usually not compatible.

RPC tools usually include:

- A language and a compiler that can be used to produce portable source code.
- A run-time facility that makes the system architecture and network protocols transparent to the application procedures.

SunSoft's general-purpose Transport-Independent Remote Procedure Call (TI-RPC) toolkit is based on source-code generation technology from Netwise Inc. The software allows software developers to create a single version of a client/server application that will run unmodified across a range of operating systems, hardware bases and networks such as TCP/IP, OSI, and NetWare's IPX/SPX.

Netwise, Inc., which sells only RPC software, offers RPC Tool, a

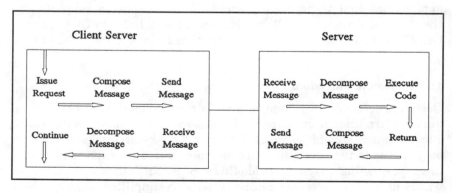

Figure 11.4 How remote procedure calls work

favorite among microcomputer and LAN suppliers. RPC Tool supports a large number of operating systems and network protocols, including Apple's Appletalk, DECnet, LU6.2, NetBIOS, Novell's NetWare, and TCP/IP.

RPCs have one major limitation. They typically require synchronous connections. If an application uses an RPC to link to a server that is inoperable or busy, the application will wait for the data rather than moving to other tasks.

11.4 Intelligent Database

Client/server applications demand more than just management of data—more than data storage, data integrity, some degree of security, and recovery and backup procedures. Client/server applications require that some of the application logic be stored with the data in the database. The logic can be stored as an integrity check, a trigger, or a stored procedure. By defining the logic in the database, it is written once and used when the "protected" data is accessed.

Most server-stored logic is vendor-dependent. The stored logic will execute only with the server database software. Some client/server application development products that are not tied to server database software allow developers to compile and store vendor-neutral logic. One such product is Ellipse from Cooperative Solutions. The logic is written in ANSI SQL and controlled by the Ellipse software. If the application moves to new server database software, the logic will still execute against the new software.

The server database software should handle referential integrity, which ensures that related data in different tables is consistent. If a *parent* row is deleted (for example, a customer), the rows related to that parent row in the *children* tables (for example, accounts such as savings, checking, and loans) should also be deleted. This centralizes the control of data integrity, ensures that the rules are followed no matter what node accessed the data and frees the developers from having to code integrity rules into the front-end programs.

Business rules should be enforceable centrally, as well. Rules can validate data or may be associated with data. The rule might use a range check or require a match against a particular pattern or against an entry in a specific list. Rules are associated with a particular column, to a number of columns or all columns of a particular data type. A special type of check is called a constraint—a passive check that only returns error messages. A constraint might be, *If a customer's title is "Mr." then the sex must be M*.

In addition, there may be procedural logic associated with the data and allocated to the server, rather than the client, for execution. This might be done for reasons of load balancing or speed.

11.5 Stored Procedures

Stored procedures are a collection of SQL statements that are compiled and stored on the server database. When an SQL command is sent to the server database, the server parses the command, checks the syntax and names used, checks the protection levels, and then generates an execution plan for the query. The comparison to interactive queries is illustrated in Figure 11.5.

Stored procedures allow developers to code queries and other groups of statements into stored procedures, compile them, store them on the server, and invoke them directly from applications. The stored procedures are parsed and checked for syntax the first time the procedure is called. The compiled version is stored in cache memory. Subsequent calls to the procedure use the compiled version in cache.

Since they are stored as compiled code, stored procedures execute quickly. They are automatically re-compiled when changes are made to the objects they affect. Since stored procedures accept parameters, they can be used by multiple applications with a variety of data. Stored procedures can be nested and remote calls can be made to procedures on other systems.

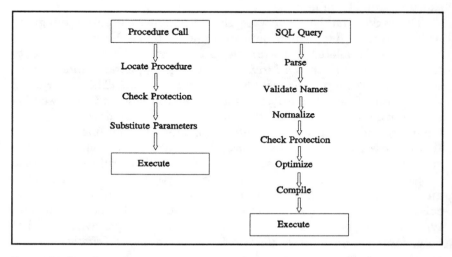

Figure 11.5 Stored procedures compared to interactive queries

Stored procedures can also be used to enforce business rules and data integrity. In the case of the banking transaction, the logic for the debit and the credit as well as a validity check to ensure that the debited account had enough funds to cover the transfer could be coded into a stored procedure called *transfer-amt*. This procedure could be used by any transaction that transferred money between accounts. The parameters used when the procedure was invoked would specify which accounts.

To comply with federal reporting requirements, this procedure could be modified to include an operation that recorded all transfers over $10,000 in a special table. The change would have to be made to the specific stored procedure only. Subsequently, any transfers made using the procedure would be checked against the $10,000 limit and recorded, if necessary.

11.6 Triggers

Triggers are special stored procedures that are automatically invoked by server database software. Stored procedures are explicitly called; triggers, which are associated with particular tables, are executed when attempts are made to modify data in those tables. Triggers and rules are both associated with particular tables, but rules can perform only simple checks on the data. Triggers can perform complex checks on the data since they can use the full power of SQL.

Triggers can be used to enforce referential integrity. In the banking example, a *delete-customer* trigger could be written to check all the open account tables for the customer number and refuse to process the delete request if any exist. The *delete-customer* trigger would be fired when a request to delete a customer from the customer table was received.

Triggers can also be used to cascade a change through related tables in a database. If a customer number is changed, all references to that customer number must also be changed. A trigger could be written to fire whenever the customer number was changed in the customer table. This trigger would check all the open account tables for the customer number and change them all to the new number.

Depending on the RDBMS, a trigger can access other databases over a network via remote procedure calls. This allows a developer to implement a referential integrity check between two or more separate databases over a network.

Business rules can be enforced through the use of triggers as well. A trigger in an order entry system might refuse to accept a new order from a customer with an outstanding balance. A trigger in a banking system might refuse to increase any credit limits more than 20 percent.

Triggers can also be used to maintain summary data. Whenever an order is placed in an order entry system, a trigger could update a sales-to-date field.

11.7 Load Leveling

One early premise of client/server computing was that all application logic should be performed on the client machine. Original implementations of client/server computing followed that premise to the letter.

However, as the technology evolved and the impact of earlier practices was felt, the idea of splitting the application logic between the client and the server—if necessary—was adopted for two reasons:

- Maximize throughput and minimize network traffic
- Number-crunching speed of server MIPS

In most instances, developers have to decide where the split between client and server processing should be and code the application logic accordingly. For example, a process that involves data-intensive sorting or multitable joins, but does not require user intervention, could be done faster on the server. Developers must also decide which server will perform which function when two or more servers are involved and how the query should be partitioned.

However, this is not a flexible approach. It does not take into account changes in:

- The size of the data being processed
- The power of the client machine
- The power of the server machine
- Fluctuations in server resource availability
- Fluctuations in the network resources

In addition to logic partitioning, network traffic and server cycles can be conserved by placing some user functions on the client machine. Two such functions are refreshing (redrawing) a screen when a window is closed and selecting the screen that satisfies a menu choice. Neither should require a network call to the server.

Tools such as Ellipse from Cooperative Solutions dynamically reconfigure the split between client and server processing.

11.8 Optimizer

A robust data server software package should provide an optimizer, which analyzes a generated SQL statement and determines the most efficient way to process the request. Most optimizers available today are cost-based. They analyze the index distribution statistics and table sizes to determine the number of disk reads required, which determines the cost, and then uses the least expensive process.

A good optimizer will check to see if the necessary data is already in cache memory before deciding to use an index. It may also choose to ignore indexes if the selection criteria matches a large portion of the rows (one-third or more, for instance). By reviewing the distribution of values in the index, the optimizer can decide whether a complete table scan or a search of the index will result in fewer disk reads.

The optimizer is an important feature of the server database when the SQL queries are generated by the front-end software (instead of embedded in front-end code). SQL queries can be written in many different ways, for instance, the order of the columns in the WHERE clause or the order of the tables in a JOIN clause. An optimizer analyzes the query and uses statistics and histograms to determine the most efficient execution path.

Server database software should also be reviewed based on the amount of data it can realistically handle. The software should be able to grow with users' requests for additional data and applications (and request they will!). Gupta's SQLBase Server is a good entry-level server database to support small-to-mid-size (50 to 200 Mbytes) databases. SQL Server from Sybase is targeted for large databases (500 Mbytes and up). It is important to talk to personnel at other sites using databases equivalent in size to the projected size of the evaluation application. The success of the project rests primarily on the reliability and responsiveness of the server database.

11.9 Testing and Diagnostic Tools

One area that still needs attention from the server database software vendors consists of testing and diagnostic tools. Data and generated indexes can be corrupted by system errors (tables sharing disk space) or bad disk sectors. Utilities that can diagnose problems and recover from them are slow in coming, as are SQL debugging tools. Mainframe development environments offer powerful debugging tools with breakpoints and real-time values of variables and support embedding of debugging commands. These types of tools are desperately needed in client/server environments.

Sybase offers **SQL-Debug**, a source-level interactive debugger to aid developers in identifying and correcting logic and performance problems in Sybase's Transact-SQL code. It offers step-level execution, breakpoint setting, conditional tracing, and variable checking. Performance bottlenecks are identified by tracking critical SYBASE SQL Server performance statistics. The developer enters commands in one window, Transact-SQL code appears in a second window and SQL Server information appears in a third. Commands, which can operate on statements, batches, or variables visible in the SQL Code Window, can be activated from a pop-up menu or a button panel.

Sybase also offers **SQL-Advantage**, an SQL programming, code checking, and debugging environment supporting Transact-SQL and APT-SQL, both from Sybase. The SQL Edit component provides a choice of default editor, EMACS, VI, EVE/TPU, or Brief. Developers can highlight a portion of a query and submit it directly to the database. The error checking provided by SQL Code Checker can pinpoint the exact location of syntax or coding errors. SQL-Advantage is also available from within APT Workbench (the SYBASE 4GL application development environment) to test APT-SQL routines.

11.10 Reliability

As mission- and business-critical applications are being downsized to client/server platforms or developed on client/server platforms, the reliability of those platforms becomes an integral part of IS planning. Even if these systems seem micro-based, the micro philosophy of "if one goes down, we'll just run it from backups on another machine" does not hold true. This might hold true for the client machines, but certainly not for the server or the network. It is important that IS have alternatives in case a server goes down or the network crashes.

Some alternatives for servers are built-in fault-tolerant resources. These could include processors, power supplies, and disk drives with disk mirroring. For networks, these could include FDDI-based networks and redundant linking devices, such as routers and bridges.

11.11 Backup and Recovery Mechanisms

There are similarities between mainframes and LANs in the area of backup, recovery, and archiving. The problems for both environments are identical but the solutions change from tier to tier.

11.11.1 Tape-Based Backups

A tape backup system, illustrated in Figure 11.6, continues to be an excellent option for backup and recovery for a number of reasons. The most obvious is cost. To store a megabyte of data on tape costs one-tenth of a cent; on a hard disk, 20 cents; on optical disk, a dollar. Another is reliability. Data is less likely to be unreadable from tape than from hard disk. Lastly, tape backup systems are more advanced than simple tape dumps. Most products have menu-driven interfaces, support unattended backups, and offer options as to whether the entire hard disk, selected files, or combination of files should be backed up.

Tallgrass Technologies offers systems that support DOS, Novell 286 and 386, XENIX, Macintosh, and OS/2. Tallgrass offers the following products:

- **FileSecure OverNet** extends the reach of the network backup system to include every user disk on any node.
- **NetSecure** integrates with Novell's operating system.

Palindrome Corp. sells **Network Archivist**, a tape backup system for NetWare LANs. It can back up files on either user workstations or file servers. File information is stored in a RDBMS and after predefined periods, the Network Archivist automatically removes unused files.

Microsoft selected **Sytos Plus File Backup Manager** from Sytron Corp. as the backup and restore utility to be packaged with LAN Manager Version 2.0. It supports a universal file format for data

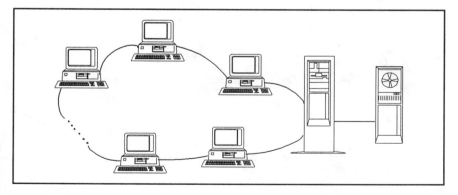

Figure 11.6 Tape backup system architecture

interchange across operating systems and storage devices, allowing tapes to be read on any drive, not just the vendor's drive on which it was created. The product supports quarter-inch tape, data cassette, 4mm Digital Audio Tape (DAT), and 8mm helical scan. Sytos Plus facilitates the backup and restore of network file and directory Access Control Lists, file permissions, and network system files.

11.11.2 Host-Based Backups

Another option is to send the LAN data over the network to a host, where the host system management products take over the storage management. This process is illustrated in Figure 11.7. This requires adequate bandwidth capabilities to support shipping large amounts of data. It centralizes the LAN data management issue with the other mainframe systems and removes the requirement for backup, restore, and archive procedures from the end users.

Organizations need backup devices that can support a heterogeneous network, but backup devices support a specific LAN and workstation operating system. Vendors have been slow in upgrading their backup system products to multiple platforms and in providing the ability to back up interconnected LANs from a central location.

The server database should support dynamic backups so the data can be backed up while the server is in use. This feature minimizes disruptions to the user community and makes it convenient to perform backups. When the backup request is received, the server software checks the transaction logs for any recently committed transactions and writes them to the database. The software proceeds with the backup at this point. The server software keeps a record of which sections of the

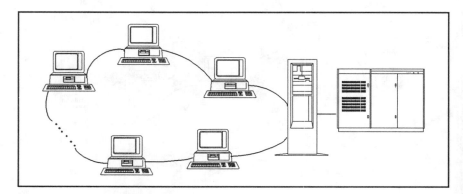

Figure 11.7 Host-based backup system architecture

database have been backed up. When modifications to the database are attempted, the server software can check to see if the affected areas have been backed up. If the area has been backed up, the modification can proceed. If the area has not been backed up, the server software reorders the backup sequence so that area is backed up next. Once the area is backed up, the transaction can be executed.

Backing up transaction logs is straightforward since transactions which are executing during the backup are added to the end of the log.

12

Server Data Management
and Access Tools

The key to a successful client/server environment is the ability to access data from any node in the network and from a variety of data sources. If the users cannot reach the data they need to be more productive, the fanciest GUI will not be enough to motivate them to use the system.

12.1 Data Manager Features

Server databases, a new class of software, reside on networked servers and are accessed by front-end tools on client machines. Ideally, server databases should provide the integrity, security, functionality, and robustness of mainframe database technology. Most provide some subset of mainframe database technology, and more features are added regularly.

12.1.1 Standard SQL Access

Structured Query Language (SQL) has become the standard language for data access in client/server applications. However, each vendor's implementation of SQL is slightly different. In order for applications to be portable, developers must be able to write SQL on one hardware/

software platform and port it without change (except system related modifications) to another hardware/software platform.

Structurally, SQL includes:

- **Data definition language**, which defines data structures and relationships
- **Data manipulation language**, which moves and updates data
- **Data control language**, which defines access and security constraints

SQL processes data in sets. This allows multiple records—and only those records that satisfy the request—to be transmitted to a client using a single call. When records are retrieved for update purposes, exclusive locks are used, resulting in possible contention for access and bottlenecks.

In addition, SQL can be used to create a results table that combines, filters, and transforms data before transmitting to the client. Only necessary rows and columns of data are sent over the network, resulting in considerable savings of data communication time and costs.

The assumption is made that most data for client/server applications is stored in relational data structures. The interface software on the client builds SQL queries that are sent to the server RDBMS. The server executes the query and returns the requested data to the client. Vendors of client/server tools are recognizing that some data needed for client/server applications resides in non-relational structures. Gateways to non-SQL databases and other data sources are now available. Whether SQL or gateways are used, the process should be transparent to the user; however, some tools are more transparent than others.

Server software must provide all of the data management services typically handled by mainframe systems, such as backup and recovery, roll forward/rollback mechanisms for transaction processing, and testing and diagnostic tools. In addition, the server software should be platform independent to facilitate machine upgrades.

SQL was initially intended to solve problems associated with database interoperability. Although vendors maintain their support of SQL-provided application portability, their proprietary extensions—intended to enhance SQL's functionality—have hindered database interoperability. In 1989, responding to the lagging efforts of ANSI's Remote Data Access subcommittee, several major RDBMS vendors (with the exception of IBM) formed the SQL Access Group. Their mission was to develop a more robust, interoperable SQL specification based upon ANSI's RDA standards. Instead of waiting for SQL2, expected in mid-1993, the SQL Access Group is basing its work on the 1989 SQL standard.

12.1.2 Distributed Database Architecture

Distributed data management, where data and the DBMS are dispersed among multiple systems, is often required in client/server applications. Organizations can spread enterprise data over multiple systems. Access across the network must be transparent to end users.

But data cannot be distributed without planning. There are some simple rules of thumb for distributing data:

- Every item of data should have a single point of update.
- Distributed updates should be kept to a minimum.
- Distributed data should be as close as possible to the processors that are likely to use it.
- Applications should use location-transparent code.

Some of these issues are being addressed by emerging industry standards such as ANSI SQL, X/Open's XA architecture and Remote Data Access from ISO. Most DBMS vendors are also involved in distributed data management and have developed their own solutions, most notably IBM.

IBM's Distributed Relational Database Architecture

Distributed Relational Database Architecture (DRDA) will provide access to distributed relational data in IBM operating environments—SAA and AIX—and in non-IBM environments that conform to DRDA. It provides the necessary connectivity between RDBMSs and can operate in homogeneous and heterogeneous system environments.

DRDA provides a common protocol that supports distributed data and client/server environments using the following IBM architectures:

- Distributed Data Management Architecture (DDM)
- Logical Unit Type 6.2 (APPC/LU6.2) Architecture
- SNA Management Services Architecture (MSA)
- Formatted Data Object Content Architecture (FD:OCA)
- Character Data Representation Architecture (CDRA)

Since it is limited to relational data, DRDA uses SQL as the common access language for defining logical connections between applications and RDBMSs. Subsets of data managed by an RDBMS can be connected separately from the entire database.

Currently, DRDA supports only remote units of work, which include remote requests and remote transaction types of distributed database processing. A remote request occurs when an application issues a single data request to be processed at a single remote site. A remote transaction allows a transaction to contain multiple data requests, but all the data must reside at a single remote location.

ISO's Remote Data Access

Remote Data Access (RDA) is the ISO protocol for multisite transaction processing. It is not an all-encompassing framework or architecture; it is a communications protocol optimized for heterogeneous data access. RDA fits into the OSI seven-layer model at the application layer and is viewed by some as an extension of OSI.

The RDA standard is divided into the Generic Model, which defines a common transfer syntax and a database access protocol, and specializations, which customize the Generic Model for use with specific data models or languages.

In the DRDA environment, an application is connected to one database at a time. Under ISO's RDA, an application can be connected to more than one database at a time. However, the RDA approach has not completely sorted out the problems related to updating multiple databases, such as failures during updating and coordinating recoveries.

DRDA and RDA are compared in Figure 12.1.

12.1.3 User Connections

One little-discussed item about server software is how it handles user

IBM's DRDA	ISO's RDA
Performance-centered	Portability-centered
Based on SNA	Based on OSI
Each server uses its native SQL	Only a common subset of SQL is supported
Maximize support for existing applications	Minimizes the effort to port tools to different servers
Focus is on IBM interoperability	Focus is on multivendor, heterogeneous database interoperability
IBM, plus nine vendors	Every major DBMS vendor except IBM

Figure 12.1 DRDA compared to RDA

connections. A connection is a single interprocess communication (IPC) channel between a client program and the server database. Server software differs in memory requirements for each connection and in the number of connections it can support. The server database treats each connection as a separate user even though a front-end program could open several connections to a client (to display multiple tables on a screen or to improve performance).

Multiple-user versions of a server database imply a certain number of connections. For example, Microsoft's five-user version of SQL Server has 20 connections. Two connections are reserved for internal use. If front-end programs habitually use more than four connections per client, five simultaneous users could not access the five-user version of SQL Server.

Each connection requires a set amount of server RAM. When adding connections, server databases using multithreaded connections require less RAM than those that require additional sets of connection logic and, therefore, can handle more simultaneous connections. By limiting the amount of RAM used for connections, the RAM cache increases, thereby increasing performance.

Some software performs its own connection management. Ellipse takes advantage of OS/2's Named Pipes to control multithreaded OLTP processes.

12.2 Data Management Software

Most of the major vendors of server data management software offer a complete package of services: client software, network software, and server software. Organizations can develop vendor-supplied or vendor-neutral solutions.

Vendor-supplied solutions offer some advantages. The products are tightly integrated. When problems do crop up, support should be excellent. However, vendor-supplied solutions violate the concept of openness and wide-reaching data access.

Vendor-neutral solutions may require more work to integrate all components of client/server architecture. However, they do support openness and allow the organization to customize the architecture.

Host-based processing client/server applications require no new server software because they interface directly with an existing application and all of the integrity and logic for the application is built into its code. Since these applications are using the host environment, they access the facilities of the host operating system.

Other classes of client/server applications require the server software to handle data integrity and security.

Organizations can choose between integrated data management software, which provides data management capabilities integrated with front-end tools and a 4GL (discussed in Chapter 16, Application Development Tools), and data management software designed for the client/server environment, which provides data management capabilities only.

The server data management software products discussed below have the following common features:

- Triggers
- Two-phase commits
- RPC support
- Stored procedures

12.2.1 SYBASE SQL Server

SQL Server from Microsoft and Sybase is a multithreaded server architecture with its own kernel and an integrated SQL control monitor. Essentially a database operating system running seamlessly on top of the machine's native operating system, Sybase's SQL Server does its own scheduling, task switching, disk caching, and locking. The product can only run on 32-bit processors.

Microsoft's SQL Server and Sybase's SQL Server are based on the Sybase technology. Microsoft SQL Server is designed for micro-based LANs. (Since most of the functionality is the same, SQL Server will be used to represent both the Sybase and Microsoft versions, unless otherwise noted.)

The SQL Server Virtual Server Architecture takes advantage of all processors on a multiprocessor machine (symmetrical if running symmetrical). To optimize performance, it uses a cost-based query optimizer, clustered indexing, shared commits, a shared procedure cache, integrated networking, multivolume tables, physical image logging, and optimized bulk data transfer.

Page-level locking and browse mode locking permit users to browse through rows one at a time and update values in one row at a time, without locking the entire dataset. Timestamping is used to detect rows that have been modified since retrieval.

SQL Server uses the named pipe mechanism and is automatically identifiable on networks as a LAN Manager service, which means it can be brought up and down remotely by LAN Manager. Because SQL Server adheres to industry standards, it can run on any network that supports OS/2, LAN Manager, and named pipes.

Two types of distributed capabilities are provided:

- **Distributed access,** a central SQL Server supports applications running on different machines.
- **Distributed data,** the data resides on different machines in a network. Multiple SQL Servers might be accessed to provide data to the same transaction.

Transact-SQL, a set of extensions to ANSI-standard SQL, is used to write stored procedures, which are compiled and stored in SQL Server's data dictionary. Online maintenance is handled by stored procedures, which are written in Transact-SQL and handled as concurrent SQL transactions.

The product has built-in security features that allow systems administrators, database owners, or owners of database objects to grant or deny access to specified users or groups of users. Data can be secured at the table, view, column, command, or stored procedure level.

SQL Server can quickly and accurately recover from system failures due to power outages or a network crash. The product uses a write-ahead transaction log—transactions are written to log before the database page is written so changes can be rerun. It logs only the offset position and byte stream rather than the logical record. In addition, using the system load and user-supplied maximum recovery times, SQL Server can calculate an appropriate checkpoint interval. At each checkpoint, SQL Server writes all the pages that have been changed to disk as backup.

SQL Server provides software-based fault tolerance. Disk mirroring is used for the transaction log to ensure that committed transactions are not lost and for the database to ensure continuous operation. Disk mirroring also allows a current read request to read from the disk whose last I/O point is the closest, speeding up response time.

SQL Server's open API allows software developers to build client applications that work with SQL Server and provides a transparent interface to networking and server protocols. DB-Library, a set of C functions, allows SQL commands that retrieve and update data values to be incorporated into an application. DB-Library routines can be used with C, COBOL, or other compilers that conform to Pascal calling conventions. DB-Library is a static link library under DOS and a dynamic link library under Windows and OS/2. Applications can also be developed using Microsoft's ODBC.

Sybase also offers a NLM called SYBASE SQL Server for NetWare that allows NetWare users to access relational databases residing on any hardware platform outside the LAN. It works with SQL-compatible front-end tools to provide familiar access to data.

SYBASE Secure SQL Server, an extension to SQL Server, supports multilevel data security. Data with multiple security classifications can be stored in an integrated database, instead of separate databases, for each classification level. This product was developed to meet stringent government specifications.

SYBASE Server/Cluster Fault Tolerant (CFT) version provides fault tolerance in clustered CPU environments. The CFT server is configured on a second CPU in the cluster but doesn't routinely use the resources of that CPU. If the CPU running the primary SQL Server fails, the CFT version is activated, connects to all the applications, recovers the database, and proceeds with normal operations.

12.2.2 Microsoft SQL Server

A component in Microsoft's integrated solution for open systems, Microsoft SQL Server is based on the Microsoft OS/2 operating system, which provides protected-mode multitasking, large memory support, interprocess communications, and a graphical user interface; and LAN Manager, which converts Microsoft OS/2 into a multiuser operating system for DOS, Windows, and OS/2 workstations. Microsoft SQL Server provides relational database services to all workstations on the network.

Microsoft offers SQL Administrator, which allows multiple SQL Server installations to be managed from a single Windows workstation, and SQL Bridge, which is a protocol gateway for accessing SQL Server data. The versatility of Microsoft SQL Server and SQL Bridge (discussed in Section 12.3.3) is illustrated in Figure 12.2.

12.2.3 SQLBase

SQLBase 5.0 from Gupta Technologies, Inc. offers plug-and-play scalability across DOS, OS/2, UNIX (currently only Sun SPARC-based computers), and NetWare platforms. SQLBase can run under LAN Manager, LAN Server, VINES, 3Com, 3+Open, and NetWare 2.11 (or higher), using NetBIOS, OS/2's Named Pipes, or TCP/IP protocols to handle communications between clients and server. SQLBase 5.0 also comes in an NLM version that runs on a NetWare 3.11 (or higher) system, which supports the IPX/SPX protocols as an alternative to using NetBIOS as the transport mechanism. SPX database routers are provided for DOS, Windows, and OS/2 clients.

In the case of SQLBase NLM, users can employ the same machine as both an SQL server database (for SQLBase) and a network server

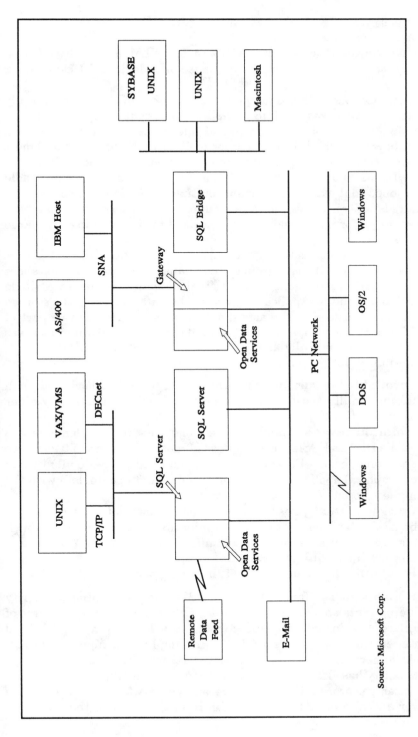

Source: Microsoft Corp.

Figure 12.2 Microsoft SQL Server architecture

189

(for NetWare). Prior to the SQLBase 5.0 NLM availability, Gupta recommended that users install SQLBase on a dedicated DOS or OS/2 machine.

SQLBase 5.0 includes a query optimizer, which can drastically reduce the time required to compile and execute complex queries, including multilevel joins and nested queries. The server performs a series of complex algorithms in order to determine the fastest and most cost-effective method for returning the response to a query.

SQLBase 5.0 can support large databases and easily handle partitioned databases that span multiple disk drives and contain hundreds of gigabytes of data. Support for partitioned database improves performance and increases capacity when working with large databases.

Access to databases that span multiple disk partitions or volumes is handled through storage groups that manage one or more database areas, which are portions of the actual data that reside in a single partition or volume. Applications access the database using the storage group name instead of the actual area names; an area can be part of multiple storage groups as well. Space allocation in the different areas is handled automatically and can grow and shrink dynamically.

Optimized for graphical application, SQLBase 5.0 includes:

- **Scrollable cursors**, which permit users to browse back and forth through multiple sets of data records and update them in any order or at any time.
- **Isolation level support** for the isolation levels implemented in IBM's DB2 and OS/2 EE Data Base Manager. SQLBase 5.0 adds two additional levels—Release and Lock, and Read Only—to allow users of graphical applications to scroll through and update data with the highest possible level of concurrency.
- **Cursor context preservation**, which allows database cursors to be used after a commit occurs, eliminating the need to re-establish application cursors for each commit.
- **Binary large objects (BLOBs) support.**
- **Read-only database support**, including those on CD ROM.

SQLBase 5.0 offers complete DB2-style referential integrity including syntax and semantics checks. Other compatibility features of SQLBase 5.0 include support for the EBCDIC character set and enhancements to Gupta's COBOL Precompiler to support COBOL programmers who use their micros as DB2 workbenches.

Security has also been enhanced through the encryption of database and user passwords. Passwords are encrypted when they are on the server and also prior to transmission from the client to the server.

12.2.4 NetWare SQL

NetWare SQL from Novell allows users to access a NetWare SQL server
from DOS, OS/2, Windows or Macintosh clients, as illustrated in Figure
12.3. The DOS, OS/2, and Windows clients communicate with NetWare
SQL through client requests, the Macintosh clients through Apple's
Data Access Language interface. NetWare SQL is implemented on the
NetWare server as a group of NLMs.

The NetWare SQL NLM is the central database engine. It receives

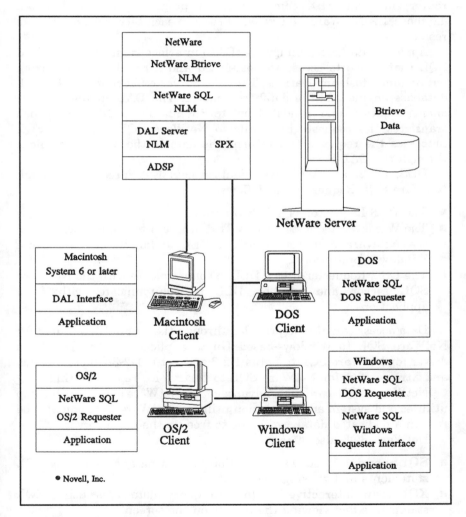

Figure 12.3 NetWare SQL architecture

relational requests, performs relational operations, and handles database security and referential integrity definitions. It also maintains the NetWare SQL data dictionaries.

NetWare SQL makes data calls to NetWare Btrieve for access to data files. NetWare SQL translates the data request into one or more Btrieve requests. Btrieve is the record manager for Novell products, such as NetWare, LANtern, LANalyzer, Communication Services Manager, and the Network Management System. NetWare Btrieve includes the following server components: the record manager, the router, and the SPX communications program. In a distributed database, the NetWare Btrieve NLM runs on each server where Btrieve resides.

Apple's Data Access Language (DAL) interface is an ANSI-standard SQL that supports access to host-based and server-based data from within Macintosh applications. The DAL Server NLM contains the DAL database engine and the database adapter. The DAL engine receives client requests and sends them to the database adapter, which translates the requests into calls to NetWare SQL. NetWare SQL processes the requests and returns the data to the Macintosh client through the DAL Server NLM.

DOS, OS/2, and Windows clients access NetWare SQL through NetWare SQL Requesters, as follows:

- The DOS Requester is a TSR program.
- The Windows Requester uses a TSR program to communicate with the NetWare SQL server and a DLL to handle requests from Windows applications.
- The OS/2 Requester uses a DLL to communicate with the NetWare SQL server and another DLL to communicate with OS/2 applications.

Data access can also be provided through the Gupta SQLRouter for NetWare SQL to Windows-based Gupta applications, the DataLens driver for NetWare SQL to Lotus 1-2-3 and Lotus 1-2-3/G applications, and Xtrieve Plus for NetWare SQL to Btrieve for report writing.

NetWare SQL can take advantage of NetWare's system backup utilities and system administration utilities. NetWare SQL can also be run on a dedicated database server to free up the main server.

NetWare SQL also offers:

- **SQLScope,** a Windows application for editing and executing SQL statements and viewing the results
- **XQLI**, an interactive product to query data files using SQL statements and viewing the results on the screen

12.2.5 Other Options

Vendors of host-based relational database products are offering server versions of their software. Many of these also offer 4GL interfaces to the data structure. These tools have many of the features discussed above, such as support for database triggers, stored procedures, integrity constraints, distributed updates, two-phase commits, and transaction processing managers. They usually support character- or GUI-based screens and, in addition, provide backup and recovery procedures. These tools are usually available on platforms ranging from micro to mainframe, OS/2 to UNIX.

ORACLE7

ORACLE7 uses a cooperative, multithreaded server technology with transparent data sharing to provide open, relational systems that support new and old systems. ORACLE7 does not perform read locks on queries, but provides row-level locking with unlimited locks per transaction, table, or database.

ORACLE7 can automatically refresh snapshots of master tables at user defined intervals. The provided security architecture is based on roles, which are named collections of privileges. Roles allow privileges on tables and other database objects to be grouped and granted to individuals or groups of individuals.

The product has an intelligent cost-based query optimizer and a resource limiter.

INFORMIX

INFORMIX Online from Informix Software Inc. provides many of the features of ORACLE7 and has the lion's share of the UNIX relational database market. INFORMIX Online supports the X/Open XA standard and ANSI SQL '89 and can handle optical disc storage of images.

To address its lack of front-end tools, Informix is working with front-end vendors to build links to INFORMIX Online.

INGRES

The INGRES Intelligent Database (from Ingres, a subsidiary of the ASK Group, Inc.) manages data; knowledge, such as business policies and integrity constraints; and objects, such as binary, fractional, and spatial coordinate data. INGRES provides a syntax-independent query optimizer and connectivity tools to link networks and gateways to other relational and non-relational data sources.

12.3 Database Gateways

Database gateways act as interface translators that move data, SQL commands, and applications from one type of database to another, as illustrated in Figure 12.4. Database gateways must know the details (syntax, data format, data types, and catalog naming conventions) of the products to be accessed and be synchronized with software releases of the data sources. The price of this accessibility is speed, because it is necessary to translate the client request and the server results.

The client, gateway, and server can reside on the same platform or different ones. This allows gateways to connect clients and servers running on dissimilar networks. They are ideally suited to bridge network protocols, such as TCP/IP, OSI, and SNA, while acting as the transportation interfaces for moving data among database platforms.

Database gateways have the following functions:

- Accept statements specified by a well-defined grammar (usually SQL) from a client application
- Translate the statements to a specific database format
- Send the statements to be executed against the database
- Translate the results back into a well-defined format
- Return the data and status information to the client

To appear transparent to the user, a database gateway must also include login validation, a cancel/interrupt/error handler, and datatype conversions; and be able to emulate the defined security. They must also be flexible enough to allow users to activate various modes of operation, such as pass-through and debug/trace modes.

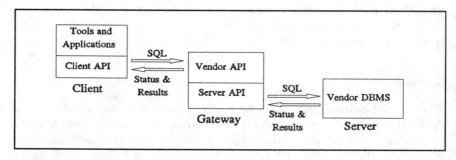

Figure 12.4 Database gateways

12.3.1 EDA/SQL

Enterprise Data Access/SQL (EDA/SQL), from Information Builders, Inc. (IBI), is a family of client/server products, based on an open architecture, that provides SQL-based access to relational and non-relational data sources on a networked multivendor system. IBM has endorsed EDA/SQL as a component of its Information Warehouse solution. Microsoft and IBI have jointly developed a product that allows ODBC-compliant Windows applications to use EDA/SQL to access data.

EDA/SQL provides a uniform, relational view of data, regardless of its storage structure. The operating environment and file location is transparent to the user. EDA/SQL can access over 45 relational and non-relational data sources.

Using a variety of end-user tools, the user develops SQL requests, which EDA/SQL distributes and processes against local or remote data, returning the results to the end-user tool. Users can join relational and non-relational data sources. EDA/SQL can directly update relational databases and uses RPCs to update non-relational databases. EDA/SQL can also be used by 3GL applications to send and receive SQL requests from anywhere in the network.

EDA/SQL consists of the following components, which run on the workstation or server, as illustrated in Figure 12.5:

- API/SQL
- EDA/Link
- EDA/SQL Server
- EDA/Extender products, including a Dynamic Extender for DB2 and one for SQL/DS
- EDA/Gateways

API/SQL, a call-level application programming interface supplied as a dynamically linkable library, supports database services, RPCs, type conversion, and record management and includes trace and debugging facilities. API/SQL also provides the necessary connection and session

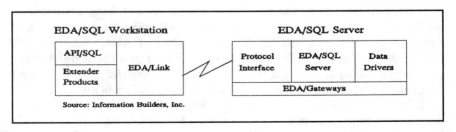

Figure 12.5 Components of EDA/SQL

commands for communications, provides control functions that allow a client application to continue processing while SQL requests or RPCs are executing on the server, and permits inquiries about the status of pending requests and RPCs. Transaction control functions support remote units of work.

EDA/Link, a modular system of communications interfaces that support over 12 communications protocols, handles the translation of protocols, transmission and routing of messages, password verification, data conversion, and detection of transmission errors, all transparently to the user. EDA/Link creates outgoing packets for the client, routes them to the server, and routes answer packets from the server to the appropriate client. Pop-up menus create the communications profiles used by EDA/Link.

At the core of the EDA architecture is the multithreaded EDA/SQL Server, a host component, which manages the flow of data; handles the interactions with communication protocols and target databases; and provides administrative functions, such as accounting and security measures. It uses a data access engine to schedule tasks, determine the network location of data, and generate trace records and accounting information.

Server-based interfaces called EDA/Data Drivers provide access to data in many different formats. Each data driver handles a particular data structure: its idiosyncracies in syntax, functionality, schema, data types, catalog naming conventions, and data representation. Included among the over 45 databases and file structures supported are ADABAS, IDMS/R, ORACLE, Rdb, RMS, INFORMIX, HP ALLBASE/SQL, SQL Server (under OS/2 EE), and Lotus 1-2-3 (via DataLens).

If the target data source is relational, EDA/SQL Server passes ANSI-compliant or dialect-specific SQL directly to the EDA/Data Driver for that relational database. If the data source is non-relational, the SQL request is passed through the Universal SQL Translator, which converts the SQL into the appropriate data manipulation language for the EDA/Data Driver.

EDA/Extender products provide direct interfaces from a variety of products, such as Lotus 1-2-3, to API/SQL, allowing these products to access data using the communication services of EDA/Link to reach EDA/SQL Server and EDA/Data Drivers. The Dynamic Extender for DB2 allows tools that support DB2 to access non-DB2 relational and non-relational data. A Dynamic Extender for SQL/DS is also available.

EDA/Gateways are used by applications with specific point-to-point data access requirements. The two initial EDA/SQL Gateways provide access to IBM's DB2 and SQL/DS databases from client/server applications on remote workstations, midrange, or mainframe platforms. The EDA/Gateways can be used to read and update DB2 or SQL/DS by products that support EDA/SQL, such as Lotus 1-2-3 and EASEL, or through API/SQL. Users of EDA/Gateways can also issue RPCs to incorporate 3GL procedures.

12.3.2 Database Gateway

Database Gateway from Micro Decisionware, Inc. (MDI) resides on an OS/2 server platform and accepts SQL transactions from client stations. The SQL transactions are redirected to DB2, SQL/DS, or Teradata DBC/1012 databases for processing. The client stations can be running DOS, Windows, or OS/2.

Database Gateway Solution includes two components:

- One component runs on the LAN under the OS/2 Communication Manager and handles communications to and from the client applications and the host.
- The second component is the host portion that links the gateway to DB2, SQL/DS, or Teradata DBC/1012.

Co-developed with Microsoft, Database Gateway for DB2 2.0 provides connectivity to a host. DB2-CICS Access Server 1.4, the host portion of the DB2 solution, running under IBM's CICS, starts a DB2 session, passes the SQL statements to the database engine, and feeds the results back through the gateway.

Database Gateway for SQL/DS interfaces with SQL/DS-VSE Access Server on the host to provide access to SQL/DS databases.

Both solutions support a remote unit of work and automatic rollback-commit or user controlled integrity. The client can initiate a Database Gateway execution of the transfer of data directly between Microsoft SQL Server and DB2 or SQL/DS.

Communication between the front-end and the gateway is achieved using named pipes, the interprocess communications mechanism used in SQL Server. The gateway will therefore run on any network that can support named pipes (such as NetWare and VINES). Communication between the gateway server and the IBM host is then achieved via IBM's APPC protocol.

Transformation levels control how much translation occurs as the commands pass through the gateway. At Level 0, the gateway makes no conversion. Levels 1 and 2 dictate increasingly higher levels of conversion.

Database Gateway supplies a data compression algorithm, which transfers data between the client and server at a fast rate because of the compression. It also permits retrieved data to bypass temporary storage within CICS, transmitting the data directly to the client application.

The Database Gateway products support such new SQL Server features as the ability to process remote stored procedures, which allow applications to communicate transparently between SQL Server and DB2. The Database Gateway products also support Microsoft's ODBC standard, as well as the cursor-control features found in the SQL Server 4.2 API.

The products feature a connection manager that balances the traffic flowing over two or more gateways to provide optimal performance, a security exit that provides different levels of access to data, and a CICS shutdown procedure that halts client transactions when the CICS mainframe application crashes.

12.3.3 SQL Bridge

SQL Bridge from Microsoft Corp. is a protocol gateway for building distributed client/server systems in Windows, DOS, OS/2, UNIX, Macintosh, and VMS environments. It allows applications to access SQL Server data through one protocol, rather than several, providing seamless integration of SQL Server applications, databases, and gateways, independent of operating systems and network protocols. It routes client/server requests across networks having different protocols, simplifying network configuration, and increasing interoperability. SQL Bridge supports all new Windows-based ODBC applications as well as current SQL Server applications. SQL Server applications can exchange information using RPCs.

SQL Bridge supports OS/2 Named Pipes, TCP/IP, and DECnet protocols on LAN Manager and Digital's Pathworks networks. (See Figure 12.2.) The next release (expected first half 1993) will add support for IPX/SPX and TCP/IP on NetWare and VINES networks. A version of SQL Bridge for the 32-bit Windows NT operating system is also planned. Using SQL Bridge, UNIX, VMS, and Macintosh, clients can access DB2 and other mainframe data sources using Database Gateway from Micro Decisionware.

12.3.4 SYBASE Open Client/Server

SYBASE Open Client/Server interfaces permit open, standards-based client/server communication among heterogeneous software and data

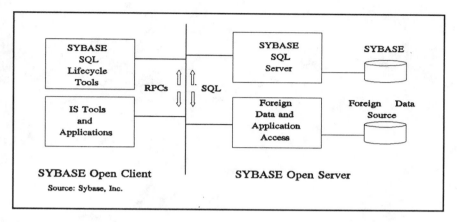

Figure 12.6 SYBASE Open Client/Server architecture

environments, as illustrated in Figure 12.6. These tools provide access to relational and non-relational data and do not require the use of SYBASE's SQL Server.

SYBASE Open Client is a client-based API for non-SYBASE tools and programs to communicate with SQL Server and Open Server applications.

SYBASE Open Server is an API for access to non-SYBASE data sources and services and does not require the use of SYBASE SQL Server. The DB-Library is an API used by client applications to pass SQL requests or RPCs to a data server, which may be a SYBASE SQL Server or, using Open Server, any other data source. Precompilers that support DB-Library are offered for many popular programming languages. Using the multithreaded Open Server API and a library of server utilities, developers can write routines that will execute within the SYBASE application and respond to calls from DB-Library as if they were SQL Servers, allowing outside data sources to be integrated into a SYBASE application.

SYBASE Open Server also includes an event notification function, which allows any data source to initiate a trigger to notify a client application of database and non-database events. The software also provides development procedures to create Open Server routines and to monitor Open Server users, application debugging tools, and configuration options, such as process scheduling and buffer size control.

The Network

Networks must be transparent to the users. The network and the distributed applications running on it must be as reliable as if they were running on a single computer. In addition, the network must provide self-healing capabilities that can reroute network traffic around broken cables and failed components and be flexible enough to react to business-related changes in its environment.

This seems so straightforward, but with client/server computing, LANs are connecting to other LANs, servers, and mainframes. Things are not straightforward anymore.

LANs used to be simple too. But now there are three different structures (LAN topologies), at least five competing standards for transmissions, and two standards for the information required to manage the network. LANs have become so complex that they require their own operating system.

Networking continues to be the least understood and most critical component in an organization's information infrastructure.

Most organizations committed to client/server computing agree that linking LANs is not the place to skimp to save money. The advice is to try not to link incompatible LANs with different platforms (hardware, software, and operating systems). An in-house pilot network should be set up to thoroughly test products before implementation.

13

Overview of Networking

Client/server computing makes utmost use of network capabilities. The internetwork transmits requests for data from client to server, routes requests for data among servers, and supports internetwork communication.

13.1 Layers, Interfaces, and Protocols

A network architecture defines the protocols, message formats, and standards used within that architecture. Products created within this network architecture (or that support it) are compatible.

The more robust network architectures use a layered structure. Each layer consists of entities that are hardware components and/or software processes. The rules and formats for communications between adjacent layers are collectively called an interface. Protocols are the rules and formats for communications within the same layer across different devices. Protocols include formats and the order of the data exchange, and any actions to be taken on the transmission and receipt of data. Figure 13.1 lists the difference between protocols and interfaces.

If two stations transmit at exactly the same time, they destroy each other's transmissions. Protocols are used to prevent this by providing rules for transmissions.

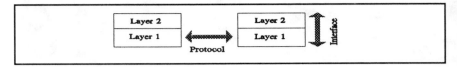

Figure 13.1 Protocols and interfaces

By using a layered structure, protocol changes can be made without affecting the other protocols (functions) in the stack (the protocols for all the layers). Each layer needs only to be aware of the services provided by the layer directly below it. In addition, different hardware and software can communicate as long as they use the same protocols and data formats.

13.2 Standard Architectures

One of the difficulties in connecting all the heterogenous equipment in an organization is the presence of multiple architectures. The network component is no different. There is no one standard architecture, there are many.

13.2.1 OSI Model

The Reference Model of Open Systems Interconnection (OSI) is one of the most popular models for networks. It is not an actual product; it represents the published standards for a common network model. Developed by the International Standards Organization (ISO), this seven-layer model, illustrated in Figure 13.2, covers all aspects of networking from the physical wiring to sophisticated application support. Layer 1 functions in one machine interact with Layer 1 functions in the connecting machine. Layer 2 interacts with Layer 2, and so on.

The lowest level is the **Physical layer,** which specifies the hardware and software necessary to place the data bits in the communication channel and transport them to their destination. This link is concerned with the physical transmission of signals. It does not provide data recognition services.

The second layer, the **Data Link layer,** is concerned with error-free transmissions and shields the upper layers from details concerning the physical transmission. This layer performs the following services:

- Data link activation and deactivation

- Transportation of data between data links
- Data link sharing
- Data link error detection, notification, and recovery
- Transparent data flow

The Data Link address, known as the local address, is used for send and receive identification. This address is used by network bridges to pass frames (blocks of data) between segments in a LAN.

The functions of these first two layers are performed by the hardware components of the network. The software on the adapter card in the micro takes the data and turns it into network-compliant packets. The transceiver located on the adapter card listens to the LAN and copies any packets addressed to it.

The Physical and Data Link layers are also addressed by the standards outlined in the Institute for Electrical and Electronic Engineers (IEEE) Project 802. IEEE also proposes a Physical layer but divides the Data Link layer into two sublayers. The Media Access Control sublayer interfaces with the Physical layer protocols. The Logical Link Control sublayer creates a logical data link between the sender and the receiver.

The functions of the layers above the Data Link layer are handled by software. The **Network layer** (Layer 3) establishes, maintains, and terminates the network connection between two users and transfers messages and data over that connection. Its services are included in X.25, the international standard for packet-switching data networks from CCITT (Consultative Committee on International Telephone and Telegraph). These services include:

Layer		Function
7	Application	Support for application programs
6	Presentation	Code and format translations
5	Session	Dialogue management between users
4	Transport	Quality control of packet transmissions
3	Network	Internetwork routing
2	Data Link	Creation of frames
1	Physical	Transmission of signals

Figure 13.2 Open Systems Interconnection model

- Network addressing
- Blocking and segmenting message units
- Data units sequencing
- Switching and routing
- Controlling local flow
- Controlling congestion
- Error detection, notification, and recovery

The fourth layer, the **Transport layer,** corrects all failures that occur at the Network layer and provides control functions between the user nodes. It takes packets of data from the Network layer and assembles them into messages.

The **Session layer** (Layer 5) creates, manages, and terminates the dialogues between the users. IBM's Advanced Program-to-Program Communication using Logical Unit type 6.2 (APPC/LU6.2) was used to develop the standards for this layer. Its services include:

- Session initiation and activation
- Session termination and release
- Dialogue control
- Synchronization and resynchronization of the session connections
- Normal and expedited data transfer

The **Presentation layer,** Layer 6, handles network security, character-code translations, and format translations. This sixth layer also creates pipes, which are areas of memory used for transferring data from one place to another.

The **Application layer** contains utilities that support application programs. This top layer does not include applications. It provides services that are not provided elsewhere in the model. The layer consists of three parts:

- **Common Application Services.** These services, which can be used by all communicating parties, provide control protocols for commitment, concurrence, and recovery and conversion protocols for specifying type and structure of conversions between user nodes.
- **Specific Application Services.** These are the protocols for user information exchanges, such as private standards or internationally recognized communication standards.
- **User Element.** If the user element (the user presentation) is defined, a user interface above this layer is not needed.

It is important to know which layer(s) network software handles. As illustrated in Figure 13.3, Ethernet and Token Ring, for example, handle the Physical and Data Link layers. NetBIOS and APPC/LU6.2

Application	Network services such as print services and database services
Presentation	
Session	LAN Support Programs such as NetBIOS and APPC/LU6.2
Transport	
Network	
Data Link	Logical Link Control
	Media Access Control
Physical	Ethernet, Token Ring

Figure 13.3 LAN software functionality

are IBM protocols for Network, Transport, and Session layers.

13.2.2 TCP/IP

Transmission Control Protocol/Internet Protocol (TCP/IP) was designed to allow military research laboratories to communicate if a land war broke out. Independent of any one vendor's hardware, TCP/IP lays out the rules for the transmission of datagrams (transmission units) across a network. It supports end-to-end acknowledgement between source and destination of the message, even if they reside on separate networks. TCP/IP is used by Internet, a large internetwork that connects major research organizations; universities; and government agencies, such as Department of Energy, Department of Defense, and National Aeronautics and Space Administration.

As illustrated in Figure 13.4, TCP/IP is a four-layer architecture

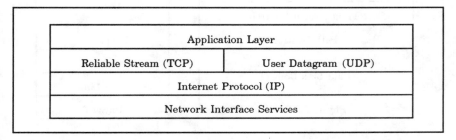

Figure 13.4 TCP/IP architecture

that is built on a physical network interface, and that specifies conventions for communications and network interconnection and traffic routing. It allows networks to communicate by assigning unique addresses to each network. Nodes in different networks can have common names. Think of each network as a state and each node as a city. Two cities can have the same name as long as they are in different states. But to find the right city, you need to know which state it's in.

The internet protocol (IP) layer deals with delivery of data packets. It provides packet processing rules, identifies conditions for discarding packets, and controls error detection and error message generation.

Data delivery, concurrency, and sequencing are handled by the transmission control protocol (TCP) layer. TCP also handles connection to applications on other systems, error checking, and retransmission. TCP uses connections between two points, not individual end points, as its fundamental concept.

13.2.3 SNA Model

Systems Network Architecture (SNA) from IBM uses a seven-layer architecture similar to the OSI model, although there is not a one-to-one correspondence between the layers, as illustrated in Figure 13.5. SNA, a mature product, was built as an open-ended architecture to accommodate newer technologies, which has allowed it to support such

SNA	OSI
End User	Application
Transaction Services	Presentation
Presentation Services	
Data Flow Control	Session
Transmission Control	
Path Control	Transport
Data Link Control	Network
	Data Link
Physical Control	Physical

Figure 13.5 Systems Network Architecture model

technologies as fiber optics, digitized voice, and distributed systems. SNA allows users in one SNA network to transparently access data and programs in other SNA networks by using SNA gateways. SNA provides resource sharing and includes reliability features such as alternate routing and backup host. Security is provided through logon routines and encryption facilities.

SNA is designed to provide networking facilities for IBM systems only. The OSI model can support homogeneous or heterogeneous networks. Recognizing the importance of OSI-compliance, IBM has been reevaluating the possibility of developing gateways from SNA to OSI-compliant architectures.

13.2.4 Other Models

DECnet from Digital is a family of products that implement Digital Network Architecture, a five-layer architecture. This architecture provides all the OSI capabilities plus additional features such as File Transfer, Management Protocol, and Virtual Terminal Protocol; distributed naming services; and domain networks. In addition to Digital networks, DECnet supports Ethernet LANs, DOS, and Ultrix (Digital's version of UNIX). Using 3270/5250 emulation, DECnet gateways can connect to SNA products. DECnet's weakness is in its limited security features.

Some other popular network architectures are Sun Microsystems's Network File System (NFS) and Xerox Network Systems, whose protocols were modified by Novell and released as Internet Packet Exchange (IPX) and Sequenced Packet Exchange (SPX).

13.3 Network Characteristics

Each network can be categorized by its communication methods used between nodes, the method used to switch data between the nodes, and its structure.

13.3.1 Network Classifications

Networks can be classified based on their communication methods between nodes. Point-to-point communication allows one node to communicate with another directly connected node. Ethernet is a point-to-point network. In a multipoint (also called multidrop) network, all nodes share one line. Each node shares time on the line, so as the number of nodes grows, the probability of delays increases. Multidrop networks are not appropriate for applications where high-speed transmission is required. Figure 13.6 illustrates the point-to-point and multidrop communication methods for networks.

Networks can also be classified based on how messages are transmitted from node to node. LANs are broadcast networks that connect each node to a common transmission channel so a single message can reach all nodes. WANs are store-and-forward networks that receive a completed message into a buffer before transmitting it to its destination. The nodes in store-and-forward networks are connected by point-to-point transmission lines.

13.3.2 Network Switching

Networks must provide methods for switching data between links to provide a point-to-point path between nodes. There are two types of switching techniques used in today's networks.

Packet-switching networks divide the traffic into small segments called packets. Each packet carries identification information that is used by the network operating system to send the packets to their final destination. After the network hardware delivers the packets, the network software at the destination node reassembles the packet. Packet-switching networks are also known as X.25 networks.

Frame relay is a faster packet-switching method for efficiently handling LANs and other applications that generate unpredictable chunks of network traffic. Frame relay allows organizations to use Asynchronous Transfer Mode (ATM) gigabyte-range switching speeds.

The message-switching routine writes messages (of any size) to the switching node's storage. Messages will be stored until the destination node wishes to receive the message. This implementation is used in E-mail applications.

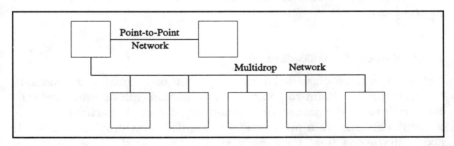

Figure 13.6 Point-to-point and multidrop networks

13.3.3 Network Topology

A network's topology is its structure of nodes and links. Links can be virtual or physical, such as phone lines, private lines, and satellite channels. Virtual links allow the network to share physical lines between multiple network programs.

Illustrated in Figure 13.7, the three popular network topologies used in LANs are:

- **Star network.** Nodes are connected to a single central switching node, for example, multiple terminals connected to a central

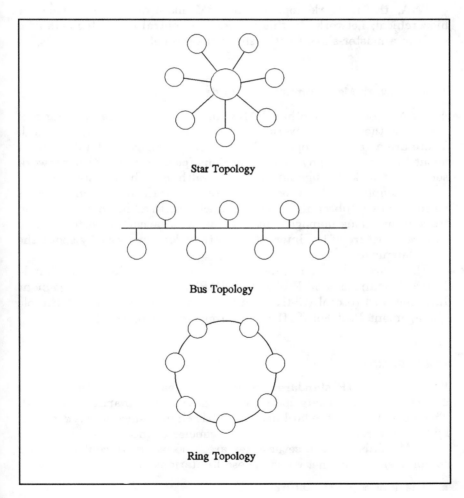

Figure 13.7 Star, bus, and ring topologies

computer. If the central switch fails, all communications stop.

- **Bus network.** Considered a broadcast network, this topology uses a shared transmission channel to connect all nodes. Each node can continue to communicate, even if one node goes down. Ethernet is an example of a bus network.
- **Ring network.** Nodes are linked to their neighbor with a one-directional loop. Transmission can be broadcast or point-to-point. The signal is regenerated at each node. Nodes whose links do not pass through a failed node can still communicate. IBM's Token Ring is an example of a ring topology.

SNA, the network topology of IBM mainframes, is a tree, or hierarchical, network. In this network, a central computer acts as a slave in a master-slave relationship with the network nodes.

13.4 Network Management Standards

As LANs connect to other LANs and host machines, the task of managing the entire network as a single entity becomes monumental. There are a variety of options for collecting management information about the internet—physical connections, performance of the network server, network throughput, and the health of each workstation.

To complicate the process, several network management tools perform only a subset of the needed functions. In addition, information from autonomous management systems must be combined to create a complete picture of the internet—and they don't necessarily speak the same language.

There are two major standards for network management: Simple Network Management Protocol (SNMP) and Common Management Information Protocol (CMIP). An improved version of SNMP, Simple Management Protocol (SMP), was proposed in late 1992.

13.4.1 SNMP

Based on TCP/IP standards, SNMP provides a format for network devices to communicate management data to the management host. The four-year-old standard has seen little change since it was designed by the universities and government agencies connected to Internet.

SNMP falls short in several key areas necessary to control today's complex enterprise networks. These limitations are:

- A lack of security features

- Inability to interconnect different network management systems
- Inability to collect network management data in bulk

13.4.2 CMIP

CMIP, combined with Common Management Information Services (CMIS), allows communications among different network systems. Based on OSI standards, CMIP and CMIS provide all the features of SNMP, as well as those it is missing.

CMIP and CMIS have their own limitations, however. As fairly new standards, products using these standards are not yet readily available. Because the OSI standards offer more functions than SNMP, products compliant with these standards are more complex and, therefore, require more time to develop. While these protocols offer more capabilities, the trade-off is in memory requirements. SNMP might need 20 kbytes of memory; CMIP might require as much as 2.5 Mbytes.

13.4.3 SMP

Four prominent SNMP software developers proposed SMP as SNMP's successor to the Internet Engineering Task Force (IETF), the official SNMP standards body. SMP remedies the SNMP problems listed earlier, supports other transport protocols besides TCP/IP, and eliminates the advantages the OSI protocols have over SNMP.

By late 1992, vendors such as Hewlett-Packard, Digital, and Hughes LAN Systems, Inc. had demonstrated prototypes of SMP on their network management products. However, these vendors are waiting for SMP to become an official IETF standard before they will commit to a delivery date for commerical SMP products.

For many organizations, support of OSI network management standards continues to be critical. Without this support, it is unlikely there will be a mass exodus by CMIP/CMIS users to SNMP or SMP.

13.5 LAN Characteristics

LANs fall into one of the following three categories:

- Interconnected LANs
- Backbone networks
- Desktop high-speed LANs

Because they replace front-end terminals, such as IBM 3270/5250 equipment, interface-only client/server applications usually run over existing networks. Other classes of client/server applications are based on newer LAN technologies.

As LANs spread through an organization, bridges and routers are used to connect them. For example, a router could be used to move information among Ethernet, Token Ring, and Fiber Distributed Data Interface (FDDI) networks. Users would most likely not realize the full 100 Mbps of FDDI throughput, though, because the router is managing all connections.

Backbone networks also connect LANs, but also provide high-speed transmission and control the flow of data among various networks. High-speed LANs connect desktop machines directly to the FDDI network and, therefore, have access to the full 100 Mbps transmission speed. This configuration is designed for high-volume, data-intensive applications, such as those that transmit graphic information and images.

The two most common LANs are Ethernet and IBM's Token Ring. Ethernet uses baseband coaxial cable or shielded pair wire and can operate at 10 Mbps. Its protocol is carrier sense multiple-access with collision detection (CSMA/CD). This requires a sending device to monitor the network and send a message only if it senses the network is not in use. If a collision is detected, the device must stop the transmission and try again when it senses the network is clear.

Token Ring uses shielded pair wire or optical cables and can operate at 4 or 16 Mbps. Its protocol is called Token Ring. A special signal code, called a token, is passed from station to station. If a device wants to transmit a message, it waits for the token to come by, takes it off the network, and transmits its message. The token is returned to the network after the transmission is completed.

14

LAN Hardware
and Software

Networks must be transparent to the users. The network and the distributed applications must be as reliable as if they were running on a single computer. The network must provide self-healing capabilities that can reroute network traffic around broken cables and failed components and yet be flexible enough to react to changes in network topology and communication loads.

14.1 LAN Hardware

LAN hardware includes the actual cabling and the infrastructure—the internetwork (internet) connections. Servers must be able to access other servers and users must be able to access information anywhere in the network. In client/server environments, servers send fewer packets per request than in other environments because only the results of requests are sent back to the client. However, this may not ultimately decrease network traffic because client/server environments usually support more users than mainframe-oriented networks.

There are five ways to interconnect LANs:

- Repeaters
- Bridges
- Routers

- Network hardware gateways
- Backbone networks

The methods are listed in order of increasing functionality. Backbone networks are connecting networks; they are not pieces of hardware that connect networks. The characteristics of the LANs to be connected determine which device (repeater, bridge, router, or gateway) should be used, as illustrated in Figure 14.1. OSI levels referenced in the figure were discussed in Chapter 13, Overview of Networking.

If the physical characteristics of the LANs are the same—the same hardware and software transports bits between nodes—a repeater can be used. If the implementations of the OSI physical layer are different but the data link layers and those layers above them are the same, a bridge can be used. If the implementations of the first two layers of the LANs are different but the software used to handle the upper layers is the same, a router can be used. If the LANs use totally different implementations, a gateway must be used.

14.1.1 Repeaters

As a signal travels along a cable, it loses strength. If communicating stations are at great distances from one another, repeaters can be used to regenerate the signal back to its original strength. A repeater can also be used to extend the reach of a LAN.

Repeaters can only be used when the LANs on both sides of the repeater are identical. They must have the same physical transmission characteristics and use the same protocols.

	Repeater	Bridge	Router	Network Gateway
Physical characteristics (OSI Layer 1)	Same	Different	Different	Different
Access and transmission control (OSI Layer 2)	Same	Same	Different	Different
Other functions (OSI Layers 3-7)	Same	Same	Same	Different

Figure 14.1 Comparison of LAN connecting hardware

14.1.2 Bridges

Bridges are used to connect LANs with different physical transmission characteristics and protocols. For example, a third-party bridge might be used to link multiple Ethernet LANs, each supplied by different manufacturers. Bridges temporarily store messages forwarded to another network in case retransmission is required. A bridged network is illustrated in Figure 14.2.

Bridges are a simpler technology than routers. They operate at the Media Access Control (MAC) sublayer of the Data Link layer of the OSI model (one layer below routers). Bridges pass frames from one segment of the LAN to another based on the MAC addresses of the sender and receiver network interface cards. All addresses, even across networks, must be unique and of the same format because bridges do not convert addresses. There can be only one route to each station because a bridge does not make routing decisions.

Bridges do not have to be configured. The forwarding database of a bridge is built and maintained automatically. Since routers base their decisions on a higher level addressing scheme, they are more flexible than bridges. However, they are more difficult to configure because they require specification of selected protocols, network addresses, interfaces, and management facilities.

Routers make efficient use of all available links in the internet by using them concurrently. Bridges depend on the IEEE 802 Spanning Tree protocol to manage redundant links and paths.

Bridge traffic must be monitored for heavy load periods, called

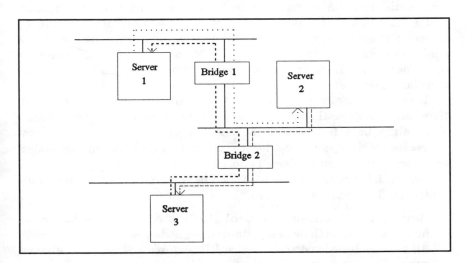

Figure 14.2 Sample bridged network

choking. Additional network processing, or additional server hardware, may be required to rectify the situation.

Bridges used to be faster than routers. Because of 32-bit CPUs, higher speed buses, and software performance improvements, routers are now as fast or faster than bridges.

14.1.3 Routers

A router is a hardware device that manages the route selection for data packets and for minimizing traffic loads on linked LANs. Routers link logically separate LANs, permitting them to share traffic loads and prevent the choking that occurs in bridged LANs. Multiprotocol routers segment the network, access wide-area networks, support diverse protocols, provide better routing capabilities, provide high network performance, and control the network.

Routers are used to connect two different networks. Each network may have been implemented independently and include stations with the same address. If a LAN message is intended for another network, the router accepts it. Each individual router understands the entire internet's topology. After a router determines the best route for a message, it is passed along with two additional addresses, the address of the next node along the route and the address of the final route.

External routers require a micro, two or more network interface cards, and router software. They support a local interface, remote interfaces, and protocols; and can handle concurrent communication among different LAN access methods, such as Ethernet, Token Ring, and FDDI. However, only nodes that use the same protocol can be linked. For example, a router can provide communications between a NetWare (IPX) user on an Ethernet LAN and a NetWare (IPX) server on a Token Ring LAN. It cannot provide communications between that NetWare user and a UNIX (TCP/IP) server.

Because routers use the Network layer address (OSI's third layer), they can determine the best internetwork path between any two nodes. This might be a function of the cheapest, most cost-effective, least congested, highest data rate, least number of hops between end nodes, or some combination of these factors.

The path between routers is decided by interrouter communications protocols. The most popular are:

- **Router Information Protocol** (RIP) is a simple, vector-based, hop-count metric (how many jumps from node-to-node are required). All routers broadcast their entire RIP database across the internet every 60 seconds, whether there are changes or not.

- **Open Shortest Path First** uses a link-state algorithm that allows a router to dynamically monitor status changes of each link and broadcast those changes immediately.
- **Interior Gateway Routing Protocol**, developed by router vendor Cisco Systems Inc., is an enhanced proprietary version of RIP.

The supported network management protocols must also be considered. Most routers support the Simple Network Management Protocol (SNMP), a management information base (MIB), and provide some MIB extensions. A MIB is a database listing of manageable objects in the internet. Support may also be provided for IBM's NetView and Digital's DECmcc Director.

Routers can usually be managed via SNMP, even in a geographically dispersed internet. A console interface connected to a terminal is used to configure the routers and provide a remote access point for service.

Some routers, such as those from Cisco Systems, NCR Corp., Proteon, and Wellfleet Communications, support the virtual terminal features of TCP/IP Telenet utilities. Routers from vendors such as Cisco Systems, Proteon, NCR Corp., 3M Corp, Ungermann-Bass, and Wellfleet Communications also integrate LANs with IBM's Systems Network Architecture (SNA) protocols (by encapsulating SNA traffic within TCP/IP or other routable packets) and in some cases NetBIOS and DECnet Phase V protocols as well.

Because each individual router understands the entire internet's topology, a router can automatically pick up a failed device's traffic load, thereby rerouting traffic around the failed router. This network partitioning also means that the separate LANs can still function as local communication paths. A routed internet is more secure than a bridged LAN because a communication device has access to the router's addressing capabilities only when needed.

Router reliability is measured in mean time between failures. High-end multiprotocol routers offer redundant power supplies, hot-swappable components, and fault-tolerant bus architectures.

Router performance is typically rated by the same two variables as bridges: filtering rate and forwarding rate, both measured in packets or frames per second. However, these do not take into account the complex process the router must go through to convert the frames of dissimilar LANs. Each LAN type uses a different frame size and frame structure. A router backplane can support virtually anything thrown at it today. However, LANs operate at a set speed (Ethernet at 10 Mbps, Token Ring at 4 or 16 Mbps, and FDDI at 100 Mbps), regardless of the speed of the interconnecting routers.

Routers come in a variety of chassis sizes and corresponding capabilities. A small chassis has a fixed configuration with one or two interface slots. A medium chassis is modular and has four slots. A large chassis is also modular and has 8, 12, or more slots.

Hybrid bridge/router software can handle both functions. If the software cannot identify the protocol for a packet-routing request, it simply bridges the packet.

Because Digital's Local Area Transport and IBM's NetBIOS do not contain routing information, they will not work (as is) with routers. Some router vendors offer bridging or encapsulation options for these protocols, but bridges are simpler to install and maintain and cost less.

Internal bridges included with such LAN operating systems as VINES, NetWare, and LAN Manager can be used for routing functions. Internal bridges require a network interface card in the file server and must notify the LAN operating system of their existence. Each network interface card in the file server supports a different logical network.

The most commonly mentioned advantages and disadvantages of bridges and routers are listed in Figure 14.3. As is usually the case with competing technologies, some of these points are disputed by advocates of that technology.

14.1.4 Network Hardware Gateways

Routers can connect networks whose physical and data link layers are different, but whose upper level layers are the same. Network gateways are used to connect networks that are entirely different.

Network gateways perform all the conversions necessary to go from one set of protocols to another, including:

- **Message Format Conversion.** The gateway converts messages of different formats, sizes, and character codes into those appropriate for the destination network.
- **Address Translation.** The gateway translates the address information to the structure of the destination network.
- **Protocol Conversion.** The control information sent with the message must be replaced with the appropriate control information for comparable functions in the destination network.

While network gateways provide great flexibility in connecting networks, they are also the most complex and expensive.

14.1.5 Backbone Networks

Many organizations are now providing connections between LANs

Advantages
Bridges • Easy to install requiring minimal configuration • Inexpensive with good price performance • Transparent to a variety of high-level protocols • Flexible and transparent to users **Routers** • Support for all topologies • Determine transmission path based on availability • Can perform load-splitting • Provide security through logical segmentation of subnetworks

Disadvantages
Bridges • Cannot handle all network problems and delays • Cannot prevent broadcast protocols from flooding every node • Can preclude some applications from running on the network • Limited functionality, such as no load-splitting • Limited support for fault isolation **Routers** • Protocol-dependent • Slower and more expensive than bridges unless compression software is used • Can be difficult to configure and install • May require additional connecting hardware for protocols that are not routable • Relocation of subnetworks requires the assignment of a new network address

Figure 14.3 Comparison of bridges and routers

using backbone networks. As illustrated in Figure 14.4, the users are not attached directly to the backbone network but to a LAN, which is connected to the backbone.

Backbone networks are of a higher quality than the connected LANs and usually use microwave-based links or FDDI. Fiber networks can span greater distances than LANs. An FDDI may be run vertically in a building to connect the LANs on each floor. An FDDI could be used to connect office buildings or buildings on a campus.

A backbone network requires a high bandwidth, the ability to transmit long distances with high reliability (because it covers such

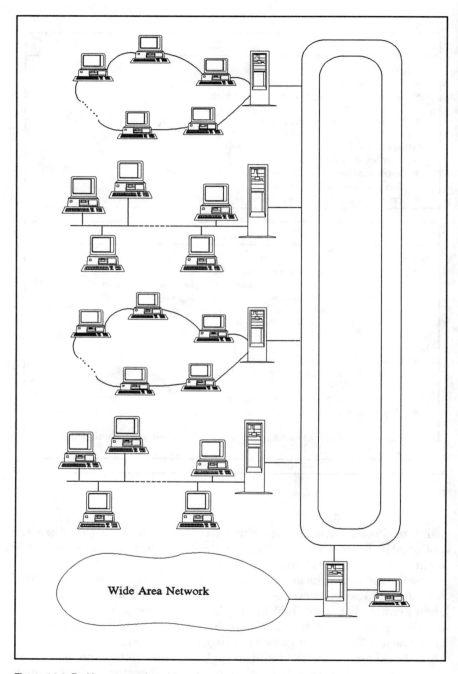

Figure 14.4 Backbone network architecture

great distances, faults are sometimes difficult to locate and repair). Backbone networks are usually built with leased wideband circuits such as T1 or T3 links operating at 1.5 and 45 Mbps respectively.

FDDI uses two counter-rotating optical fiber rings, in which two networks actually run on one set of cables. One ring is set up as the primary ring and the other ring is the backup ring. If the primary ring encounters a problem, the other remains in operation. The backup ring wraps around, isolating the failure, as illustrated in Figure 14.5.

A backbone network allows the individual LANs to operate in parallel, for optimum processing efficiency and reliability (each LAN can continue to operate no matter what goes down in the rest of the network, including the backbone). The individual LANs are connected to the backbone with a bridge, router, or gateway.

14.2 Network Operating Systems

As networks become more sophisticated, they need operating system software to shield application programs from direct communication with the hardware. A network operating system manages the services of the server in the same manner that an operating system manages the services of the hardware. Today's leading network operating systems offer the reliability, performance, security, and internetworking

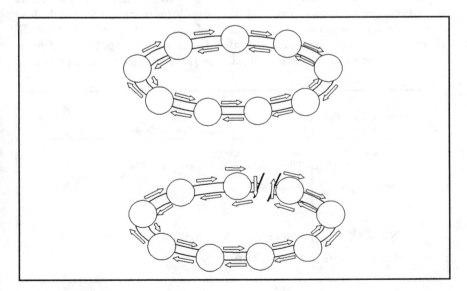

Figure 14.5 FDDI failure recovery

capability once associated primarily with mainframe and midrange computers.

A network operating system exists at the Session and Presentation layers of the client machine's network management software and provides links to upper layer network management software, as shown in Figure 14.6. GUIs are an overlay to the network operating system.

When an existing network is used to support a basic client/server application, no new software should be required. Care must be taken, however, to ensure that the resulting network traffic does not bring the network to its knees.

Developed as server-enablers, LAN operating systems have evolved into a network management tool, an enabler of other software packages, and a platform for GUIs and other presentation standards.

The most popular LAN operating systems are:

- NetWare from Novell
- LAN Manager from Microsoft
- OS/2 LAN Server from IBM
- VINES from Banyan

There are some DOS-based LAN operating systems, such as Novell's NetWare Lite, Artisoft's LANtastic, and Performance Technology's POWERLan. They use DOS to manage the hard disk in the server. Excellent in performing single tasks, their lack of a multitasking environment does not allow them to run multiple applications simultaneously. These products for small networks are much less expensive and less complex than LAN Manager, NetWare, or VINES. However, if the organization's goal is to set up a compatible network away from the main operation site, high-end network operating systems

Network Operating System	Upper-layer Software
NetWare	Novell proprietary Third-party links to NetView, SNMP, proprietary
LAN Manager	Proprietary NetView Alerts SNMP
VINES	Third-party links to NetView, SNMP, proprietary
OS/2 LAN Server	NetView Alerts

Figure 14.6 Network operating system links to upper-layer network management software

now have reasonable start-up versions for almost the same cost as the DOS-based products.

IBM's OS/2 LAN Server represents a very small market share at the time of writing, but due to Microsoft's incorporation of LAN Manager capabilities into Windows NT, OS/2 LAN Server may inherit LAN Manager users. For that reason it is discussed in this chapter.

14.2.1 NetWare

One of the most popular LAN operating systems today is Novell's NetWare. NetWare's architecture is illustrated in Figure 14.7. The newest member of the family, NetWare Lite, is designed for small

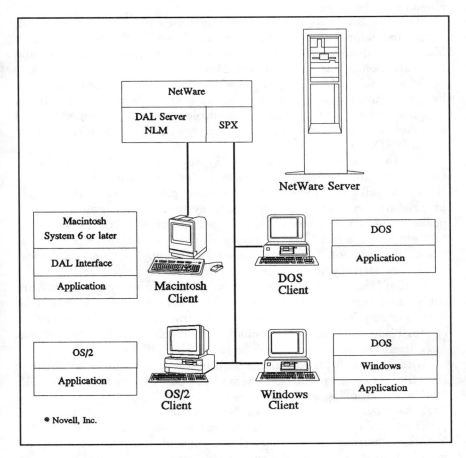

Figure 14.7 NetWare architecture

offices and is a peer-to-peer system. In a server-based system like NetWare, the network operating system, applications, and files are stored on a dedicated machine that manages file traffic across the network. In a peer-to-peer setup, the network operating system is installed on each machine that has access to the network.

NetWare can be used with bus (such as Ethernet) or token ring (such as Token Ring) architectures. It supports file and printer sharing, E-mail, remote access, and inter-LAN communication via a NetWare Bridge or a gateway to IBM's SNA, and it can emulate NetBIOS. Utilities are provided for adding users, changing passwords, and maintaining system security. NetWare is supported by software vendors ranging from micros to UNIX-based to IBM hosts. A single NetWare server can seamlessly integrate DOS, OS/2, Macintosh, and UNIX clients on a network.

NetWare 3.11 supports TCP/IP and its native IPX/SPX protocol. Additional support can be provided via Novell's NetWare Loadable Modules, such as NetWare Asynchronous Communication Services and NetWare Communication Services Manager.

As with LAN Manager, NetWare's ability to run multiple protocols lies in a driver specification (in this case Open DataLink Interface), which allows a client to attach to multiple networks. Using additional software, a DOS client can simultaneously attach to a NetWare server and a UNIX host.

NetWare (and Banyon's VINES) uses a technique called IP tunneling to allow clients to access their devices across the IP network. Network software in the client takes packets with the native proprietary protocol of the operating system, wraps them inside IP packets and moves the encapsulated packets across a TCP/IP backbone for delivery to a node that can strip away the outer envelope and use the native protocol. Tunneling allows TCP/IP applications and devices to use network-specific routers and other network services.

Unlike Microsoft LAN Manager or VINES, an entry-level NetWare server can run on a 386SX CPU with 4 Mbytes of RAM. But most networks require a more powerful configuration. NetWare can run on a multitude of platforms, including VMS and UNIX. Novell has announced plans to port NetWare to OS/2.

With Version 3.11, Novell has built network management functions into the network operating system. Data can be passed up to IBM's NetView and, using an SNMP agent, to SNMP management stations such as Novell's new NetWare Management System (NMS). NMS provides an open and extensible environment for managing the NetWare environment (as well as hubs, routers, and WAN links), which is tightly integrated into the server platform.

NetWare Name Service simplifies multiple server management. Each group of servers, called a domain, includes a name server to keep track of user passwords and network privileges. As the system administrator makes changes to the user's data, the name server copies the user database to the other servers on the domain. However, currently, unlike LAN Manager and VINES, NetWare does not allow user privileges to be set on one server for the entire network.

As for fault tolerance, Novell currently offers disk mirroring and disk duplexing. Novell System Fault Tolerance Level III (SFT III), an enhanced version of NetWare, creates mirrored servers, allowing a backup server to take over if the primary server goes down.

However, NetWare was not designed to support multiple LANs and as such contains a serious weakness. Because NetWare is a combined operating system and network operating system, it runs in Ring 0, the execution mode associated with Intel 80286 and higher micro-processors. Small ring numbers indicate greater privilege and less protection than higher ring numbers. APIs called NetWare Loadable Modules (NLMs) can be written to link applications and resources to NetWare. During the linking process, the NLM code is physically linked to NetWare code and, therefore, also runs at Ring 0. Because NetWare lacks a preemptive scheduler, the NetWare kernel cannot get control of the CPU back from an NLM until the NLM surrenders control. So if an NLM crashes, it brings down the server.

Novell is expecting to begin shipping NetWare 4.0 mid-1993. NetWare 4.0 will provide a distributed directory and naming service that can be automatically replicated and synchronized across all NetWare servers on a LAN. This first release of Version 4 will not contain large LAN support, the ability to run application in protected memory (which would minimize crashes due to NLMs), virtual memory, optional pre-emption, or multiprocessing support.

14.2.2 LAN Manager

Microsoft's LAN Manager works across multiple protocols, supporting either NetBIOS or TCP/IP (but not both concurrently), and has connections to the mainframe environment through its compatibility with IBM OS/2 LAN Server. It is also tightly integrated with Windows and offers interoperability with NetWare through its NetWare Connectivity Program. LAN Manager requires that the server run OS/2 but it can be accessed by clients running other operating systems, including the Macintosh.

LAN Manager's features include:

- **The concept of a domain**. Servers can be grouped into a domain and treated as a group. This feature facilitates adding and deleting users and applying security authorizations.
- **OS/2 Named Pipes facility**. A named pipe is a connection that transfers data between processors, usually on separate computers. Under LAN Manager, a Named Pipe is a logical structure that redirects communications across the network. As a shared resource, it is available to any user and can be used by developers as an interface for their API development.
- **Support for multiprocessing**. Processors can be dedicated to specific operations. All requests for that operation will automatically be routed to that processor.
- **A preemptive scheduler**. The operating system can cut off one process to give the CPU to another process with higher priority. NetWare, by contrast, relies on the designer of an NLM or VAP to return control to the scheduler.
- **Remote access service**. This feature allows users to dial into a LAN Manager network.

LAN Manager can connect the client and the server with any number of a wide range of transport protocols, including LAN Manager's NetBEUI (NetBIOS Extended User Interface) and TCP/IP. Above the transport protocol lies the NetBIOS API, which receives server message block packets and delivers them across the network. With a common API, applications are shielded from the nuances of different transport protocols.

Below the transport protocols lies NDIS (Network Driver Interface Specification) and 3Com's DPA (Demand Protocol Architecture), which enable LAN Manager to run multiple protocol stacks on a single client. The combination of DPA and NDIS enables users to load and unload alternate protocols, such as Novell's IPX, 3Com's XNS, or the OSI transport layer.

Since LAN Manager's native protocol, NetBEUI, cannot be used to route NetBIOS, Microsoft supports NetBIOS over TCP/IP, which provides the necessary network layer information to be interpreted by the routers. Since most UNIX hosts do not understand NetBIOS, LAN Manager clients can only access other LAN Manager servers. Microsoft offers a set of TCP/IP utilities that will allow DOS or OS/2 clients to access UNIX hosts.

Microsoft's fault tolerance consists of disk mirroring, where two hard disks on the same controller replicate each other, or duplexing, where two hard disks are on separate controllers. Previously, LAN Manager provided a hot-fix capability, which checked for bad sectors but provided no mirroring or redundancy. In the current version of LAN Manager, error and status information can be sent to a NetView management host or SNMP can be used to give the information to a network management system on a TCP/IP host.

But LAN Manager's continued success is dependent on Microsoft's commitment to the OS/2 server platform. Although Microsoft recently released LAN Manager 2.2 with centralized management capabilities, Microsoft has already announced plans to move LAN Manager to Windows NT. Such a move can be interpreted to mean that Windows NT, rather than OS/2, will be Microsoft's development platform of choice. OS/2 shops running LAN Manager will have to look to IBM and OS/2 LAN Server for alternatives.

14.2.3 OS/2 LAN Server

Because IBM's OS/2 LAN Server 2.0 code is based on LAN Manager 2.0 from Microsoft, LAN Server and LAN Manager can work together on the same LAN. However, due to OS/2 LAN Server's compatibility with LAN Manager APIs and Named Pipes, applications written for LAN Manager can be run on an OS/2 LAN Server network. IBM has added two enhancements—aliases and dynamic resource sharing—that facilitate the administration of large networks using OS/2 LAN Server.

OS/2 LAN Server allows administrators to create a dynamic resource. When LAN Manager administrators create a shared resource, the program enters the share name into a static table, with a maximum of 500 active shared names on a server. File servers with large hard disk subsystems or numerous shared resources can quickly reach this limit.

In OS/2 LAN Server, the share is not created until the user requests it. When the user is finished with and unlinks from the resource, OS/2 LAN Server removes the share from the table and frees up the slot.

Another enhancement OS/2 LAN Server offers over LAN Manager is to extend alias name support to shared resources. The administrator can define a one-word alias for any resource in the domain, regardless of where the resource resides, and the domain controller will complete the link. Users just have to remember what they want to use, such as choosing PPLOTTER instead of //PRIMESERVER/IBMPLOT1.

Still missing from OS/2 LAN Server is support for Macintosh clients (although a version is due for release mid-1993), which is offered by LAN Manager. IBM also does not include support for TCP/IP in the base OS/2 LAN Server package, but a separate package is available that includes support for TCP/IP connections with other LAN Manager servers, but not for non-LAN Manager servers.

With the current uncertainty concerning the future direction of Microsoft's LAN Manager, IBM's efforts ensure that the capabilities of LAN Manager will continue to be available and enhanced under OS/2. IBM recently announced LAN Server 3.0, which is a 32-bit LAN operating system and includes all the functionality of LAN Manager (version 2.1) in addition to IBM-developed enhancements such as remote installs. LAN Server 3.0 comes in two versions. The Entry version is targeted for department use. The Advanced version also includes a high-performance file system, support for the multiprocessing capabilities of IBM's PS/2 Model 295, and enhanced fault tolerance that supports disk duplexing and disk mirroring. IBM also announced a Macintosh version of OS/2 LAN Server for mid-1993 availability.

Organizations that are committed to OS/2 as a server platform should readily accept OS/2 LAN Server (2.0 or 3.0) as an alternative to LAN Manager. The alias support for shared resources and Dynamic Resource Sharing make administering the LAN a much easier process. With the addition of Macintosh support, the differences between OS/2 LAN Server and LAN Manager are minimal.

14.2.4 VINES

Designed for larger networks, Banyan's VINES (VIrtual NEtworking System) integrates directory, security, and network management services on interconnected servers, each of which can support one or more micro-based LANs. In addition, as illustrated in Figure 14.8, it can run over WAN server-to-server interconnections to provide a single, global view of the enterprise network.

Because VINES is based on a UNIX kernel, a VINES server can be a 286, 386, or 486 machine running a POSIX-compliant version of UNIX System V. Clients can be running DOS, Windows, or OS/2. VINES Symmetric Multiprocessing takes advantage of powerful servers that distribute tasks dynamically across multiple processors.

VINES Internet Protocol (VIP), its native protocol, is a derivative of TCP/IP (and XNA). VIP supports:

- 3270/5250 emulation
- X.25 Packet Switching, TCP/IP and LAN Manager protocols
- Named pipes
- Application programming interfaces

An RPC interface allows applications to be developed independently of the specific communication protocol. Data transferred through the RPC interface relies on a proprietary transport layer program called the VINES Interprocess Communications Protocol.

VINES also uses the IP tunneling technique used by NetWare. In addition, tunneling can also be used to move TCP/IP traffic across VINES networks by encapsulating IP packets within VIP packets.

VINES provides easy-to-use configuration and monitoring tools and authorization routines for network-wide security. Standard functions include file and print services and VINES Network Mail.

The naming convention used by the Banyan StreetTalk distributed global directory can set up an organizational directory of all networks, identifying users within groups and groups within organizations. The StreetTalk database, stored at every server, details the name, location, and attributes of every network user and resource, including shared volumes, printers, lists, nicknames, host gateways, and integrated third-party products worldwide. The VINES servers pass updates of the

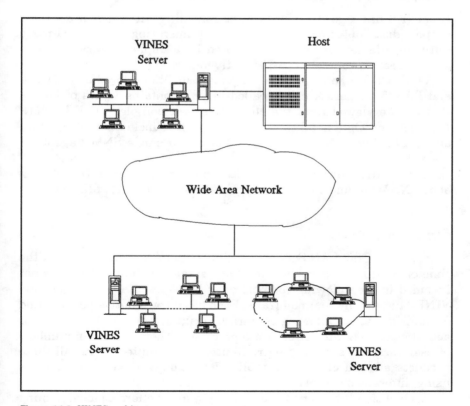

Figure 14.8 VINES architecture

StreetTalk database among themselves regularly. In addition, StreetTalk can direct local servers to connect automatically to remote servers and update the master directory of StreetTalk users, thus incorporating individuals added to the system as recently as the day before.

For mixed networks, Banyan plans to link StreetTalk to the X.500 standard. It has developed an NLM that provides StreetTalk services to NetWare platforms, making it easier to link VINES and NetWare servers in a common network environment.

Complementing StreetTalk is VANGuard, VINES's security system. In addition to the expected password verification and access rights, VANGuard provides a number of unusual security features, which include the following:

- It authenticates a user's ID before VINES performs a significant event.
- It provides password encryption with no session replay.

VINES has a good reputation for reliability. Although it does not support disk duplexing, it does allow disk mirroring. With third-party software, file services can be mirrored by a duplicate server; if one server crashes, control is passed to the other.

VINES lacks the separate management utilities offered by NetWare and LAN Manager. A utility called MNET contains layers of menus that can be viewed from the client or server console. VINES SNMP Proxy Agent Option takes data from MNET, including information about all active VINES servers, and acts as a single SNMP agent for the network.

Despite these difficulties, VINES's multiserver capabilities place it above NetWare and LAN Manager in the extended network market.

14.2.5 Comparisons

(Note: Since OS/2 LAN Server is so similar to LAN Manager and at the time of writing holds such a small percentage of the market, it is not included in the following comparisons.) NetWare, LAN Manager, and VINES have many common traits. Each has its own native protocol and is multithreaded allowing security, print-server, and file access activities to be treated as separate processes. They are sold in number-of-user versions, such as 5-user, 25-user, or unlimited users. All three products allow a client to establish a session with multiple servers using different protocols.

Each of the three network operating systems offers a global naming service, which groups servers into domains—groups with a common interest. One logon server typically handles security control for all servers within its domain. Within the domain, users access all resources through resource names instead of complex multilevel names linked to specific servers.

VINES' StreetTalk, the most comprehensive global naming service, supports domains across extended networks. Novell's NetWare Name Service is an option; a naming service is built into LAN Manager. But the NetWare and LAN Manager services handle user and group names. They do not provide the network resource information or the directory service features provided by StreetTalk. In addition, VINES is the exclusive provider (of the three products) of a global lookup service for locating a specific resource.

All three network operating systems are beginning to include fault-tolerant features, such as monitoring the operational status of an uninterruptible power supply attached to the server; mirroring disk drives or drive controllers; duplicating servers; and disk duplexing, which maintains mirrored disks by using separate controllers, eliminating another potential point of failure. NetWare 3.11 includes all these features except server duplication, which is planned for Novell SFT III. VINES has little built-in fault-tolerant capability, but third-party vendors offer products that add strong fault tolerance to it. While LAN Manager provides many fault-tolerant features, they are not as easily managed as those in NetWare.

To manage the network, all three products support SNMP. LAN Manager and NetWare also support IBM's NetView management system. In addition, NetWare also supports CMIP.

Network operating systems are headed toward combining the network operating system with the server operating system. The next-generation server operating system will have built-in networking hooks. The network operating system will exist as part of the server operating system, and the client software will include hooks to the network software. This is the approach Microsoft has taken with Windows New Technology. The idea of a universal Windows client integrated with the server software, as in the Macintosh today, certainly appeals to Microsoft. It also benefits Banyan with its unique enterprise architecture. To Novell, however, this approach means defending its presence in the LAN market.

14.2.6 Network Routing Software

There are also third-party vendors offering software to cross the boundaries of network operating systems.

SQL*Net from Oracle supports a wide variety of networking protocols, including IPX/SPX, TCP/IP, DECnet, APPC/LU6.2, OSI, OS/2 Named Pipes, NetBIOS, AppleTalk, and VINES, with a different version of SQL*Net for each supported protocol. Our discussion will use SQL*Net TCP/IP as an example.

SQL*Net uses layers of hardware and software. At the bottom is a physical network, (for TCP/IP, usually Ethernet). The network protocol (TCP/IP) transfers packets of information between nodes on the network. SQL*Net uses the protocol (TCP/IP) to make a connection between a front-end client running on a personal computer and a back-end database server.

SQL*Net is installed as part of the database server installation process. Once SQL*Net is installed, clients can access the database on the server by appending what Oracle calls a "connect string" onto the end of an application logon.

IBM's Advanced Program-to-Program Communications (**APPC**) and **OS/2 Named Pipes** have the communications facilities to connect DOS workstations to IBM hosts via an OS/2 communications server. This architecture offers such advantages as access to existing host data and facilities from DOS workstations, efficient use of resources, and maximum use of existing LAN-connected DOS workstations for integrated applications.

APPC is an SNA facility for peer-to-peer communications across DOS, OS/2, AIX, OS/400, VTAM, CICS, and other IBM systems. OS/2 Named Pipes is an interprocess communication service, which uses a programming interface to allow bidirectional communication between two programs, running on either the same or separate systems.

APPC itself supports OS/2 Named Pipes and the workstations use the APPC connectivity in the OS/2 communications server, keeping memory requirements on the DOS workstations to a minimum. Because APPC is used to communicate with most IBM platforms, micros can access data and facilities throughout an organization without the users' knowing or caring what platforms are being accessed.

In order to communicate via APPC, a program must identify itself to the local SNA network management facility (OS/2 Communications Manager, for example) as a transaction program (TP) and is then assigned a unique TP ID. Each TP accesses the SNA network via an SNA software socket, referred to as a logical unit. A TP issues APPC calls to its local logical unit in order to communicate with a partner logical unit. This communication requires the allocation of a conversation between the two logical units over an SNA session, or logical connection. Multiple conversations, usually short in duration, can serially share the same session. Conversations can be either basic or mapped. Mapped conversations are relatively less complex than basic conversations and are used by application programs.

APPC conversations use a half-duplex, flip-flop protocol based on send and receive states. At any given time in the conversation, one partner should be in send state and the other in receive state. Applications that flip-flop often must avoid getting into an invalid state. The working model seeks to avoid invalid-state problems by using a simple send request/receive response protocol.

Open Windows Connection from Cogent Data Technologies, Inc. allows users to transparently connect to dissimilar network operating systems and automates the process of logging on to different servers.

Using a menu-driven Windows interface, users define combinations of connections and assign an icon to the group, called a server group. The server group can be modified, deleted or expanded by including other groups. Users activate and deactivate connections by clicking on the group's icon.

Open Windows Connection supports popular network operating systems such as NetWare, LAN Manager, and VINES. It supports popular protocols such as IPX/SPX, TCP/IP, SNMP, NFS, NetBIOS, DECnet, and Digital's Local Area Transport, which is a nonroutable, terminal-server protocol used on Ethernets that permits terminals to connect to an entire LAN.

Development
and Deployment

Organizations envision client/server computing as an opportunity to re-engineer their business—rethinking and redesigning their workflow, customer service, and other aspects of the business to gain a competitive advantage. These companies are making strategic use of this new technology.

Client/server applications require new skills from developers and an expanded focus from IS. Developers need to integrate GUIs, distributed applications, relational databases, and networks. They need to start thinking in terms of objects and become comfortable with the object-oriented paradigm. The tools that help developers build applications for client/server environments assume that the developer has acquired a new skill set based on GUIs, desktop computing, and SQL databases.

There are options for downsizing applications to smaller platforms without totally redesigning and coding an application. Converting 3270/5250 screens to GUIs offers immediate benefits in end-user productivity. COBOL-to-COBOL conversion tools can convert CICS screens to GUI screens and mainframe COBOL to micro COBOL. CASE tools can be used to re-engineer existing applications. These options automate existing processes so if inefficiencies exist to begin with, they will be transferred to the smaller platform.

IS now has to contend with distributed application software, distributed data, distributed transactions, multivendor environments, and a geographically dispersed information infrastructure. The walls of the glass room are tumbling down.

15

Development Methodology

The current evolution of computer-based systems is forcing major changes to IS processes and procedures. In the past, applications ran on one machine, regardless of size; now applications are partitioned and data distributed so more than one machine could be executing the processing for an application. The network (and its health) has become a critical component in the information infrastructure. In a distributed environment, the network is no longer as simple as cables connecting terminals to a box.

Applications are evolving from character-based systems, to which users are accustomed, to graphical-based systems. Data is no longer stored and controlled by the mainframe with a high-level of security and backup. Instead, data is spread organization-wide on servers that require security and backup, and is the responsibility of IS. Adopting open systems means maintaining links between components of a distributed system, which introduces new technologies to the IS staff, such as UNIX, Windows, OS/2, LAN operating systems, RPCs, gateways, and DME/DCE.

After spending years with structured and top-down design and programming techniques, developers now have to jump to GUI generation and object-oriented analysis and programming techniques. The transition to new techniques is not easy and it is not done overnight.

But it is worth the effort. The desktop machine provides a user-friendly interface (most client/server application development tools use GUIs), local autonomy, subsecond response time, and a personal prototyping workstation. All analysis, design, prototyping code generation, testing, emulation, execution, and maintenance can be done on the desktop. The finished product can then be ported to the appropriate environment.

The focus is changing from application development to application construction. Traditionally, application development required trained, specialized IS professionals who met with users to define system requirements. IS then went away for some period of time (always too long from the users' point of view, never long enough from IS's point of view) to develop the specifications and build the application. Often, the IS solution was not quite what the users wanted or thought they asked for. In addition, during the time required to develop the application, the business may have changed so that the original specifications no longer fit the current requirement.

Application construction uses tools to automate the analysis, design, prototyping, generation, and build phases of application development. These tools allow users to do more of the development themselves. Using a GUI, users can specify their data requirements, data entry criteria, and business rules. Multiple users can participate in the analysis. To encourage user input, prototyping tools simulate the look-and-feel of the application. Users can react to what they see and use. The tools can be used to make changes to the prototype rapidly and efficiently.

Once the design or prototype is complete, the development tool can generate forms, menus, and reports for the application. This goes far beyond the code generators that IS has worked with over the last five years. New generations of development tools build the necessary links from the menus to the forms and reports. At the push of a button, out comes a complete and executable application.

Another advantage of application construction tools is that the final product (the application) is easily maintained by the same software that created it. Developers can make changes to the high-level specifications for the business model and regenerate the application automatically.

As the characteristics of the applications change, so does the appropriate development methodology or at least the combination of the methodology tasks. The development of a single-user, single-location application should not require the same rigorous techniques as the development of a multiuser, multilocation, multidata-source application.

There are currently four methodologies for generating client/server applications to replace or augment existing applications:

- Convert 3270/5250 screens to client-based GUI screens and make no modifications to the host-based application.
- Downsize the application by converting the mainframe COBOL-based application to a server COBOL-based application. Emulate existing, host-based database management systems on the server.
- Convert the host-based application to a server-based application by re-engineering and rebuilding the application software.
- Re-think the business process, then design and build applications to support the new approach: re-engineer the business.

15.1 Convert Existing Screen Interfaces

By putting a GUI front-end on 3270/5250 screens (illustrated in Figure 15.1), organizations provide an easy-to-use interface to familiar processes without requiring additional power from the host. In addition, since the client software converts the 3270/5250 data streams to a GUI screen, there are no changes required of the host application. It is a fairly easy step to improve productivity using existing (often underutilized) equipment. It also provides a common graphical interface to host applications.

In order to realize some of the benefits of client/server computing, organizations must go beyond simply adding a GUI front-end to an existing application. With the easy-to-use micro-based development tools for converting 3270/5250 screens, developers can add micro-based error checking to the client application (just translating screens is considered an application, though it performs no other functions than translation). Micro-based menus and help routines can be built to aid the user in working with the host application.

Many corporations find that this is just window (no pun intended) dressing. It is a low-risk venture into GUI territory and is technically considered client/server computing because the screen building is performed on the client. But host processing requirements are not reduced. The host is still generating the screen and performing edit

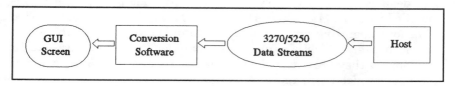

Figure 15.1 GUI front-end to 3270/5250 screens

checking on incoming data—which may have been edited by the client software.

One other disadvantage of this approach is that MIS personnel must support and maintain the host application code as well as the micro-based code.

15.2 COBOL-to-COBOL Migration

One option with a high success rate is the migration of mainframe-based applications to LANs with a COBOL-to-COBOL conversion.

15.2.1 COBOL Workbench

Micro Focus Inc. offers a micro-based environment that provides a mainframe-like development environment and relies on existing skills, such as expertise in COBOL and CICS. Its reasonably priced COBOL programming tools for building software run on the smallest desktop micro or the largest mainframe.

COBOL Workbench from Micro Focus is a suite of development tools for creating, debugging, and testing applications on DOS, Windows, OS/2, and UNIX environments. Version 3.0 offers a runtime environment for Windows, improved file management tools, and a Probe utility that lets developers examine the structure of COBOL applications and how they interact.

The newest release of the Micro Focus COBOL 3.0 compiler runs on DOS, Windows, and OS/2. It features productivity enhancements to Animator, a graphical debugger, as well as support for Novell's Btrieve file format. The company also plans to release versions of the compiler for IBM's AIX and The Santa Cruz Operation Inc.'s SCO Unix 386 operating system. In addition, Micro Focus has OEM agreements with Microsoft and IBM; their PC COBOL compilers are actually Micro Focus COBOL compilers.

Micro Focus Toolset is a collection of tools and utilities that help build portable COBOL applications under DOS, Windows, and OS/2. Version 3.0 includes Micro Focus's Operating System Extensions, which provide a common set of system functions that allow applications compiled with the Micro Focus COBOL 3.0 compiler to be easily ported to various operating environments. Two of these tools are the Micro Focus Checker, which is a full-screen compiler that allows users to fix problems as they are detected by the software, and Animator, which is a full-screen debugger and unit testing tool.

Micro Focus's new product, Fileshare, a file server for COBOL applications, runs as an NLM with the NetWare 386 LAN operating system. It is designed to improve the performance of COBOL file processing on Novell networks, and performs record locking, file update logging, roll-forward recovery, and transaction processing.

Micro Focus also offers:

- **Common Communications Interface** (CCI), a COBOL-oriented, protocol-independent application program interface (API) that shields developers from the intricacies of communications programming
- **CICS OS/2 Option**, used to migrate CICS applications to smaller platforms

Micro Focus's Dialog System 2.1, another COBOL tool, lets developers create graphical user interfaces for COBOL programs running under DOS, OS/2, Windows, and UNIX. Dialog System supports point-and-click development of graphical and character-based user interfaces. It isolates screen and keyboard logic from COBOL applications, replacing lines of screen definition code with a simple CALL statement. User interfaces can be prototyped, developed, and updated without impacting the application logic.

15.2.2 CA-Realia COBOL

CA-Realia COBOL from Computer Associates (formerly from Realia, Inc, which was acquired by Pansophic, which in turn was acquired by Computer Associates) provides many of the features included in Micro Focus's COBOL Workbench but in a simpler environment and for less money. With the marketing and development resources of Computer Associates behind the product, it may catch up to Micro Focus, the current market leader.

15.2.3 UniKix

UniKix from Integris can port IBM CICS/VSAM applications to a variety of UNIX platforms without code modifications. Once UniKix is initiated, the user does not deal directly with UNIX, but is under control of the UniKix executive and needs no detailed knowledge of UNIX. UniKix also provides a development environment for OLTP applications.

UniKix uses Micro Focus COBOL and Animator to provide an interactive development and debugging facility. UniKix supports SNA networks on UNIX. Its XPU4 product connects 3270 terminals and cluster controllers directly into the UNIX system and the UniKix application. Its XPU5 product allows the UniKix system to act as a domain within the overall SNA network.

15.3 Re-Engineering Existing Applications

Software re-engineering examines and alters existing code into a new form. Nearly three-quarters of an organization's programming efforts go toward maintaining and enhancing existing systems. As existing applications have been modified to incorporate the changing needs of the business, their code becomes unwieldy and hard to maintain. Re-engineering the code results in an application that has the original features but uses a simpler code structure.

The two steps in software re-engineering are:

- **Reverse engineering.** The code is analyzed to determine the physical and logical design of the application—what are the components and how do they interact. Ideally, the information about each component should be stored in a repository. The output is an application with its original features and platform support but with an easier code structure for maintenance.
- **Forward engineering.** Traditional CASE tools could then be used to forward engineer the system, adding functionality and cleaning up data relationships and data objects in the process. Forward engineering generates the necessary code for the cleaned-up application to run on a new platform or with a new data source.

Software re-engineering can be used to convert an application to another DBMS, source-code language, operating system, or hardware platform. Ideally, reverse engineering should generate specification information that can be used by CASE tools to generate the code. Specification information required by a CASE tool for forward engineering includes data structure diagrams, entity-relationship diagrams, functional decomposition diagrams, and data flow diagrams.

However, the software re-engineering tools only provide some of this specification information.

- **Documenters** read code and generate high-level information about what the application is doing.
- **Restructurers** replace spaghetti code with structured code.
- **Analyzers** evaluate the logical complexity of a program and search for redundant data definitions.
- **Diagrammers** read application code and produce structure charts, or read database code and produce data model diagrams.

However, most re-engineering tools simply produce reports. Only a few tools use a repository to store the results. Consequently, rekeying or manual transformation are usually required to pass information from one re-engineering step to another. Software re-engineering tools can handle the lower-level CASE functionality. Currently, there are no products that can automate the process of extracting data flow and entity-relationship information from existing applications. This is still a manual, labor-intensive process.

15.4 Business Re-Engineering

The 1970s term popularized by James Martin and Clive Finkelstein is being revitalized: *information engineering*. In essence, information engineering focuses on business knowledge (what is to be achieved and how to achieve it) rather than technology. It represents a change from the *process with data* paradigm to *data-based process* paradigm. When an information-engineering approach is followed, a development team is made up of more business users than IS professionals. Systems developed using this approach can respond faster to business changes because the system architecture did not focus on technology—it was not forced to fit a particular data model or the idiosyncrasies of a particular processor. The architecture of the system was based on business needs. This has given rise to the current phrase *business re-engineering*.

Business re-engineering involves rethinking and redesigning the entire business system—processes, management systems, organizational structures, jobs, beliefs, and values. Instead of simply automating existing processes and procedures, the old processes are replaced with new ones that have a positive impact on the business and affect every worker in the organization.

Organizations are considering business re-engineering as a means of reducing cost, improving customer service, and streamlining operations. The downside to business re-engineering is disruption in the workplace and the need to manage the resistance to change.

Although the evaluation of business processes is not new, business re-engineering is becoming important in light of increasing global competition, slim profit margins, rapid changes in the business climate, and the need to improve customer service. Information technology is becoming an enabler in the design of more efficient business processes.

Business re-engineering is not an IS task and should not be proposed or led by IS. An executive champion should inspire the effort and lead the process. The business process planning requirements need to be determined before the enabling technology is selected. Managers should understand how the redesigned business process will add value to the organization and develop performance measures for that process. IS is part of the team that designs the new business system. IS professionals should be technological visionaries who contribute insights into the current technology and future trends.

Systems re-engineering redesigns the workflow of the organization's information systems. This redesign is not likely to disrupt the organization, although it requires teamwork on the part of IS and users. Two examples of systems re-engineering are the use of electronic document interchange (EDI) and imaging systems to replace paper-based systems.

To effectively re-engineer a process within an organization, there must be strong (and visible) commitment from upper management, a willingness to see the process to completion, and excellent interpersonal communication—to re-engineer the processes, manage change, and control rumors. Business re-engineering does not require outside assistance (other than perhaps a consultant knowledgeable in new information technologies). The organization's staff is the best source for the critical information required to support re-engineering.

Business re-engineering is not an easy task—to redesign the processes or to implement them. However, organizations that have re-engineered their businesses have reaped dramatic benefits that made the effort worthwhile. These benefits include increased competitive capabilities, increased access to data, greater flexibility in business operations, and a dramatic reduction in the cost of computer systems.

15.5 Methodology Tools

Methodology tools need to address the following areas in GUI-based computing environments:

- Support for the migration of legacy systems and applications to the new environment.
- Generation of portable GUI source code so that the same code can be deployed on different platforms.
- Support for a mix of platforms, such as Windows clients linked to UNIX servers.
- Generation of fairly complete application code from prototypes.

The tools discussed in Chapter 16, Application Development Tools, provide a CASE-like environment for developing client/server applications and can be used to prototype applications quickly, as well.

15.5.1 Prototyping Tools

Computer-based tools now allow developers, working with business users, to develop application specifications on-the-fly in the form of running prototypes. Prototypes, rather than specification documents, become the communication medium in organizations that use joint application design (JAD) or rapid application development (RAD) methodologies. To support this kind of interactive development, vendors of 4GLs are coupling their products with computer-aided software engineering (CASE) products. Other vendors are adding prototyping capabilities and CASE-like features to their products.

As illustrated in Figure 15.2, the prototype process facilitates communication between users and IS, making the users an integral part of the process. The users generate a first pass at specifications for the application. IS then uses a prototype development tool to create and test the prototype (mock-up). The users review the prototype of the system and modify their specifications, which are then coded into the prototype and tested. This process continues until the users are satisfied with and accept the prototype. Depending on the application and the development tool, the prototype could become the production version of the application or the specifications would be used to code the application in some other language.

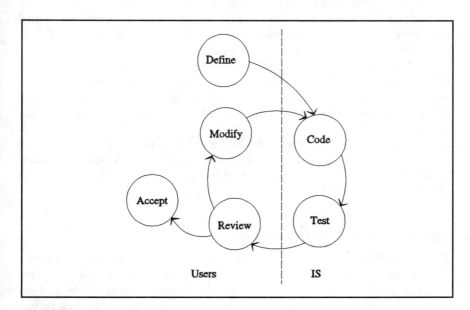

Figure 15.2 The prototype process

15.5.2 CASE Tools

CASE products are evolving rapidly. GUIs have changed the way users interact with computer applications. The shift toward client/server networks and distributed computing has created new application requirements. RAD tools and techniques, such as prototyping and JAD, must incorporate contemporary graphical interface requirements.

GUI-based systems require more functionality than CASE tools have provided in the past. They must generate applications that are platform-independent for the client interface and the server. They must be more graphic-oriented, using a WYSIWYG approach. In addition to producing the code for GUIs, CASE tools have to support the client/server computing paradigm.

The resulting applications must support user queries to the data sources in the application, ideally resulting in fewer requests to IS. In addition, IS organizations need tools to help them migrate legacy applications to the rightsized platform.

CASE tools have been used by IS professionals to improve the quality of their applications by formalizing communication between developers and users in the early stages of development. High-end CASE tools use data-flow diagrams, functional decomposition diagrams, and entity-relationship diagrams to implement structured design methodologies. Low-end CASE tools, such as screen editors and application generators, support rapid prototyping and automatic code generation. Conventional CASE tools assume that the application and the data are on one machine and the user interacts with it via character-based screens on terminals.

Client/server environments are not that simple. Applications now take advantage of distributed computing, use GUI front-ends, and run on programmable machines. In addition to the presentation logic, the client machine performs some database access and application processing.

However, CASE tools are just beginning to provide limited support for client/server computing. However, most CASE vendors have announced plans to have full support for the client/server paradigm in the next release of their product.

Application Development Workbench

KnowledgeWare's integrated CASE product, Application Development Workbench (ADW), combines integrated, graphics-based modules (called workstations) with optional host-based tools. Information collected during development is stored in a central encyclopedia, ensuring consistency among specifications and designs.

As illustrated in Figure 15.3, ADW is comprised of the following components:

- **Planning Workstation** is used to establish a framework for system development throughout an enterprise. The enterprise model defines the organizational structure, business functions, goals, critical success factors and information needs of each organizational unit.
- **Analysis Workstation** creates detailed data and process models for each business area and their interrelationships. Consistency is automatically maintained among diagrams and updates are made as changes occur. All information is presented in the form of diagrams and reports.
- **RAD Workstation** provides prototyping based on the information collected in the Analysis Workstation. Using a screen painter, developers create screen templates and hierarchical screen models. The prototypes can be animated to allow users to verify the interface and screen flow before design work is started.
- **Design Workstation** is used to build high-level program logic, design data definitions and databases, and create screens and reports. Applications are illustrated graphically to facilitate understanding.
- **Documentation Workstation** automates systems documentation by managing diagrams, reports, and text files collected and produced

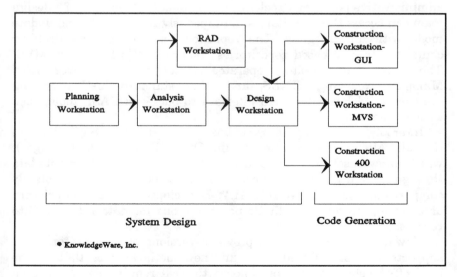

Figure 15.3 Application Development Workbench architecture

by other ADW workstations. It also incorporates text and graphic files from external sources, such as word processing packages. Documents can be organized, formatted, and viewed on the screen prior to printing.

- **Construction workstations** use the developed specifications to generate code. Currently there are individual workstations for MVS, AS/400, IBM's Cross System Product (CSP), and GUIs. The Construction Workstation-GUI also provides additional design tools for laying out GUI screens and defining help files. The current release of Construction Workstation-GUI supports Presentation Manager. The next release will support Windows and a future release will support Motif.

Excelerator II

Intersolv Inc. provides a client/server version of Excelerator, the application analysis and design tool that is a re-implementation of Excelerator for OS/2-based LANs. To address the challenge of supporting teams of software developers with shared access to common design components, Excelerator II (XLII) OS/2 is built around an active LAN-based repository. XLII uses an object-oriented design to combine the original Excelerator capabilities with LAN support. Intersolv terms the product as a full multiuser, multitasking, multithreaded, planning, analysis, and design tool.

The Intersolv LAN Repository provides central storage and an administrative point for Excelerator components. Members of a design team can access the repository simultaneously in read-only and update mode with full integrity. The repository can operate by itself or connected to host-based repositories such as IBM's Repository/MVS. The LAN-based repository operates on top of LAN Server, LAN Manager, NetWare, VINES, and other standard LAN operating systems. LAN Repository can interface to back-end CASE tools, such as code generators.

Intersolv's LAN Repository is based on a standard SQL database (initially Microsoft's SQL Server and OS/2 EE Data Base Manager), which allows users to store and access application development data through standard SQL tools for quick reports and specification lists. By comparison, KnowledgeWare's ADW Encyclopedia uses a proprietary data storage format that limits users' options for data retrieval into reports.

Upwardly compatible with previous versions of Excelerator, XLII supports a library of traditional and new methodologies that can be used off-the-shelf, or can be tailored to local requirements using an expert system called Customizer. Users can choose from a library of popular development methodologies that support data-driven, process-driven, and event-driven design approaches (client/server applications are event-driven). An optional feature authorizes modifications to the graphical objects and rules defined in the Intersolv LAN Repository.

XLII comes with a database reporting tool from Pioneer Software called Q+E, which allows users to access the repository directly to perform queries or generate reports. A DDE link built into XLII inserts information from XLII into Microsoft Word documents.

To facilitate the design of GUIs, XLII also includes a Graphical Application Workbench tool, which models GUIs for OS/2 and Windows applications, as well as 3270-type data-entry screens. Support for the generation of GUI code, through Intersolv's APS code generator, was available late 1992.

XLII for Windows is expected by mid-1993. Versions for UNIX and Sun's SunOS are expected by the end of 1993.

Information Engineering Facility

Information Engineering Facility (IEF), an integrated CASE tool from Texas Instruments, supports the development of GUI applications. Developers design and build the mainframe/server portion of an application, design and build the client portion, and then tie the two together.

The IEF product provides full integration within each stage and across all stages of the development life cycle by way of the IEF Host Encyclopedia, a comprehensive repository of sharable information. The IEF architecture is illustrated in Figure 15.4.

The IEF Planning, Analysis, Design, and Construction Toolsets are used by developers to create business system specifications for the data and business activities. When the specifications are complete and the target environment is chosen, COBOL or C code for the application is generated by the IEF Construction Toolset. The Construction Toolset also compiles and links the application, generates the documentation, and builds the databases.

Developers create GUIs with Window Designer, which is fully integrated with the IEF Encyclopedia and the other IEF toolsets. The code necessary to create and manipulate window objects is generated by Window Designer. Current GUI support is for OS/2 PM and Windows. Motif support will be available in the next release of the IEF product.

The IEF product can also generate the required communications

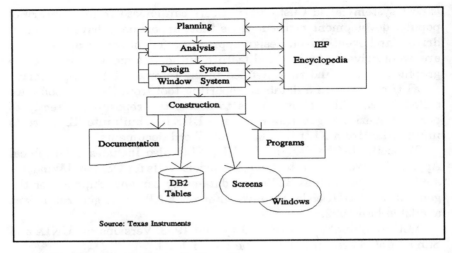

Figure 15.4 Information Engineering Facility architecture

components for a client/server application, using industry standard protocols.

The next version of the IEF product, due for release in mid-1993, will support runtime specification of the target environment, a LAN-based repository, and additional target environments.

SUPRe/DAISys

SUPRe/DAISys (Developer's Assistant for Information Systems with Secure User Programming by Refinement) from S-Cubed, Inc., uses familiar business icons such as forms, documents, and rules to describe the application, unlike the technically-oriented structured diagrams used in other CASE tools. Developed applications can run in both mainframe and client/server environments, enabling developers to build on one platform and migrate to another. SUPRe/DAISys supports ANSI-standard SQL databases, such as DB2, ORACLE, and XDB. It supports APPC/LU6.2 in the mainframe world, NetBIOS-compatible networks in the micro world, and TCP/IP in the UNIX world.

The DAISys component is comprised of three independent modules:

- **Research and Analysis Assistant**. Designed to help developers determine business requirements, this module provides cross-checking facilities for consistency and completeness, uses symbols and terminology that users can understand, and transforms business requirements into a logical model of data and processes.

- **Design and Simulation Assistant.** This module transforms the logical model into a technology-specific physical model. The developer specifies the target environment and clicks on a few buttons. The software performs all the process partitioning between the client and server and generates a test system, which can be reviewed by the users for completeness.
- **Code Generator.** The software will generate the client side and server side of the application in the appropriate language. System-level commands and embedded SQL will be included, if appropriate. The generated code must pass through the appropriate DBMS's precompiler before the application can function in production.

The SUPRe module allows users to customize their windows in the application without jeopardizing database security or integrity. Users can modify their screen by:

- Moving display objects around
- Adding buttons
- Changing colors
- Inserting local calculations
- Linking other applications

However, they are unable to bypass any of the data validation rules for the application, which are stored on the server. At runtime all transactions are validated before they are committed to the database.

In order to minimize network traffic and server processing cycles, SUPRe/DAISys stores a synopsis of the rules on each client, where they are checked each time a user enters or accesses data. This provides fast response for erroneous or unauthorized transactions and does not expend network or server resources for data integrity and security checks. The client's version of the rules are checked when an application's execution is initiated. If the client is not using the current version of the rules, a revised synopsis is passed to the client from the server.

A scripting feature allows users to record and playback keystrokes and mouse moves, just as they would macros in word processing and spreadsheet software. SUPRe/DAISys also includes a query facility for *ad hoc* queries against SQL databases.

16

Application Development Tools

One of the primary requirements of business users is simplified access to data. Business users don't care if the data access is implemented via client/server, distributed, object-oriented, terminal-based, LAN-based, or carrier pigeon. Business users just want to access their data with tools *they* find easy to use and that are responsive. To most users, that means GUIs—menus, buttons, icons, and dialog boxes with point-and-click operations. These tools should also support those users who want to develop their own simple applications.

IS professionals need tools that support the development of complex, mission-critical applications as easily as they support the development of simple applications and that allow them to build easy-to-use interfaces to those applications. It is important that application development tools be able to support team development. There should be a repository for objects, definitions, and reusable code. There should also be version control to synchronize module development.

16.1 Application Development Environments

The easy-to-use tools discussed below go beyond application design; they generate complete applications. To build a client program for an SQL server database using a 3GL such as COBOL, C, or C++, a programmer or programming team has to understand not only the 3GL itself, but networks and relational databases. To further complicate matters, many companies are building applications with GUIs. IS professionals are then required to understand GUIs, networks, and relational databases. Even for IS professionals with expertise in these three areas, building client/server applications that are written in a 3GL and use GUIs, networks, and relational databases is difficult and time consuming.

Two basic strategies minimize the requirement for such expertise. One strategy is to use simple query-and-report tools that require no knowledge of programming and a minimum of database knowledge, so that the tools can be used by business users. Such tools permit users to get information quickly and easily, without programming. These tools are discussed in Chapter 12, Server Data Management and Access Tools.

The second strategy makes even complex programming tasks easier by providing easier-to-use programming tools. Products that support this strategy are discussed below.

16.1.1 EASEL Workbench

EASEL Workbench, an evolution of the EASEL product that is used to build front-end interfaces for existing 3270/5250 host applications from Easel Corp., expands the EASEL capabilities to include support for creating client/server applications. An OS/2 development platform product, EASEL Workbench can generate client/ server applications for DOS, Windows, and OS/2 environments with dynamic SQL access to SQL Server, OS/2 Data Base Manager, ORACLE Server via SQL*Net, and DB2 via MDI's Database Gateway.

EASEL-developed applications are made up of objects, events, and responses. The supported object types are the visual and interactive components of an application: windows (called regions), keys, dialog boxes, and dialogue controls.

All functions provided by EASEL Workbench are accessible through a menu in the main Workbench window. These functions are illustrated in Figure 16.1.

Easel has announced two products that are expected to be available by the middle of 1993. The EDA/SQL Option for EASEL Workbench enables OS/2 and Windows EASEL clients to link to data sources supported by EDA/SQL, which is discussed in Section 12.3.1. The EASEL Transaction Server Toolkit provides EASEL Workbench developers with high-speed, static SQL access to all SAA databases via an OS/2-based transaction server.

Workbench Project	Identifies the EASEL source code for a project, the most recently compiled version of the program, information about the state of the program and its target platform
Layout Editor	Creates the application objects
Drawing Editor	Creates images using vector graphics
Attribute Editor	Specifies the attributes of an object
Text Editor	Creates and edits text-form objects and responses
Incremental Compiler	Compiles only the modified source code for the application
Program Execution Controls	Controls the execution of the application within EASEL Workbench such as start, pause, continue, abort, and restart
Interactive Debugger	Debugs the operation of a program within the EASEL Workbench environment
Parts Catalog	Retrieves objects and responses from a central repository of all objects and responses
Project Views	Groups related objects and responses that are to be viewed together

Source: Easel Corp.

Figure 16.1 Functions of EASEL Workbench

16.1.2 Ellipse

Ellipse, from Cooperative Solutions, was developed specifically for distributed client/server online transaction processing applications. Cooperative Solutions uses the term client/server transaction processing (CSTP) instead of online transaction processing (OLTP). Much of the mainframe system software necessary to maintain the integrity of OLTP applications is currently not supported by conventional client/server software. Consequently, Ellipse was designed to include the system-level software required to support OLTP in the Ellipse-developed applications. Ellipse-generated code includes error handling and process-to-process communication, and can handle transactions that are distributed across multiple LANs and databases. Ellipse's architecture is illustrated in Figure 16.2.

Developers use Ellipse after a database schema has been prepared and business transactions defined. The application is then broken into activities, which are a set of transactions that share a common user interface. Activities (also referred to as objects) also contain definitions of data types, variables, and constants used by the activity and definitions for reports and procedures for data manipulation or calculations.

The Ellipse Development Environment (Ellipse/DE) is used to define the application activities and their components. Ellipse/DE provides the following editors:

- An **activity overview editor** illustrates the overall structure of an activity: a user interface for initiating transactions, procedures that execute the transactions, and working storage for storing data temporarily.
- A **WYSIWYG forms editor** facilitates the definition of GUI-based interfaces.
- A **template-based procedure editor** is used to specify procedure

---

Ellipse Application

Ellipse Production System

OLTP Services
- Integrity
- Availability
- Security
- Scalability
- Performance
- Concurrency
- Manageability

CSTP Services
- Distributed transaction management
- Multiple database access
- Set-oriented transactions
- Application partitioning
- Graphical user interface
- National languages

Standards-based Services

Communications Services
- Named Pipes
- TCP/IP
- Novell

SQL DBMSs
- SQL Server
- Database Manager
- ORACLE

Operating Systems
- OS/2
- DOS
- UNIX
- NetWare

Presentation Services
- Presentation Manager
- Windows 3.0

Source: Cooperative Solutions

Figure 16.2 Ellipse architecture

statements selected from a pull-down menu. Using a template for the statement, the developer fills in the blanks to specify the complete procedure statement.

After the activities and related interfaces of the application are defined, the application can be generated and installed on a LAN. As part of the installation process, the installer provides configuration information (such as addresses for databases and external procedures and location of printers) and describes the production environment (such as operating system(s), number of servers, types of DBMSs, and presentation services). Individual procedures can be coded to execute on the client or the server. The installer can also specify where specific application activities, such as stored procedures or reports, will execute on the network. Ellipse can also assign locations to application objects using an algorithm designed to reduce network overhead and optimize performance.

Among the headaches that developers of client/server applications (or any distributed applications) have is installation of the same application software on a variety of platforms: different presentation services, operating systems, LAN technologies, and DBMSs. Added to this problem is the lack of standard system services for client/server applications. Even if the application functioned exactly the same way in each installation, customized versions of the application (containing system-level code) would have to be created and maintained.

Users of Ellipse are not concerned with the topology of the LAN or the partitioning of the application objects until the application is installed. Consequently, the same application can be deployed at hundreds of different sites, each site possibly configured differently without customizing application code. This facilitates maintenance, version control, and software integrity, not to mention decreased development time.

The Ellipse Production System (Ellipse/PS) is installed on clients and servers. At runtime, Ellipse creates a process on each client and an application process on each server. The application process on the servers communicates with the client processes. As transaction volume increases, more application server processes are added automatically. The end-to-end control provided by these processes allows Ellipse to handle application error recovery and transaction management in the distributed environment. To accomplish this, Cooperative Solutions developed its own remote procedure call (RPC) called Application Procedure Call.

The two major features of the Ellipse transaction manager are:

- It is designed to handle transactions that involve multiple databases and processes that are distributed between client and server.

■ It handles aborted transactions using the rollback and recovery mechanisms used by a variety of DBMSs.

The transaction manager uses the *optimistic* database concurrency control model. With this control model, database records are not locked while data is in use at the client; they are only locked during retrieval and update. Before a record is updated, Ellipse rereads the data to determine if it has been changed. If no change occurred between retrieval and update, the update proceeds. If a change did occur, an exception error is transmitted to the application so the application can determine how to proceed.

Ellipse currently supports Microsoft Windows and OS/2 clients on OS/2-based servers. A version that supports Sun platforms and VMS is due for release in mid-1993.

16.1.3 SQLWindows

SQLWindows from Gupta Technologies, Inc. is a development system for Windows or OS/2 Presentation Manager applications. SQLWindows supports multiuser access to data stored in any SQL database on the network and supports simultaneous access by a single application.

Development in SQLWindows is performed in the Design Window and the Outline Window. The Design Window is a screen painter used to create or modify objects such as data fields, multiline fields, push buttons, radio buttons, check boxes, lists of values, and BLOBs. Objects can be customized using the Object Customizer. Code can be shared among applications as objects that are public and can be included by any application (includable object). When an includable object changes, applications can be manually or automatically refreshed.

Each time an object is selected for display in the Design Window, a sequence of procedural statements appears in the Outline Window. Using SQLWindows Application Language (SAL), the developer works in the Outline Window to add or edit objects, define actions, and specify logical procedures. Changes in the Outline Window are automatically reflected in the Design Window.

Messages drive SQLWindows applications and are triggered every time an action takes place on the screen. For example, when data in a field is changed and the cursor leaves the field, a SAM_Validate message is fired and the SAL code within the SAM_Validate message does the validation.

SQL database access is controlled in the Table Window, which displays relational tables in row and column format. From within a Table Window, a user can display a query, browse through rows of data, insert, update, or delete rows of data. Any actions done in the Table Window automatically generate procedural code, which can be modified. An intelligent editor checks the procedural code for syntax errors.

Connectivity to data sources, such as ORACLE, SYBASE, SQLBase, DB2, OS/2 EE Data Base Manager, ALLBASE/SQL, and Teradata, is provided through Gupta's family of SQLRouters and SQLGateways. Client support is provided for both Windows and Presentation Manager.

SAL supports both internal functions written in SAL, and external functions via dynamic link libraries. In addition, SAL supports declared variables and one-dimensional arrays and accepts values from called functions and procedures. SAL also supports the DDE and Clipboard Windows interfaces.

Runtime versions of an application are distributed in compiled form. Gupta's SQLWindows Developer's System includes the following modules:

- SQLWindows for online applications
- Express Windows for generating applications
- ReportWindows for simple reporting requirements
- SQLTalk for database administration
- SQLBase, a single user version of Gupta's DBMS

Gupta's application generator, Express Windows, allows a developer to quickly build data entry and query applications for master and detail tables using default information stored with the tables. An Express Windows application permits users to do queries-by-example, add new data, update data, or browse data. Record validation, field formatting, range checking, and lookup routines are supported within the product's interface. Express Windows generates a complete SQLWindows application which can be further customized with SQLWindows.

The types of SQLWindows applications can be built using Express Windows are:

- **Express form**, a single-record form display application
- **Express table**, a multi-record tabular display application
- **Master/Detail**, a combination single-record and tabular display based on a two-table, one-to-many relationship of the data

Windows-based ReportWindow has an on-screen, object-oriented WYSIWYG designer for designing report templates, which may then be produced with data accessed from SQLBase Server or any SQL database supported by Gupta's SQLNetwork.

SQLTalk, a data manager for SQLBase Server and databases supported by SQLNetwork, comes in two versions. SQLTalk/Windows contains menus and dialogues for a wide variety of data management operations and provides a point-and-click interface to those operations. SQLTalk/Character is a DOS command-line interface.

Future releases of SQLWindows will support picture buttons, Object Linking and Embedding (OLE), object-oriented extensions, and ultimately, a CASE module.

16.1.4 PowerBuilder

PowerBuilder from Powersoft Corp. combines object orientation with 4GL and CASE techniques to provide a client/server development environment for building production-quality applications. The software was written for and extensively uses the Windows environment. Currently, there is no support for the Macintosh, UNIX or OS/2, although Powersoft is moving towards support for the Macintosh and UNIX.

The developer creates *scripts* to define the response to a specific object/event occurrence. Scripts, written in a high-level, graphic, object-oriented language called PowerScript which has hundreds of built-in functions, are used to define the application. Scripts can accommodate external C and C++ code and can link to other application software through OLE, DDE, and dynamic link libraries. Once the scripts are defined, the developer uses PowerBuilder to compile them and then generate executable code, which runs under Windows. PowerBuilder applications provide transparent access to several approved back-end databases—ORACLE Server, SQL Server, SQLBase, XDB, and ALLBASE/SQL. DB2 can be accessed using MDI's Database Gateway. The result is an .EXE file that is distributed with runtime versions of PowerBuilder.

PowerBuilder features an object-oriented, event-driven architecture called Object Easy. Object Easy supports inheritance, which allows many programs to be updated at the same time, and reusable objects, which consists of predefined code that can be used across several platforms.

PowerBuilder's functions are accessible through a central menu called the Power Panel, which displays each function as an icon. Figure 16.3 describes PowerBuilder's default functions called Painters. The Power Panel can be customized for each installation.

Database	Provides interactive facilities for creating and maintaining SQL databases.
Application	Describes the application, its defaults, and object libraries.
Window	Graphically positions and edits all objects that can be placed in the window, such as window controls, text, edit fields, check and drop-down list boxes, user-defined objects, and DataWindows.
Menu	Creates top-level action-bar commands, drop-down lists, multi-level cascading menus, and pop-up menus. Menus are attached to a window, either when the window is defined or dynamically from a script at runtime.
DataWindow	Creates intelligent database interaction objects that allow database access without actually coding SQL. A DataWindow, an SQL-smart object, is an interface for presenting, manipulating, and updating data from a RDBMS, which insulates the user from the database interface. There is a separate DataWindow for each database. An application can have several DataWindows active (its database open) at a time. A DataWindow object can also process data from internal files, DDE interfaces, and other desktop facilities such as dBASE and spreadsheets.
User Object	Creates user-defined objects from standard objects or other user objects, objects inherited from existing PowerBuilder objects, user-defined attributes, events, and functions. User-defined objects may be used in the Window Painter as though they were standard PowerBuilder objects.
Picture	Allows developers to initiate and execute graphic packages that are supported by PowerBuilder and include bitmap graphics or pictures in application windows.
Function	Extends the functionality of PowerScript with customized functions accessible by PowerScript.
Script	Defines scripts by pasting object names, variables, and functions or painting SQL statements. Traditional graphic text-editing capabilities are also provided.
Preference	Customizes PowerBuilder to a user's preferences.
Library	Creates and maintains libraries of objects, scripts, and sharable PowerBuilder programs in a central repository which is automatically used by PowerBuilder applications as defaults.
Structure	Creates complex data structures at the global or object level and provides communication with external functions written in C.

Source: Powersoft Corp.

Figure 16.3 PowerBuilder's default Painters in the Power Panel

16.1.5 SQL Toolset

SQL Toolset from Sybase Inc. uses a point-and-click interface for development of Windows-based applications. Applications built with SQL Toolset can be deployed on character-based terminals or bit-mapped workstations, without conversion. Character-based terminals will look like bit-mapped workstations.

Sybase's Adaptable Windowing Environment allows applications to run under a variety of presentation services without recoding for each windowing system or platform. This layer of software insulates SQL Toolset and applications built using it from vendor-specific windowing systems. A platform-independent interface allows window-based applications built with APT Workbench (Application Productivity Tools Workbench) and Data Workbench to adopt the same look-and-feel of the host windowing system.

APT Workbench is organized into modules, as illustrated in Figure 16.4. The modules are:

- APT-Edit
- APT-Build
- APT-SQL
- APT-Execute
- APT-GUI

Used to build forms and menus, APT-Edit includes the following features:

- Provides constructs for handling grouped objects on a form
- Can attach processing to forms, groups, and other objects
- Can call other forms and application components

APT-Edit supports single choice, multi-choice, and rotating choice fields, can automatically generate value lists and has context-sensitive help. Specifications written in APT-Edit can be converted to APT-SQL.

APT-Build can be used to automatically generate the code for a complete application that can browse and edit a database. Code can be modified within API-Edit. Generated application code is ready to use.

An extension of Transact-SQL, APT-SQL supports flow-of-control statements, can process a group of data as an object, and can make calls to other SQL Servers. APT-SQL procedures are reusable and can be written, tested, compiled, and modified from within APT-Edit. APT-SQL supports RPCs via the SYBASE Open Server product.

APT-Execute, the standalone, runtime module for deployment of compiled APT Workbench applications, eliminates the requirement for development copies on each user's workstation.

Module	Features
APT-Edit	Creates forms using a visual editor
APT-Build	Builds a baseline application prototype using a visual dictionary-driven generator
APT-SQL	Builds the application using an object-based 4GL
APT-Execute	Executes the application
APT-GUI	Converts applications to native Motif or OpenLook widgets
Source: Sybase, Inc.	

Figure 16.4 APT Workbench components

APT-GUI translates GUIs to native Motif or OpenLook GUI widgets, automatically incorporating the native look-and-feel of those presentation methods. A feature of this component is APT-GUISE (GUI Style Editor), which translates a character-based representation of a screen to a graphical representation and then takes advantage of GUI capabilities.

APT Workbench uses a forms-based and event-driven development methodology. Development processes are based upon the forms themselves. All processing is triggered by screen events, such as entering or leaving a field, a menu item or a form.

17

Managing the
Production Environment

Once all the components of client/server computing are in place and the communication between them is reliable, IS must turn its focus on managing the flow of data between equipment from multiple vendors and ensuring the integrity of the data and its transactions.

17.1 Distributed Transaction Management

Updating a distributed database adds a set of complicated problems to data management. These problems include:

- Keeping the databases in sync when updates affect more than one file and/or database
- Distributed locking and deadlock detection
- Local and global backup/recovery

The mainframe world has proven there are advantages to separating the transaction management from the DBMS. CICS is an example of a mainframe transaction manager of IBM's proprietary environments. Transaction managers for open systems are currently UNIX-based and specifically address the major open systems benefits—interoperability and portability.

In heterogeneous distributed client/server environments, transaction processing managers (TPMs) must:

- Support global transactions that impact multiple distributed databases, including backup and recovery of global transactions
- Send and receive messages between the clients and servers in the network
- Manage the flow of transactions and distribute the workload
- Deal with resource managers, such as DBMSs, using standardized interfaces
- Interface with data entry systems to create and manage interactive data entry forms using presentation software
- Provide a powerful and flexible system administration facility

Several representative transaction managers for open systems are described below.

17.1.1 Tuxedo

Tuxedo from UNIX System Laboratories (USL), formerly a division of AT&T and now a subsidiary of Novell, requires that applications and resource managers running under Tuxedo adhere to standard interfaces. The Application Transaction Manager Interface (ATMI) supports client/server computing by providing network independence, service location transparency, load balancing, transparent data format conversion, context-sensitive routing, and priority processing. The X/Open XA interface, a component of the Distributed Transaction Processing (DTP) Reference Model, handles the communications with the resource managers. All major UNIX DBMS vendors have built XA-compatible interfaces. In addition, by using UNIX System V Transport Layer Interface (TLI), which supports TCP/IP, NetBIOS, OSI protocols, and APPC/LU6.2, Tuxedo is separated from underlying network technologies.

Nearly 10 years old and now in release 5, the Tuxedo system consists of the following components:

- **Transaction manager**, which includes such facilities as Name Server, Communications Manager, Transaction Control, and routines for operations, administrations, and maintenance
- **System resource manager**, which includes server applications and their database access interfaces and remote application access
- **High performance file system**
- **Data entry system**

The Tuxedo architecture is illustrated in Figure 17.1. The Tuxedo transaction manager and resource manager components use standard interfaces, such as ATMI and X/Open XA, to communicate with the system's resource managers.

Global transactions are made up of several local transactions that access a local resource manger under control of the local Tuxedo TPM. The Tuxedo ATMI treats transactions that involve more than one resource manager and more than one physical location as one logical unit of work. For a global transaction to be successful, all local transactions must be successful.

In order to ensure the ACID features of the transaction, which are discussed in Chapter 13, Overview of Networking, Tuxedo:

- Creates transaction identifiers
- Tracks the status of all participants
- Detects and resolves deadlocks
- Coordinates transaction recovery
- Acts as the coordinator for its two-phase commit process

A recent addition to the Tuxedo family of products is Tuxedo Enterprise Transaction Processing, which consists of Tuxedo/WS (workstation) and Tuxedo/Host. Tuxedo/WS supplies APIs that allow DOS, Windows, OS/2, and UNIX workstations to be Tuxedo clients. Tuxedo/Host allows legacy (existing) mainframe applications and data to be integrated with UNIX products by providing a framework for building gateway servers.

17.1.2 TOP END

TOP END is a fairly new product from NCR and is based on the company's years of experience in OLTP and point-of-sale applications. It is also based on X/Open's DTP environment and uses XA interfaces to UNIX-based DBMSs. Key enhancements to DTP include:

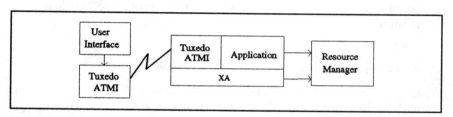

Figure 17.1 Tuxedo architecture

- **Intranode and internode communications**
- **Security authentication** (using Kerberos Authentication system), which permits user authentication across the network and the exchange of encrypted messages, and includes security audit capabilities, such as security modifications—locally or globally
- **Dynamic workload balancing**, which includes transaction routing and alternative routing
- **Advanced system administration facilities**, which include start-up and shut-down routines, status reporting, control of the number of client terminals allowed on the network and initial logon screen specifications for local and remote clients
- **Distributed debugging facilities**
- **Support for UNIX-based and DOS-based workstations**

TOP END splits the transaction processing into modules that can be distributed across the network for flexibility and efficiency or replicated for concurrency and location autonomy. The X/Open-compliant two-phase commit protocol, which is transparent to the user, ensures global transaction integrity. TOP END has direct support for UNIX TLI, OSI, and APPC.

As illustrated in Figure 17.2, the major TOP END modules include:

- **Transaction manager**, which regulates execution within a processing node and handles transaction routing, scheduling, commit/rollback coordination, security, and timer functions
- **Application server** instances, which execute application programs
- **Resource manager**, which interfaces with the resource managers on the network
- **Communication resource manager**, which supports cooperative processing for the applications
- **Network interface**, which allows network-connected TOP END transaction managers to communicate

The TOP END modules can be distributed across the network. TOP END keeps track of their distribution and uses the information to perform dynamic load balancing. Transactions are sent directly to the specified node whenever possible but can be routed to the less busy components.

Compared to Tuxedo

As is often true in the software world, the newer TOP END is similar in architecture and functionality to the older Tuxedo. Having the advantage of time, NCR incorporated enhancements that compensated for the weak areas in the older technology in the design stage of TOP END, whereas USL must force-fit enhancements into Tuxedo's existing code.

The major differences are in the following areas:

- **Security.** TOP END supports the Kerberos security system; Tuxedo offers little authorization functionality.
- **Administration.** In TOP END, resource definitions can be created interactively and stored in the DBMS repository. Tuxedo uses the UNIX editor to create the definitions and the UNIX file system to store them.
- **Communications.** TOP END has direct support for major UNIX network protocols. Tuxedo uses UNIX TLI.
- **Workload balancing.** In TOP END, workload balancing is dynamic and network-sensitive. In Tuxedo, it is predefined.

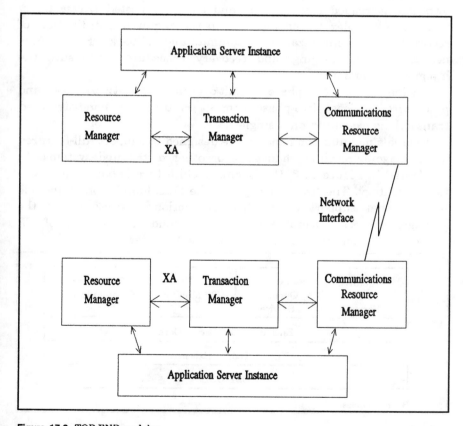

Figure 17.2 TOP END modules

As the dust from the AT&T and NCR merger settles, one of these competing products will gradually be phased out. Industry analysts are betting that TOP END will be the survivor.

17.1.3 Encina

Based on the technologies from the X/Open Consortium and OSF's DCE, the Encina (Enterprise Computing In a New Age) product line from Transarc Corp. provides a high-quality, highly reliable, and easy-to-use transaction processing environment for open systems and client/server and distributed computing environments.

Encina combines DCE's strengths, such as resource location transparency, security, and communication and management tools, with application development tools. In addition, Encina provides its own multithreaded environment and supports nested transactions, which are complex to manage due to the required coordination of recovery and synchronization of commits and rollbacks. Encina uses nested commits, logging, and recovery procedures to ensure the integrity of the data.

Encina supports two-phase commit over multiple network nodes and processors. A local two-phase commit is used for nondistributed transactions executing on a single node.

Encina's modular components are designed to support full-featured TP managers, resource managers, or other distributed systems. As illustrated in Figure 17.3, the Encina architecture is based on a two-tiered strategy. The first tier expands the DCE foundation to include services that support distributed transaction processing and the management of recoverable data. The second tier consists of TP services based on facilities provided by the first tier.

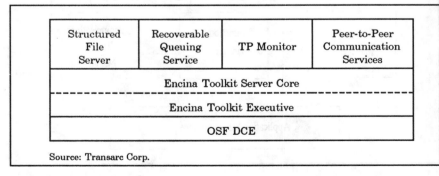

Source: Transarc Corp.

Figure 17.3 Encina components

The first tier, the Encina Toolkit, when coupled with OSF DCE, provides standards-based, distributed services for creating and managing reliable, distributed applications. The Toolkit consists of:

- The **Encina Toolkit Executive** extends the services of OSF DCE to support client/server transaction processing. It includes Transactional-C, a high-level API that provides transaction demarcation and concurrency management. It extends the DCE RPC technology to ensure transactional integrity over distributed transactions. The Executive also provides a distributed two-phase commit engine.

- The **Encina Toolkit Server Core** extends the services of the Executive to support the storage and maintenance of recoverable data. It includes a locking library to serialize data access, a recoverable storage system based upon write-ahead logging, a common log, and an XA interface to permit interoperability with compliant databases.

A wide variety of tools to support distributed systems can be built using the foundation services of the Encina Toolkit and DCE, such as TP monitors, DBMSs, CASE and other application development tools, recoverable memory managers, and administrative tools. Transarc has developed its own family of TP products built on the services provided by Encina and DCE. These tools, which are illustrated as a second tier, include:

- The **Encina Monitor**, a full-feature TP monitor, provides an easy-to-use development environment for programming and integrating distributed TP applications, a reliable execution environment that provides load balancing and scheduling services across heterogeneous platforms to provide high performance and transactional integrity, and an administrative environment that treats the configuration and management of the distributed system as a cohesive unit.

- The **Encina Structured File Server** is a record-oriented file system that provides full transactional integrity, high performance, log-based recovery for fast restarts, and broad scalability for large databases. It can participate in two-phase commit protocols across multiple servers.

- The **Encina Peer-to-Peer Communication Services** support transactional CPI-C peer-to-peer communications over TCP/IP and LU6.2 (for IBM's SNA) transports.

- The **Encina Recoverable Queuing Services** provide transactional queuing of data. Tasks may be queued for later processing. The service provides multiple levels of priority and can support large numbers of users and high volumes of data.

17.1.4 Retix

A newcomer to this market, Retix Corp., offers a suite of products that combine UNIX Transaction Processing (TP) and Remote Database Access (RDA) to address open online transaction processing (OLTP) and database connectivity. Retix TP-920 for OSI Transaction Processing and Retix RD-930 for RDA enable manufacturers and software developers to build interoperability and open systems compliance into their transaction processing and database products.

Retix TP-920 provides interoperability between proprietary transaction processing monitors (TPMs) and OLTP systems. Retix TP-920's generalized solution allows vendors to build products that can operate in open, heterogeneous transaction processing environments. TP-920 supports the X/Open Distributed Transaction Processing model, which provides vendors with industry standard APIs and architecture.

Retix RD-930 provides interoperability between database servers and user applications. The product supports the SQL Access Group '91 and '92 formats and protocols, is compatible with both OSI and TCP/IP, and supports the SQL Access Group call-level interface (CLI) APIs.

Retix also offers core OSI stack products designed specifically for software and systems vendors who are developing open networking products based on UNIX System V. Products include applications such as X.400, X.500 Directory Services, File Transfer Access, and Management and Virtual Terminal.

In addition, Retix provides an integrated OSI communication software platform or core stack that supports all of the industry standard APIs that have been endorsed by UNIX International. These include TLI, Data Link Provider Interface, and the new programming interface, ACSE/Presentation Library Interface (APLI), which is the OSI Presentation and Session layers technology developed by USL. The core stack utilizes a kernel-based STREAMS implementation of APLI.

17.2 Integrating Multivendor Environments

Managing large networks in single-vendor environments is difficult in itself. As organizations adopt open systems and distributed processing, managing the multi-vendor platforms becomes a nightmare.

As discussed earlier, Simple Network Management Protocol (SNMP) and Common Management Information Protocol (CMIP) are used to gather management data from communication devices such as bridges, routers, gateways, and terminal adapters. This data is stored in a management information base (MIB).

However, each vendor supplies its own network management system that is designed to support the devices they sell. When a large network contains devices from many vendors, the operators in the network management control center must review multiple consoles to monitor the state of the network. In addition, although data captured in MIBs can be viewed by an SNMP network management station, values are meaningful only to that vendor's network management system. Unless the values are translated, the customer has no way of knowing if displayed text means trouble or not. In effect, this keeps the MIB proprietary and defeats the purpose of open systems.

Network management is the focus of IBM's Systems Network Architecture (SNA), which supports network management and the NetView family of network management products. However, it is a single-vendor solution. It does not address multivendor environments or provide an open system solution.

17.2.1 Distributed Management Environment

To overcome this hurdle, OSF has proposed a vendor-neutral platform that promotes network manageability for multivendor environments. The Distributed Management Environment (DME) creates standard APIs that can be used to develop network management software and a consistent user interface to network management systems from multiple vendors. It also addresses management of the computer hardware (clients and servers) on the network. The ambitious goal of DME is to combine the management of systems and network, so they can be monitored as a single node.

OSF is taking an object-oriented approach to this monumental task. A network management system—the manager—interacts with network elements—objects that are managed. Objects that share common traits can be grouped into classes. Using the concept of inheritance, all objects in a class have traits common to that class. For example, all routers have IP tables and emit certain types of alarms. When a new router is added to the network, it inherits these traits and the code created for that class is used to manage that router.

The manager needs the following information about a managed object:

- **Operations** that are performed on it, such as start, stop, and test
- **Events,** such as the messages sent when an error occurs

- **Associated data,** such as configuration parameters and tracked statistics

With this information stored in a software library of managed objects, a manager can supervise the network and its nodes.

Recognizing that an object-oriented environment uses a very different paradigm from a procedural-oriented environment, OSF has two sets of APIs in DME—one for each environment.

The components of the DME architecture are shown in Figure 17.4 and discussed below.

User Interface

A consistent user interface simplifies the use of resource management applications from different vendors. DME provides a user interface toolkit for creating screens that access vendors' applications. This technology, derived from HP's OpenView and TIVOLI System's Tivoli Management Environment, supports the following interfaces:

- Map and collection
- Dialogue view
- Command

Application Services and Management Applications

DME includes a defined set of utilities called application services as

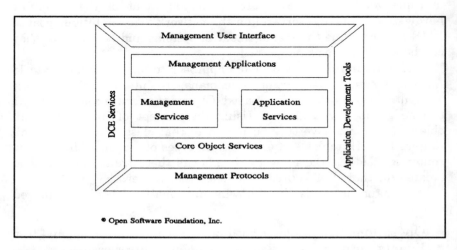

Figure 17.4 Distributed Management Environment architecture

well as a management application for each service. These services include:

- **Distributed print services** track down printing problems and provide security support.
- **Distributed license services** track software licenses and their users.
- **Software distribution and installation services** include utilities to package, install, and distribute software on heterogeneous and possibly incompatible systems. They can support disk, tape, and CD ROM as distribution media and display the distributed services in visual form.
- **Distributed host services** include utilities for determining internet addresses and starting up files. They are based on technology from TIVOLI Systems.
- **PC integration** addresses the architectural limitations of DOS-based systems to ensure downward scalability and enables micros to participate in host management activities.

Management Services

Management applications are visible to and utilized by end users, whereas management services are used by developers to write applications and to ensure consistency between applications produced by different vendors. DME offers guidelines to be followed when developing DME-compliant applications. These include facilities for:

- Grouping managed objects together to be treated as an entity
- Partitioning views of the network into manageable pieces
- Specifying rules that govern individual objects
- Assigning administrative privileges
- Maintaining a class dictionary that serves as a repository for management information

Development Tools

DME includes tools to simplify application development and support applications written in standard C language or object-oriented C++ language. These tools include:

- Dialogue language and compiler
- Event language and compiler
- APIs: a low-level Consolidated Management API, which provides

direct access to CMIP, SNMP, and OSF's RPC; and two object-oriented APIs

Object Services

To bring together the network and system management services, DME includes two modules:

- Management request broker
- Object server

The management request broker (MRB) ensures that tasks are routed and handled properly using standard APIs that allow objects to talk to one another. It is similar in functionality to the Object Request Broker proposed by OMG and X/Open.

To initiate and control management tasks, the DME supports two object servers. One object server supports short-duration tasks, such as changing a printer configuration or a user password. IBM's Data Engine, an internal object server, supports long-duration tasks, such as network monitoring. The Data Engine is a multithreaded server and, since each operation (object) is a thread, operations can execute in parallel and communicate between objects very efficiently. The Data Engine uses a process called *versioning*, which maintains historical data about an object. If necessary, the Data Engine transparently replicates this information for access by network management systems when attempting to isolate and solve problems.

Management Protocols

To transmit management data between nodes, OSF modified HP's version of CMIP to use a DCE stack instead of an OSI stack of protocols. Support for SNMP and IBM's Query Engine is also provided.

Summary

Some points to keep in mind about DME. Although it does not require DCE, DME is more effective if used in tandem with DCE.

DME addresses the complexities of UNIX-based systems but it can also manage other systems. As more organizations standardize on UNIX-like open systems, the management of legacy platforms (usually proprietary) will need to be addressed by more specific DME functions.

Complete DME specifications are not expected until mid-1993 and products that are completely DME-compliant are expected early 1994.

As pieces of the specification are complete, OSF does release snapshot versions of DME to its members.

The OSF premise is that network device manufacturers will gladly give up the responsibilities of creating and maintaining network management systems and will concentrate on the software required to manage their equipment. If OSF can stick to these dates, DME could provide the technology necessary to manage the open systems that organizations are envisioning.

17.2.2 Object Management Architecture

Object Management Group's Object Management Architecture (OMA) combines distributed processing with object-oriented computing to help build cooperative-processing applications within a heterogeneous, distributed, networked environment. It provides a standard method for any type of object to be created, preserved, located, and communicated with on a network—objects can be anything from entire applications to pieces of applications, such as graphical screens or complex number-crunching algorithms.

OMA backers say distributed object management can be used to easily integrate new and existing applications and have them work cooperatively. Several OMG vendor members plan to offer development tools that will enable developers to encapsulate legacy applications turning them into objects so that they, too, can use OMA services and communicate with other objects via the Object Request Broker.

The OMA is layered on top of existing operating systems and the communication transports that support standard RPCs such as SunSoft's Open Network Computing (ONC). As illustrated in Figure 17.5, the OMA consists of four main components:

- **Object request broker** (ORB) specifies the interface that must be used and the information that must be presented when one object

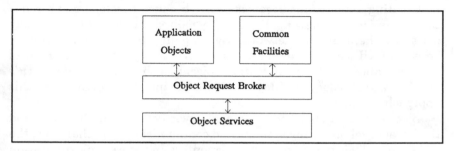

Figure 17.5 Object Management Architecture components

is communicating with another.

- **Object services** consist of utility objects that help perform object-oriented housekeeping chores such as creating, deleting, or copying objects, and storing them temporarily or permanently. Services provide for consistency, integrity, and security of objects and of the messages that pass between objects.
- **Common facilities** provide the functions commonly used by applications such as printing and spooling or error reporting.
- **Application objects** are applications or parts of applications created by independent software vendors or in-house software developers.

ORB links the other OMA components using its Interface Definition Language (IDL), an OMG-developed language with its roots in C++. The OMG provides mappings between IDL and common programming languages such as C or COBOL so developers can write to the ORB interfaces. So far, only a C mapping has been specified.

ORB allows objects to communicate dynamically or via a set of faster, preprogrammed static facilities. To manage interobject messages, the ORB provides features such as name services (similar to an object directory) and exception handling. ORB is the foundation for OMG's Common Object Request Broker Architecture (CORBA) discussed in Chapter 4, Understanding Client/Server Computing.

OMG maintains that object management makes programming cooperative applications easier and more flexible. Rather than creating one-to-one RPC connections between applications, developers could access any application on the network as an object without knowing its physical location. Interfaces to complex RPC APIs would be provided as a basic service of the object architecture itself. The concept is to allow any object to communicate with any other object simply by sending a message to the common RPC interface. So, OMA backers say, application developers could forget about dealing with complex, low-level RPC APIs.

Creating applications becomes easier because developers can reuse code in assembling new applications by calling on objects that already exist anywhere on the network. By dragging and dropping pointers between GUI icons, even end users can create objects, such as reports that are called by other application objects on the network. Both HP's NewWave technology and Microsoft's OLE interface already use this approach.

By creating an object management layer between applications and the lower-level operating systems and communication mechanisms, the OMA can deliver true application portability. In theory, any application that conforms to the OMA's interfaces could run in any OMA-compliant environment.

However, the OMG has been unable to achieve a consensus among its members on interoperability. While the current ORB specification supports portability of objects between ORBs and communication between heterogeneous systems using the same ORB implementation, it does not guarantee that messages passed between different ORB implementations will work. The initial ORB specification did not define how messages between objects are to be coded when passed along the network. Without that information, different ORB implementations cannot exchange messages.

The OMG is working on a second ORB specification that will deal with interoperability but it won't be available until mid-1993 at the earliest.

There is no widespread support in the micro community for the ORB and the rest of the OMA object model. Microsoft is working on object management features for its upcoming Windows NT operating system, but no mention has been made regarding how—or if—it will interact with ORB.

As stated earlier, OSF has not endorsed the OMA and has specified its own MRB and IDL as part of DME. OSF expects that its MRB will some day converge with the ORB and the other OMA components. But, for now, the two groups are moving on separate tracks.

17.2.3 UI-Atlas

UI-Atlas, the framework for open systems presented by UNIX International Inc. (UI), defines how to build open system architectures using hardware, software, networking, and other standards-based components. The framework is illustrated in Figure 17.6.

UI-Atlas incorporates the OSI seven-layer network model, a GUI that supports both OSF Motif and OpenLook under one API, and an expanded version of Sun's Network File System (NFS) that will operate over wide area networks and support file replications. UI-Atlas also includes a global naming support system, a system management framework, and a distributed object management model that complies with OMG specifications.

Like DME, the UI-Atlas system management service is based on technology from TIVOLI Systems, Inc. UI-Atlas can manage DCE environments, as well as existing environments, such as Sun's ONC and micro-based LANs. Using an intermediate definition language that is based on the Class-Definition Language from the OMG, programmers can execute any supported RPC (UI-Atlas can handle multiple RPCs; DME addresses only one) to provide interoperability between LAN environments.

There are a few differences between DME and UI-Atlas:

- UI-Atlas uses Tuxedo for transaction management services. DME uses Transarc's DCE-based OLTP Toolkit. Tuxedo is a mature product that has been retrofitted for distributed environments. OLTP Toolkit was designed for distributed environments.
- UI-Atlas supports the OSI networking standard. DME promises to migrate to it.
- DME/DCE uses the Andrews File System. UI-Atlas uses Sun's Network File System.
- UI has provided DCE support in the UI-Atlas framework but DME/DCE can be incorporated into non-UNIX operating systems.

UI-Atlas is expected to base much of its distributed applications and management environment around the ORB and the OMA. UI will first focus on system management applications for the object management built into UI-Atlas, which is expected mid-1993. UI will then layer the ORB and OMA services on top of UNIX System V Release 4 running with a graphical user interface on the desktop.

Although UI-Atlas is available only for UNIX, it could create a degree of object interoperability between UNIX SVR4-based

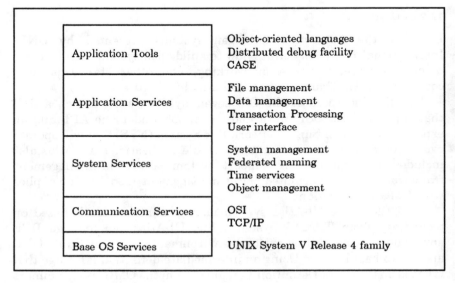

Figure 17.6 UI-Atlas framework

applications and operating systems from various vendors if UI's members license the object-based UI-Atlas technology.

Production Requirements

When a client/server application is in production, one of the most
obvious requirements is reliability—of the hardware, the software, and
the network. The reliability of each of the components of client/server
computing has been discussed in sections related to those components.
This chapter deals with global issues, those that pertain to the internet
itself.

18.1 Systems Management

Systems management tasks in the mainframe world center around
control. They include configuration management, change control,
performance monitoring, console management, problem management,
and security.

Enter the world of client/server computing. There are heterogeneous
(different) platforms, multiple copies of software, and multiple
operating systems. Desktop machines can access data anywhere on the
network. Users are responsible for protecting the data accessible from
their desktop machines. The user has as much authority over the
system as IS does.

Now there are network functions that also have to be managed,
including such tasks as print services; licensing, creating, and deleting
user accounts; naming and directory services; and backup. The term
networked system management indicates the blending of network

functions and mainframe systems management. OSF's DME addresses these tasks.

Users can manage their systems with standard utilities and specialized tools that vendors have tailored to their products. Emerging third-party tools can manage entire heterogeneous networks of systems. One such tool is Tivoli Management Environment from TIVOLI Systems for the UNIX environment. The product uses a Macintosh-like interface and has an object orientation, which supports the integration of system management applications from different vendors.

As illustrated in Figure 18.1, Tivoli Management Environment consists of the following components:

- **Tivoli Management Framework** uses an object-oriented system management framework. Resources and operations are encapsulated as objects. By using the common object services, applications can be integrated without modification.
- **Tivoli/Works** manages the fundamental system resources, including the Management Framework.
- **Tivoli/Sentry**, an optional package, performs resource monitoring.
- **Tivoli/Courier**, an optional package, manages the distribution of software.

TIVOLI Systems also offers two toolkits for its Management Framework. Tivoli/AEF can be used to customize and extend Tivoli Management Applications. Tivoli/ADE, another tool from TIVOLI Systems, is used to develop new management applications.

Tivoli Management Environment is currently available for workstations running Sun's SunOS. Support for other UNIX versions is expected by the middle of 1993.

18.1.1 Security

Security is one of the least understood and least discussed issues of client/server computing. The security issue is that micros are capable

Tivoli/Works	Tivoli/Courier	User Applications
	Tivoli/Sentry	Other Vendor Applications
Tivoli Management Framework		
Source: TIVOLI Systems, Inc.		

Figure 18.1 Tivoli Management Environment

of accessing data anywhere in the internet. How secure is a micro, its data or any data accessible to that micro? Not very. Micro operating systems and LAN networking software were not written with security in mind. Yet these two layers of software are major building blocks in client/server computing.

Security affects everyone who uses a system. The level of security that must be implemented depends on the people and the organization and how they view the value of data. Every level of system security requires dollars and additional steps for the users. The cost and inconvenience (to users) associated with security must be balanced against the cost and inconvenience of corrupted or insecure data.

The security functions included in Novell's NetWare are:

- Authentication
- Authorization
- Auditing
- Accounting
- Administration

System administrators for NetWare can use all, some, or none of these functions.

The DBMS products usually offer their own security. Sybase uses stored procedures to define, limit, and authorize user access. By storing the security with the database, no data can be accessed without going through the security checks.

Server database software vendors are extending their products to include government specifications for multilevel data security. There seems to be little interest from commercial users for this degree of security.

Vendors of security products need to address a host of customer needs based on such factors as hardware platform, software, type of business, and varying levels of protection. Some mainframe-based vendors, such as Computer Associates, are porting their mainframe security packages to LAN environments. Others are developing products specifically for LAN environments.

For example, IBM offers the following security products for the client, the server, and the network:

- **Secured Workstation Manager/DOS** for DOS and Windows provides authentication, access control, and security management, and can be used with OS/2.
- **Transaction Security System** for DOS, OS/2, and MVS supports the exchange of encrypted data throughout an organization. It provides signature verification, encryption, and administrative

services, and conforms to IBM's common cryptographic architecture.
- **LAN Network Manager** provides physical security and controls access to an IBM Token Ring network.

ACE/Server from Security Dynamics controls network access through its SecurID Card, a visually readable, credit card-sized token that generates a unique and unpredictable access code every 60 seconds. To access a protected network, a user enters a personal identification number and the access code displayed on the SecurID card. ACE/Server authenticates the individual's identity and, if authorized, allows access to the network resources. ACE/Server currently runs on SunOS and Ultrix.

SunSoft offers **Account Resource Management**, which allows systems administrators to set the number of attempts a user has to correctly enter a password, and **Automated Enhanced Security Tool**, which allows administrators to set security levels. Both run under SunOS, Sun's version of UNIX. SunSoft also plans to incorporate the data encryption technology from RSA Data Security, Inc. in further releases of these products.

Pyramid Development Corp. offers **PC/Dacs**, which provides protection of system ports, floppy and hard drive files (including directories and subdirectories), and **Net/Dacs** for the NetWare environment, which integrates file server and workstation security.

Third-party security firms offer software and hardware security options. Fischer International Systems Corp. offers **Watchdog PC**, a software product that provides access control, data protection, data encryption, and system administration. Watchdog Director allows a central administrator to manage access control, grant user permission, and collect audit data from networked micros.

As discussed in Chapter 16, Application Development Tools, **Ellipse** from Cooperative Solutions is a client/server transaction processing application development product that runs on 386- and 486-based clients and servers. Security, configuration management, and version control tools are integrated into both Ellipse subsystems: a development environment and a production environment.

18.2 Network Management

Before client/server computing, most large installations had relatively homogeneous centralized mainframe and midrange processors and networks. Networks were managed with a variety of third-party terminals, recovery and backup systems, and tools supplied by the hardware vendor. Systems were managed separately.

Today, the network with all its nodes is "the system" and comes with a diversity of vendors and components. Organizations have to monitor the physical network and network performance, and then analyze performance data and traffic bottlenecks, despite the diversity.

An effective LAN management strategy incorporates multiple vendors, network topologies, operating systems, and applications. It also must be flexible enough to support an ever-changing environment.

A variety of tools aid network administrators in cutting through the dissimilar products to fine-tune network performance, reduce downtime, and cut costs by reducing the need for LAN consultants. These products fall into four categories:

- Protocol analyzers and monitors
- Intelligent wiring hubs
- Network management software
- Network performance monitors

18.2.1 Protocol Analyzers and Monitors

Protocol analysis views and analyzes traffic on the network in order to observe a particular protocol within a specific architecture. Protocol analyzers monitor network traffic and allow the network administrator to watch and inspect packets on a LAN segment. These products are available in dedicated, portable, and remote versions. Remote analyzers plug into a particular segment of the LAN and allow the data to be read from another location on the network.

The functions of protocol analyzers (capture, view, analyze) are divided between the software in the probe (monitor) attached to the LAN and the manager software running at the operator's end. The manager software may do everything from collecting and processing data to alerting the operator, handling the graphic presentation, and providing graphic, mouse-and-menu control of the distant software agents.

At one end of the product offerings is software-based **LANwatch** from FTP Software, which costs $1,200. At the other end of the range are hardware/software products, which range in cost from $5,000 to $40,000. These products, from familiar vendors like Hewlett-Packard and Novell, might include a 386 with 4 Mbytes of memory and 40 Mbytes of hard disk storage. These products can analyze packet streams, communicate using multiple protocol stacks, and handle distributed client/server architectures.

Novell's **LANalyzer** identifies problems on client machines in distributed LANs. It can decode most major protocols and can interface with most network topologies. In addition to protocol analysis, the server-based LANalyzer monitors LANs by displaying packets per second, network utilization, and errors per second on a dashboard-image screen with speedometer-style dials. Users can graph packet traffic and other variables over time to assess network usage trends and plan for backups. LANalyzer includes predefined, customizable, computer-aided test programs for almost all of the industry's network protocols. It has a Windows interface and supports Novell's Open DataLink Interface driver. Unlike many other protocol analyzers, it is a software-only solution that eliminates the need for proprietary hardware.

Hewlett-Packard offers two versions of **LanProbe II**, a network monitoring system that supports existing and emerging standards. One version supports the Remote Network Monitor (RMON) Management Information Base as well as HP's OpenView network-management scheme. RMON is a recently finalized standard that allows SNMP systems to collect LAN traffic and protocol analysis data from remote monitoring systems. The RMON-compatible probe supports large corporate users who mix and match network components from different vendors.

HP's other version requires a Windows-based network-management console package called ProbeView, which provides tools for examining data from LanProbe. These tools include network and segment maps, statistics, packet trace, event log, cable test, and alert manager.

HP's products monitor the number of packets sent across a LAN and build a database of events such as collisions, errors, runts (devices that send very small blocks of data), and jabbers (devices that continually send corrupted data) that can be displayed in graphs. They can also capture packets and decode them. The products can display a logical map of a network and network-use statistics graphically. Network administrators set alarm thresholds for notification before a problem causes a network crash.

The **Sniffer** product line from Network General Corp. collects and processes data on network performance, behaving as a protocol analyzer and as a probe. It supports all major protocol suites and network topologies, including FDDI, but does not currently support a GUI interface. The Distributed Sniffer System permits protocol analysis to be performed on multiple subsections of an internetwork and permits the network to be monitored from a central point.

Network specialists generally suggest that organizations install a monitor on each LAN to report alarms. In addition, each site should have an analyzer that can be quickly connected to a LAN segment as needed.

18.2.2 Intelligent Wiring Hubs

Intelligent wiring hubs, also called smart wiring hubs, provide the central connections required for managing star network topologies. They allow the network to be segmented into manageable chunks, which makes it easier to isolate problems, enforce security, and track configuration changes.

More intelligent hubs include 386/486 processing power, RISC (reduced instruction set computer) CPUs, and software to analyze hardware, cabling, and adapters. Low-end hubs can be mixed with high-end hubs, allowing a network to be configured with an intelligent hub for every five or six low-end workgroup hubs. Hubs can be run from local consoles or central management stations.

Prominent vendors of intelligent hubs are Cabletron Systems Inc. and SynOptics Communications Inc. These systems are cost effective, extremely easy to maintain, and include management schemes for a constant, day-to-day support strategy for the physical and logical network.

Cabletron has also implemented some management techniques in its network hub products. Cabletron calls its integration system of hardware and software products Integrated Network Architecture, which incorporates a management software package platform with two main components.

- **LANVIEW** interfaces with the architecture to provide real-time data at the physical layer.
- **SPECTRUM** is a sophisticated management platform for internetworking environments.

SynOptics supports multitopology configurations. Its **LattisNet** network management software captures real-time data on the network and allows for automatic reconfiguration of certain operational parameters. The software views the LattisNet system at the physical board module level. This allows operators to monitor, log, and analyze all areas of network activity.

Network operating systems are appearing as components in smart wiring hubs. Putting the wiring hub inside the server reduces costs because the server's CPU runs the hub management software. Wiring hubs also allow vendors to ship ready-to-run networks, complete with preconfigured file servers. Integrating the hub and server, however, creates a central point of failure and precludes on-the-fly insertion or removel of hub cards from the file server.

Novell's Hub Management Interface (HMI) bundles low-end hub cards into its servers. HMI integrates the wiring hub (the center of many Token Ring and Ethernet cabling schemes) and the file server into a single device.

Ungermann-Bass, Inc. (UB) and Network, Inc. are migrating NetWare and its associated applications into their wiring centers. With the hub and the server running NetWare, management of devices is integrated. UB recommends moving communications-related services, such as routing and messaging, to the hub, although any NLM or other NetWare application could reside there.

The new features offered by network hubs are actually network management tools that allow MIS to be continually aware of the health of the network and, simultaneously, focus on troubleshooting daily LAN problems.

18.2.3 Network Management Software

As a network grows, it becomes critical for network administrators to monitor and analyze the entire network from a central point. Their workstations should support windowing software and high-resolution graphics. The network management software that runs on these machines should analyze operations at remote workstations and servers and analyze network cabling. A topological layout of the network must be maintained. Some vendors of network operating systems are integrating network management capabilities into their products.

LAN inventory software is appearing on the market. This software automatically collects and records information about hardware and software serial numbers, registration, processor type and speed, memory capacity, video system type, ports, add-ins, and versions of system software. Trends in this emerging market include software tracking, multiplatform support, wide-area networking, and the ability to provide server as well as workstation information.

Most network management software uses a MIB (management information base) to hold statistics and SNMP to transport data to a central site for testing against threshold rules. Since each machine generates its own set of data, the amount of data can be overwhelming.

The UNIX-based **DualManager** family of products from NetLabs, Inc. allows users to set parameters and gather information on remote resources. When the parameters are violated, DualManager triggers an alarm. One version of its product manages heterogeneous networks of up to 100 nodes; the other version, 200 nodes. The Discovery product searches TCP/IP to determine the network components and topology. NetCAD is a planning tool for accessing data to simulate existing networks, run simulations, and interpret the results.

Trellis Inc.'s **Expose** products can be used to manage Banyan's VINES networks. The family of products consists of the following:

- **Expose Draw** is a diagramming package that automatically sketches the network's topology based on data from the routing tables. LAN segments and connections can be color-coded for easy identification. The software cannot discover individual nodes on a VINES LAN, but it can find servers, asynchronous communications links, backbones, and remote links.

- **Expose Network Observer** is a monitoring system that is used as an early-warning device, with alarms and graphs of network performance. Network Observer collects simple server statistics in 12 categories and displays them on a dedicated PC. LAN managers can set alarm thresholds for each category.

- **Expose Network Manager** is a Windows-based product, which tracks 90 statistical categories, ranging from network performance to service, disk, serial, and LAN interface parameters. It also includes "smart alarms," a tool that identifies problems and recommends solutions.

LANlord, from Client Server Technologies (CST), manages and controls resources across multiple heterogeneous LANs, running Novell's NetWare network operating system, from a central location. This product allows managers to collect statistics on LAN resource utilization to manage and control remote workstation hardware and software across networks and multiple locations. It gathers SNMP data, which can be viewed by other SNMP systems such as HP's OpenView and SunNet Manager.

LANlord provides a remote-access module that acts as a traffic cop, facilitating the identification of communication problems, and provides file-transfer routines for uploading and downloading data. This module is based on Carbon Copy, a remote control software package from Microcom. CST, which was recently acquired by Microcom and operating as a subsidiary, continues to focus on software for the top four layers of the OSI communication model.

NetDirector, a network management product from Ungerman-Bass Inc., supports centralized control and has recently been enhanced to allow the product to be tailored to a hierarchical, distributed or centralized architecture. The enhancement, Adaptive Internetwork Management, uses an SNMP agent on the NetDirector server.

HP's **PerfView** is based on HP's OpenView framework, which supports the management of multivendor networks from one location and was accepted by OSF as part of DME. OpenView focuses on managing network resources; PerfView focuses on monitoring and managing the performance of distributed systems across a WAN.

PerfView addresses two categories of performance management:

- Online performance management, which is reactive
- The planning side of performance measurement, which is proactive

PerfView allows network managers to isolate and characterize system performance problems in complex systems by first narrowing the problem down to one node, and then using lower-level node systems to isolate the specific problem.

PerfView performs management-by-exception. Data is collected and fed into alarm algorithms. The monitoring system then determines if an exception condition exists. If it does, PerfView issues a notification via the alarm system. The network manager, in response to the alarm, may look for supporting information from the central site or identify the problem using HP's node-specific tools.

PerfView is currently available for HP/UX platforms, proprietary MPE systems, and Sun SPARCstations. By the end of 1993, HP plans to have support for all major Unix environments and for NetWare.

Sybase offers **SA Companion** to provide operational control for SYBASE SQL Server client/server environments. By automating complex SQL syntax and system procedure calls associated with operation control, system administrators can focus on what needs to be done instead of on how to do it.

SA Companion includes the following modules:

- **SQL Server Management** module handles the management and analysis of the SQL Server machines in the network. Routines are provided for establishing server connections, installing new servers, configuring SQL Server software and examining error logs.
- **Device Management** module manages the devices, such as databases and database objects, known to a selected SQL Server.
- **User Management** module handles the administration of SQL Server user accounts and database-level user management.
- **Database Management** module provides tools for the database and system administrators to manipulate databases and their objects, and manage user access to them.

In addition, SA Companion prints reports to facilitate system and data administration.

18.2.4 Network Performance Monitors

It is important that a network administrator be able to monitor (ideally from a central location) the network's performance and reconfigure resources to offset problems and bottlenecks.

Auspex Performance Monitor from Auspex Systems, itself a client/server application, gathers data on network servers and analyzes it on the network administrator's desktop machine. It can be set at a variety of time bases to check for maximum utilization. It can look at moment-to-moment or steady-state utilization and reconfigure resources for maximum performance by spreading the workload among multiple drives.

IBM's **Distributed Console Access Facility** (DCAF) allows a network administrator to take control of a machine on a LAN from a remote site so application software problems can be diagnosed.

IBM's **LAN Administration Manager**, an adjunct to NetView, can report network topology-related errors and automatically or manually react to those errors. It provides alarm indication and operations management but has no support for protocol analysis.

Novell's **LANtern** supports remote monitoring and can manage multiple LANs from a central point, using SNMP to communicate with a central console. It also includes the RMON protocol. Also available as an NLM, LANtern allows NetWare servers using the RMON NLM to capture and filter network packets and send the results to a central SNMP-based network management system for analysis. The LANtern Services Manager provides a graphical user interface to LANtern.

18.3 Runtime Specifications

Flexibility is one of the major benefits of client/server computing. To maintain that flexibility, an application should run, with little or no modification, on any platform combination. One way to achieve this goal is to use software that supports runtime specifications.

18.3.1 Network Characteristics

Client/server application software should adapt to changes in the network. If the network is reconfigured and nodes are moved, the access software should not require modifications.

18.3.2 Application Partitioning

In the simplest models, GUI and application logic are stored and executed from the client machine. But, as discussed earlier, there are situations where the application processing should be shared between the client and the server. The basic rules-of-thumb are that all user-interface processing belongs on the client, all report processing belongs on a server, all data validation should be done first on the clients, all shared business rules should be processed on the server, and so on.

However, these rules do not *always* apply. Processes that typically run on a client may be allocated to a server, or vice versa. A client machine may be too busy with an advanced interface facility to perform data validation. Conversely, the client and the network may have excess processing capacity that might be used by an overworked server to perform math and sorting functions for a report run against a seldom-used table. Many applications have exceptions to the rules.

Ideally, the software should recognize the bottlenecks in the infrastructure and reroute processes as needed. The entire process should be transparent to the user. Many of these load-leveling functions are provided automatically by the runtime facilities of products such as Ellipse from Cooperative Solutions.

18.3.3 Application Platform

Client/server applications are typically developed for a specific GUI and for specific data sources. But if those choices change, the application must adapt to those changes.

Current application development environments for client/server computing support multiple GUIs, such as Windows, OS/2 Presentation Manager, Motif, and OpenLook; however, the application specifications must be recompiled before moving from one target environment to another. For example, a Windows interface for an application is developed and populated on the users' micros. However, if users prefer using Motif, they should be able to initiate the application through Windows and, through the Windows menu, change the GUI to Motif.

Current application development environments for client/server computing support transparent access to multiple server database management systems. For example, an application is designed for SQLBase. The user wants to do analysis that requires data that resides in SQL Server. With a few menu picks and required specifications, the SQL Server data should be accessible to the application.

18.4 Distributing Software Updates

With software distributed to every user machine, there has to be a central point that monitors what software and what version (applications and packages such as Lotus 1-2-3) resides on each user machine to ensure that the installed versions of software components of the system are compatible.

Some client/server application development tools automate version control. When a user initiates the application, the server software checks the version on the user's machine and if the software is out of date, the server software downloads a current copy.

Software that is used to manage software package distribution is now available. One such product is **Synchrony** from Telepartner International, which manages software updates in distributed systems by scheduling software changes, performing automatic installations, and providing an audit trail. It can collect data and deliver it to micros from the mainframe or vice versa. For UNIX platforms, **WizardWare** from TIVOLI Systems uses object-oriented technology to provide both centralized and distributed management. Lotus is working on a product, code named Lynx, that will automate and manage software distribution.

18.5 Vendor Support

In a multivendor environment, support becomes a big issue. When front-end software and back-end software are from the same vendor, they are usually tightly integrated. The downside of that marriage is that the front-end doesn't always link easily to other data sources and the back-end only works with that front-end software. Oracle provides its own front-end software, Oracle Card, that only accesses Oracle databases. Gupta Technologies offers SQLWindows to access its SQLBase Server as well as ORACLE and SQL Server. Interface software that works with multiple data sources is usually not well integrated.

Future Trends

The use of computers has gone from automating individual processes, such as accounting, to becoming a critical component in an organization's ability to create and maintain a competitive advantage. IS has evolved from its initial role as a provider of services to its current role as a partner with the user community.

Trends in technology have allowed organizations to take advantage of changes in the business climate. In some cases, the technology itself has forced those changes.

Predicting technology and its impact is difficult. The importance of enhancements under development can be discussed but prediction of their impact is risky. Look back at the literature that predicted that micros would never have an important presence in businesses or that OS/2 would be the premier operating system for micros by the end of the 1980s.

Some advances in hardware technology that are available on high-end machines will find their way down to the low-end machines. Current high-end machines will become tomorrow's low-end machines.

The same holds true of software. Some features currently available in expensive software will soon be available in less expensive versions.

Chapter

19

Hardware and
Software Trends

It is difficult to say how many industry analysts might have predicted
the current state of client/server computing based on the technology
available five years ago. It is equally difficult to predict where
technology will be in five years—or even three years. Some hardware
and software advances will enhance the functionality of client/server
computing. Others will affect the evolution of client/server technology.
Such advances in client/server computing will continue to improve the
competitive capabilities of the organizations which choose to take
advantage of client/server computing.

19.1 Mobile Computing

Smaller, lighter machines are supporting the computer needs of the
mobile worker. As the vendors of these new computers search for a
"killer application," their primary focus is on automating two very
manual processes: completing forms and capturing data.

19.1.1 Smaller Machines

The automation of data analysis was a focus of the 1980s. In the 1990s,
due to increased competitive pressures, organizations are looking for
ways to quickly capture data so it can be analyzed. Organizations are
evaluating client/server computing as a means of capturing data, in

machine-readable form, at its generation point.

Client machines are getting smaller and less expensive, more powerful and more portable. Notebook computers, weighing about six pounds, have a *de facto* minimum of 4 Mbytes of memory and fast hard disks with capacities as large as 120 Mbytes. Minimum configurations use chips that are equal to Intel's 386SX, 386SL, and 486SX products. Current battery life is about two hours but is expected to reach to eight hours (and require less recharging time) by the end of 1993.

Although earlier notebook computers had inadequate nine-inch displays, current notebook computers come with ten inch diagonal LCD displays with VGA resolution. Easier-to-view active-matrix screens are also available at a higher price.

Other categories of machines in this smaller-footprint technology are:

- **Clipboards and tablets.** These machines are generally micro-compatible and industry watchers expect them to be used to automate forms processing. They usually run Intel 386 (or higher) chips, have small hard drives or use flash memory cards. They are less powerful and smaller in size than notebook computers. Sample products are GRiD Systems Corp.'s GridPad and IBM's ThinkPad.
- **Palmtops.** These machines have smaller screens and less power than clipboards and are expected to be used to automate blue-collar tasks. A sample product is GRiD's PalmPad.
- **Convertibles.** These machines, also called pentops, combine palmtop technology with pen technology (a combination pen and keyboard machine) and are being evaluated as a means of supporting business applications. Major vendors of convertibles are GRiD Systems and Toshiba Corp.
- **Personal digital assistants** (PDAs). These hand-held, limited-purpose consumer devices are targeted at personal management applications, such as simple note-taking, address book maintenance, calendar scheduling, and letter-writing. They have some connectivity features for transmitting files to a host. Apple's PDA and a similar unit from Sharp Electronics, both expected to be released mid-1993, will be entirely pen-based (no keyboard or physical buttons) and feature a combination touch and LCD screen interface. These units will run Apple's new Newt/OS operating system, which has four key elements: recognition algorithms for text and graphics, intelligence and software agents (intelligent "servants" that anticipate users' needs based on the specific command), intelligent format options, and a multitasking architecture.

Docking stations may ultimately replace desktop machines. A docking station is a CPU-less box with an opening for the notebook. It becomes a complete system when the notebook is slid into place. The docking station contains a desktop monitor, full-size keyboard, and a table chassis with expansion slots and drives.

19.1.2 Pen-Based Computing

A significant new technology is pen computers. Pens were first introduced as pointing devices. They have since evolved into a self-contained architecture. Pen-based operating systems store *ink*, a new datatype that displays the strokes of the pen and stores them as they are created by the user. Ink field values can be cut and pasted like normal computer text. Pen computing is aimed at supporting mobile field and office workers.

The original concept of using a pen as an interface focused on the elimination of keying hand-written data into an application. However, current handwriting recognition software is not yet industrial strength for the following reasons:

- It is limited to recognizing handprinting rather than handwriting.
- Users have to stop midstream to reprint unrecognized characters.

Consequently, most successful pen applications today take a forms approach. Users check an item, fill in boxes, write notes to themselves (which are stored as-is in a text field), and use the pen to draw. Machines that use pen-based technology must be able to travel easily and take a lot of banging.

Another advantage of pen computers is the ability to do electronic signature capture. The signature is then retrievable like any other piece of data.

The major pen operating systems—Go Corp.'s PenPoint and Microsoft's Windows for Pen Computing (Pen Windows)—run on Intel-based CPUs, store text in ASCII, and can output in many standard file formats. Due to its memory and storage requirements, Pen Windows cannot run on as small a palmtop as PenPoint can. Currently Pen Windows uses pens as pointing devices (mouse replacements). As palmtops become more powerful, more robust applications will follow.

Software for the pen environment is beginning to appear on the market. Slate Corp. offers PenApps, a program development software for PenPoint and Pen Windows, which uses PenBasic, a programming language similar to Microsoft's Visual Basic, and supports DDE under Windows and Embedding under PenPoint. Penware, Inc. offers PenCell, a spreadsheet product that runs under Pen Windows.

It is difficult to predict how successful pen computing will be. Some industry watchers say never, some predict 1995, and others will only say it is worth watching and, for the right applications, worth trying.

19.1.3 Connectivity

Have computer will travel. And these traveling computer users want to connect to the rest of the world. Consequently, most notebooks and laptops have a serial and a parallel port, a slot for an internal modem (or FAX/modem), and connectors for a desktop monitor, external keypad, and also Personal Computer Memory Card International Association (PCMCIA) devices.

The portability has given rise to wireless LANs and pocket LAN adapters, which allow mobile users to plug their computer into the LAN without taking the back cover off of the machine.

Some notebook computers are communications-ready and bundled with a cellular-capable FAX modem and built-in E-mail software. Most notebook computers offer an optional wireless FAX/modem with rates of up to 9600 bps. These machines can be linked with one- or two-way pager technologies, connections over telephone or cellular networks, infrared LANs, and local and wide-area radio networks.

Recognizing the need to support portable communciation, Go Corp. is developing a version of its operating system that will allow communications devices to transmit phone calls, data, and images. The interface, different from the one used by PenPoint, will use a metaphor with standard communications formats, such as an envelope and fax cover sheet for incoming and outgoing messages. Designed to work with mail-enabled applications, it is targeted at handheld micros and will contain built-in protocols for a fast serial port, parallel port, modem, and Mobitex network.

19.2 More Robust Servers

More and more features of fault-tolerant computers are becoming available on micro/servers. The distinction between a micro/server and a midrange computer is becoming as blurry as the distinction between a midrange computer and a mainframe. As client/server applications become company-critical, the reliability of the components also becomes critical. Servers will offer standard dual processors, redundant buses, redundant arrays of inexpensive disks with error correction capability, and backup power supplies.

Multitasking, multithreading, and parallel processing will be common features of server machines. Symmetric multiprocessing, where processing can be assigned to any processor, will become the norm. Transparent support for symmetric multiprocessing will be built into operating systems and database management systems.

I/O throughput and storage and memory capacities will continue to increase and their costs will continue to decrease. As the processing bugs are worked out of supercomputers using RISC chips and parallel processing, these features will find their way into server machines.

The advances in technology will, in general, make servers faster, and more reliable. Many of the increases in speed and reliability will be achieved through the use of parallelism.

19.3 Network Management Standard

As internetworks incorporate more diverse networks, management of the internet requires standards for reporting the health of the networks. SNMP is becoming the most popular method of integrating network management information from different suppliers. Its rise to *de facto* standard is based on:

- Low licensing costs
- Ease in developing software that conforms to the specifications
- Simple to use

As SNMP (and its proposed successor, SMP) is accepted as a standard, additional network management software will become available. The end result will be that organizations will be able to manage the network from central or remote locations.

Mid-1992, a collection of vendors that includes Intel, Microsoft, Novell, SunConnect, Synoptics, and Ungermann-Bass began to outline APIs that would allow SNMP and other network management protocols to monitor application software. The group plans to address application monitoring, software licensing, and configuration management.

As discussed in Section 17.2, Integrating Multivendor Environments, OSF's Distributed Management Environment, UI's UI-Atlas, and OMG's Object Management Architecture address the management of multivendor environments. As these products evolve, an organization will finally be able to use one piece of software to manage its entire computer infrastructure as a single entity.

19.4 Intelligent Wiring Hubs

As discussed in Chapter 18, Production Requirements, intelligent wiring hubs have auto-configuration capabilities that allow network administrators to move network nodes among workgroups without having to rewire the network. By providing a central management site and tools for analyzing the hardware, cabling, and adapters in the LAN, wiring hubs simplify network management tasks. Intelligent wiring hubs allow administrators to manage a network from a logical point of view as well as a physical view.

As hub vendors begin to add network operating system software to their products, the complexity of client/server computing will diminish. Vendors can ship ready-to-run networks with preconfigured file servers.

19.5 Wireless LANs

Wireless LANs allow portable computer users to connect to a LAN without a fixed address and without a phone jack. Executives and mobile personnel equipped with portable computers and wireless modems can access their host or peer computers on the network.

Wireless data messages are sent in digital form over a wireless packet network. Network messages are addressed to individual devices with unique identification codes. Due to the proprietary APIs for wireless networks, network users are only able to communicate with others on the same wireless network.

The portable computer must be outfitted with a wireless modem, such as Ericsson GE's Mobidem product. Currently, the two major wireless packet network service providers are New York-based RAM Mobile Data and ARDIS, a partnership of IBM and Motorola, which also supports in-building and on-street data communications between hand-held terminals and host computers.

The availability of cost-effective wireless data communications combined with hand-held computers and pen-based computing is expected to impact personal and corporate computing the way cellular telephones revolutionized phone use. According to industry analysts from Workgroup Technologies, the installed base of radio-frequency-equipped personal computers could exceed two million units as early as 1996.

SplitSecond RF from Simware Inc., a support product for wireless LANs, improves wireless network response time, reduces data communications costs, simplifies micro-to-host connections and replaces cryptic mainframe screens with a user-intuitive interface. Because SplitSecond RF is based on a client/server architecture that takes advantage of the intelligence on both computers, the host application requires no changes. SplitSecond RF works with Mobidem portable wireless modems and networks from RAM Mobile Data and ARDIS.

19.6 ATM Switching

Asynchronous Transfer Mode (ATM) use switching technologies rather than shared-medium to link LANs to high-speed networks. This emerging gigabit-speed-capable technology is more suited to the high-bandwidth requirements of delay-sensitive voice and video applications than the emerging 100 Mbps FDDI technology. ATM supports frame-relay traffic and Switched Multimegabit Data Service traffic and uses industry standard-size cells for transmission across the network.

Because LANs require multiple users to share a fixed amount of bandwidth, network performance can degrade as users are attached. Consequently, network administrators continually segment the networks to keep local performance high—at the expense of interLAN performance—as traffic travels through more bridges and routers.

ATM expands proportionally as computer speeds rise. This frees network administrators from continually segmenting and fiddling with networks in response to bottlenecks. ATM may ultimately eliminate the boundaries between LANs and wide-area networks.

Advancing beyond the auto-configuration capabilities of smart wiring hubs, ATM technology relies on a virtual network, where LANs are configured in software instead of physical media. Physically moved nodes automatically appear in their virtual workgroup with no new addressing or management requirements. In addition, temporary, point-to-point, secure network connections can be built during a transfer at full network speeds (which brings new meaning to the term *on-the-fly!*).

Although multimedia applications can run over local LANs, problems arise when transmitting across the internetwork where traffic is aggregated in bridges and routers. To minimize this negative effect on speed, networks use a feature of ATM referred to as its isochronous capability, which guarantees that equal-length traffic packets arrive at their destination in a steady, deterministic fashion, and a high bandwidth.

Internetworking vendors are introducing interfaces, switching modules or full switches to allow organizations to convert to ATM infrastructures. The most common migration to ATM is expected to be gateways in routers and wiring hubs that feed LANs into ATM networks. The hold-up is price. At the time of writing, per port prices for an ATM connection were five times higher than FDDI prices. But, as the ATM vendors and ATM-networked organizations are quick to add, once the infrastructure is in place, the technologies do not have to be upgraded.

In order to accelerate the implementation of high-speed networks, a group of vendors has already formed the ATM Forum to create standards for this new technology.

19.7 Integration of Network and Server Operating Systems

One of the biggest impacts on client/server computing will result from the integration of server software and network software, as indicated in Microsoft's plans for integrating Windows NT and LAN Manager. Since the two operating systems (system and network) are interdependent, the integration of their functions makes the platform more reliable and easier to maintain and support. The evolution will probably place some network-oriented software on the client, as well.

The evolution reflects how micro software is beginning to parallel the software structure of larger machines, such as the AS/400 which has a fully integrated operating system and does not require a separate network operating system. This trend is also a result of corporate America's demands for more from client/server technology and vendors' developing products to specifically support client/server architecture.

19.8 Use of Object Technology

Object-oriented analysis and design tools will allow software and application developers to design and build software from reusable components. The most successful client/server application development tools are object-oriented. Object technology can be used to quickly produce applications that contain easily maintained code.

Another book would be needed to describe object technology but an overview is necessary to understand its impact on client/server computing. An object class is any thing, real or abstract, that has a specified behavior. In object software, a class is a data structure definition, the code (functions) for operating on that data, and a list of services that can be performed on, by, or for the class. Instances of a class are called objects. The software representing the object contains the data structure and methods (procedures) that express its behavior. Encapsulation combines data and the functions that operate on that data into a self-contained object.

An object may consist of many other objects, which in turn may consist of other objects, and so on. Object-oriented design tools store the software for the objects in a repository as reusable objects, which include screens, icons, tables, coded procedures, and dialogues.

The methods in an object can manipulate only the data structures of that object. This protects the object's data from corruption by other objects and simplifies design requirements because each object tracks its own data.

An object can send a message to another object in order to use its data structures. The message causes the invoked object to behave in a specified way, which may include returning a value to the calling object. This aspect of object technology, called polymorphism, allows single functions to behave differently, depending on the context in which they are used. For example, if the OPEN function is sent to an application object, it would start up the software and begin the application itself. If the OPEN function is sent to a file, it opens the file for access.

Another important concept of object technology is inheritance. Objects belong to hierarchical classes, such as *parent* and *child*. The child inherits the properties of the parent and may have additional properties of its own. Some classes inherit properties from more than one parent. A subclass does not necessarily inherit all the methods and data structures of its parents.

Most application and software designs require that reusable code be modified to fit the current application. (A case of *it's the same as...except...*) Developers need to be able to override some inherited characteristics. The same message can communicate with the object even if some of the parameters contained in the message are changed. The object would adjust its actions based on the content of the message.

At this point, most people say *So what?* An example of the use of objects may help. As illustrated in Figure 19.1, the object class of FIELD, which is used to build SCREENs and DIALOGs, has a COLOR attribute and two subclasses, INPUT-FIELD and NON-INPUT-FIELD. Subclasses of INPUT-FIELD are PART-NUMBER and PART-NAME, both of which inherit the properties of FIELD (as subclasses of INPUT-FIELD), including its COLOR. When the designer overrides the color in INPUT-FIELD, the new value of the attribute is inherited by both PART-NUMBER and PART-NAME.

19.8.1 Object-Oriented Databases

As the next generation of applications incorporates increased use of unstructured data, such as text, compound documents, bit-mapped images, and graphics, relational technology begins to fall short.

Unstructured data does not fit neatly into tables. Data cannot always be represented as entities, attributes, and relations.

Relational databases require data to be broken into separate tables for efficient retrieval. For example, an order might be broken into header information, which is stored in one table, and detail for each order item stored in another table. To review an order in its entirety, these two tables must be joined before data can be pulled from each one.

Object technology keeps the data and its processes together. They depend on each other. Rarely do we think of an order without thinking of its detail items and its status (open, back-ordered, closed, payment due, etc.).

Object-oriented database technology is evolving rapidly. One of the major stumbling blocks is the retraining required to change from a procedural, row/record-oriented paradigm to an object paradigm. Despite the long learning curve, most industry analysts predict that object-oriented databases will replace relational databases just as relational databases have replaced hierarchical databases.

19.8.2 Object Development Tools

Object-oriented analysis and design defines classes (the data) and their objects, structure, attributes, and services (functions). Techniques are

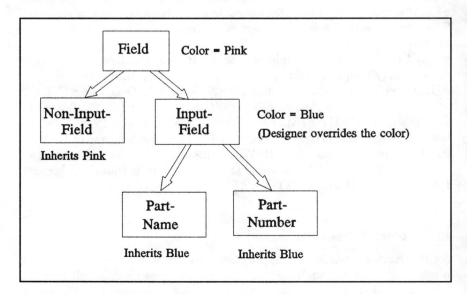

Figure 19.1 Inheritance concept in object technology

being developed to aid in the definition of classes and objects, some with built-in artificial intelligence. Expert systems and class browsers are being developed to assist the developer in navigating the class structure. Indexing and cataloging are also used to pinpoint reusable objects.

These libraries of classes and objects may be stored in a repository for future use in the same or a new application, or can be sold as a product to developers. For example, Microsoft's Foundation Classes is a library class of Windows interface and system objects.

19.8.3 Standards for Object Technology

Currently, the major group that is focusing on object technology is the Object Management Group. The OMG's goal is to have its members (mostly software vendors) agree on:

- A standard messaging format and method for how objects talk to each other
- The model and specification language for the structure of the data
- Common interfaces
- Methods for handling security and containment
- Standards for linking and embedding

19.9 Support by CASE Tools

CASE tools are used by IS professionals to improve the applications they develop. CASE tools were one of the first technologies used by IS to formalize communication between developers and users during the design phase of an application, a process called prototyping. However, these tools assumed that the end user interfaced to the application via character-based screens and the application ran on a single machine. In addition, the leading CASE tools, such as IEF from Texas Instruments and ADW from KnowledgeWare, require more discipline and create more cultural change than corresponding client/server development tools.

The major CASE vendors have recognized that applications need to support GUIs. Most now support the client/server model but still require the developer to decide what processing is done on the server and what is done on the client. When CASE tools can make that determination, they will greatly benefit client/server application developers.

In addition, application development tools must be able to generate code for multiple platforms from one specification. Multiple platforms include multiple GUI environments, server operating systems, network operating systems, and server databases. The platform configuration that provides the services to the user should be incidental to the application's specifications. Only then will applications be truly portable.

Recognizing that the CASE paradigm has increased productivity, many client/server development tools are adding CASE-like features to their products to help develop the system specifications with the users. These tools are usually object-oriented, which closely parallels the thought processes of most users.

19.10 Repositories

When DBMSs were first evaluated by organizations, a great selling feature was the data dictionary, which provided standardization for the data and consistency for the programs that used the data. Repositories are an extension of the services provided by data dictionaries.

A repository is a collection (or warehouse) of objects, in object-oriented terminology; or definitions, in CASE terminology. It stores common building blocks for applications and facilitates understanding and consistency of data and processes. An organization uses many tools to build applications: CASE software, 4GLs, DBMSs, and application development software. Since a repository is a warehouse, it should support the efforts of all development tools. However, today that is not the case. For example, it is difficult to find a CASE tool whose repository specifications can be used by another development tool.

IBM, with AD/Cycle, and Digital, with CDD/Repository, have tried to provide a common metadata model for repositories from multiple vendors. Neither product has been very successful in the marketplace.

However, as more tools provide repository support and integration, applications will be easier to develop and maintain. New applications will be quickly built based on proven methods used in existing applications. The meaning of data will be consistent for all users on all nodes, an important tenet of client/server computing.

19.11 Multimedia

Multimedia, the use of voice and images (video and graphics), is finding its way into application portfolios as organizations re-engineer their business processes. Imaging allows an organization to convert paper files into computer images that can be searched, sorted, and retrieved and is a relatively inexpensive way to process documents while they are in an active cycle. Imaging is being used by insurance companies and banks to support their paper-oriented processes. Other industries are now using the technology to automate the paper process across LANs and WANs.

Imaging can use standard micros and run on standard networks. Industry standards are already in place and the price of imaging is coming down, both for installation and per-transaction (retrieval) cost. But there is a down side. Multimedia applications require large amounts of storage and high-bandwidths for transmission, and the application development tools are just now emerging. The justification of multimedia lies beyond just seeing and hearing video and voice. Multimedia's benefit is that it provides access to information that is available in video or voice form.

Users are finding that the client/server architecture is perfect for supporting multimedia applications. The network is in place and the concept of a server and as-needed data access from any node is accepted and supported. Relational and object-oriented databases offer support of binary large objects (BLOBs) to accommodate the storage of images. The pieces are there; the key is finding the right project that will truly benefit from multimedia.

19.12 Workgroup Computing

In the broadest sense, groupware is software that can improve the coordination and communication among employees working in groups. It removes geographical and organizational barriers that exist in a group. Workgroup computing (which uses groupware software) is a natural evolution from personal computing. It acknowledges that employees do not work alone, they work in groups. As organizations group workstations into networks, individuals can easily communicate with others in their group. Groupware facilitates and formalizes that communication.

Groupware goes far beyond E-mail communication, which is one-to-one (regardless of how many cc: copies are sent). For example, a project leader prepares a status memo which details areas of the project that are behind schedule. Under the E-mail paradigm, the project leader sends a copy to every member of the team. They each respond. But unless each member sends a response to all the other members, there is no peer-to-peer communication. If the response is copied (via E-mail) to all the other members, the network is tied up sending the same document to many people, and disk space is used to store redundant copies of each member's memo and the project leader's memo.

Under the groupware paradigm, the project leader sends the memo to the group's database, where each member can access it, read it, and respond to it. Each member can read the other members' responses and, if necessary, respond. A log of the documents, which contains sender identification and the links for the responses, is maintained for future reference.

A groupware product can replace face-to-face meetings with computer-based conferences. Telephone conversations can be replaced with real-time computer-based discussions. In addition, spreadsheet, images, graphics, and other data can be included as part of a conference message. Groupware keeps all data (typically text or bit images) in a shared storehouse that can be organized from a number of different perspectives. Groupware software also supports private communication.

Workgroup computing facilitates a change in corporate culture and the way people do business. The written word becomes more important than the spoken word. It softens the natural hierarchy of groups because managers and executives are readily accessible via the computer links. All members must participate through groupware for the benefits to be realized. Benefits are mostly intangible (shorter, more-efficient meetings) but some tangible benefits can be attributed to travel cost savings.

Groupware applications depend on an E-mail system to route messages. They rely on client/server architecture and distributed environments to provide the necessary division of data and labor.

As the importance of collaborative environments is recognized, the word *workgroup* is making its way into product names and marketing literature. For example, Microsoft's Windows for Workgroups provides a peer-to-peer network for file and printer sharing, but requires no separate network operating system. However, this product should not be considered groupware software.

Lotus Notes from Lotus Development Corp., one of the major players in workgroup computing, uses a distributed and automatically replicated database to give multiple users access to the shared files. It accepts a variety of data types and supports DDE, OLE, and the DataLens interface to RDBMSs. Lotus Notes users can circulate documents, incorporating changes as they go. Multiple users can work on one or more documents simultaneously. Notes automatically controls the flow of the information. A Notes API, currently under development, will allow Notes to be incorporated with and accessed by other applications.

Each Lotus Notes database is stored on multiple Notes servers on the network. The database contains documents that can be categorized and linked according to users' needs. Filters can also be used to facilitate faster location of specific documents.

Groupware software and the concept of workgroup computing is not new. Every organization would benefit from a collaborative working environment that takes advantage of individual expertise. However, its success continues to be slow in coming. Although most organizations would agree that workgroup computing is the wave of the future, they are waiting for some of the obvious bugs to be worked out:

- Support for cross-platform conversions
- Lack of interoperability between groupware software
- Degradation of network speed
- Limited links to other software
- Application independence
- A new set of user dynamics

19.13 Dealing with Legacy Applications

Many IS organizations are evaluating the migration of host-based systems to smaller platforms, often as a COBOL-to-COBOL conversion with converted front-end interfaces. This frees up host resources and is an excellent option for an organization which does not wish to modify or redesign the application code.

However, most legacy (existing) applications have been modified so often that the code should be reviewed and restructured. Reusable components should be identified and stored in a repository. It is important to determine if the application is broken or just out of touch with current technology or organizational structure.

As discussed earlier, software redevelopment involves the following steps:

- **Reverse engineering**. This step produces the physical and logic design of the application independent of the target environment. It produces a design deliverable for the application which, ideally, should be stored in a repository.
- **Forward engineering**. This step identifies reusable components, cleans up data relationships, and adds enhancements to the design of the application. The deliverable is executable code re-engineered for the target environment.

Although existing software applications may not achieve the same level of benefits as re-engineering, the process itself, the ability to extend the life of an application and plan for its replacement, is benefit enough for many organizations.

19.14 Overall Trends

Organizations are changing the way they view their information infrastructure and are modifying their computer systems architecture to support that view. Software is constantly evolving to take advantage of new capabilities in hardware.

19.14.1 Software Technologies

As personnel become more expensive and computer power less expensive, developers are using the increased computer memory capacities to experiment with user interfaces and new data-handling techniques. Gone are the days of writing programming overlays to manage memory. No longer do features have to be justified based on whether or not they fit into memory. Now users can be working with many applications and their related data at the same time. Even the notion of one application per machine is gone.

GUIs have taken the software industry by storm and have become the *de facto* interface standard. We can expect to see smarter interfaces and the exploitation of pen technology for pointing and data entry. Operating system and application software will handle more administrative duties, such as file and memory management.

19.14.2 Multitiered Architectures

The computer architecture in many organizations is becoming multitiered as illustrated in Figure 19.2. The first tier supports a LAN-connected group. Personal files may be stored on the client machine and the shared data stored on the server. The second tier supports a group of LANs and the third tier, the enterprise. Each tier can transparently access data from the others. To those used to glass rooms, this architecture is unnatural. To business users, it seems very natural. It is, after all, the way data and information actually flow within an organization. It reinforces the need to place the computer power and data access in the hands of the users.

19.15 What Next?

Users are clients (customers) of IS. Client/server computing and distributed environments allow IS to provide its clients with the tools to help them do their jobs better and faster. As every successful consultant knows, a happy client generates more work. And so it is

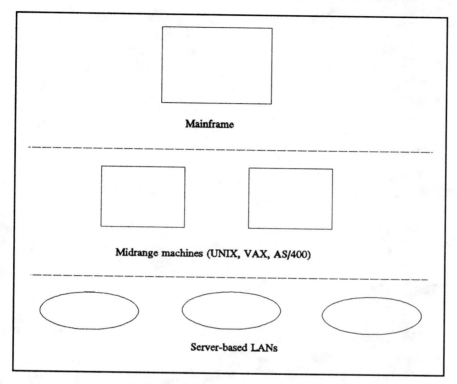

Figure 19.2 Multitiered computer architecture

with client/server computing. Users are pushing IS; IS is pushing vendors; vendors are pushing for technology advances.

This is not the technology for a *sit back and wait* attitude. Start small or start big, but start! Or watch your competitors start taking your market share.

List of Abbreviations

3GL	Third-generation language
4GL	Fourth-generation language
ADW	Application Development Workbench (KnowledgeWare)
ANSI	American National Institute of Standards
API	Application programming interface
APPC	Advanced Program-to-Program Communication (IBM)
ASCII	American National Standard Code for Information Interchange
ATM	Asynchronous transfer mode
CASE	Computer-aided software engineering
CICS	Customer Information Control System (IBM)
CISC	Complex instruction set computing
CLI	Call-level interface
CMIP	Common Management Information Protocol
CMIS	Common Management Information Services
CORBA	Common Object Request Broker Architecture
CPI-C	Common Programming Interface for Communications
CPU	Central processing unit
CSTP	Client/server transaction processing
CUA	Common User Access (IBM)
CUI	Character-based user interface
DAL	Data Access Language (Apple)
DBMS	Database management systems
DCE	Distributed Computing Environment (OSF)
DDE	Dynamic Data Exchange (Microsoft Windows)
DDEML	DDE Management Library (Microsoft Windows)
DFS	Distributed file systems
DLL	Dynamic link libraries
DME	Distributed Management Environment (OSF)
DOS	Disk operating system
DRDA	Distributed Relational Database Architecture (IBM)
DSS	Decision Support System
DTP	Distributed Transaction Processing (X/Open)
E-R	Entity-relationship diagrams
ECC	Error-correction code
EDA/SQL	Enterprise Data Access/SQL (Information Builders)
EIS	Executive information system
EISA	Extended Industry Standard Architecture

FDDI	Fiber Distributed Data Interface
GOSIP	Government Open Systems Interconnection Profile
GUI	Graphical user interface
HLLAPI	High Level Language Application Programming Interface (IBM)
HPFS	High Performance File System (IBM OS/2)
I/O	Input/output
IDL	Interface definition language
IEEE	Institute of Electrical and Electronic Engineers
IEF	Information Engineering Facility (Texas Instruments)
IP	Internet protocol
IPC	Interprocess communication
IPX	Internet Packet Exchange (Novell)
IS	Information Systems
ISO	International Standards Organization
JAD	Joint application design
LAN	Local area network
LU6.2	Logical Unit 6.2 (IBM)
MAPI	Messaging Application Programming Interface
Mbps	Millions of bits per second
MCA	Micro Channel Architecture
MIB	Management information base
MIPS	Millions of instructions per second
MIS	Management Information Systems
NFS	Network File System (Sun Microsystems)
NLM	NetWare Loadable Modules
NTFS	NT File System (Windows NT)
OBDC	Open Database Connectivity (Microsoft)
OLE	Object Linking and Embedding
OLTP	Online transaction processing
OMA	Object Management Architecture (OMG)
OMG	Object Management Group
ONC	Open Network Computing (SunSoft)
ORB	Object Request Broker
OSF	Open Software Foundation
OSI	Open Systems Interconnection
PM	Presentation Manager (IBM)
POSIX	Portable Operating System Interface for UNIX
PROFS	Professional Office System (IBM)
PTC	Prepare-to-commit
RAD	Rapid application design
RAID	Redundant arrays of inexpensive disks
RAM	Random access memory
RDA	Remote Data Access (ANSI)
RDBMS	Relational database management system
RISC	Reduced instruction set computing
RPC	Remote procedure call
SAG	SQL Access Group

SFT III	System Fault Tolerance Level III (Novell)
SMP	Simple Management Procotol
SNA	Systems Network Architecture (IBM)
SNMP	Simple Network Management Protocol
SPX	Sequenced Packet Exchange (Novell)
SVR4	UNIX System V Release 4
TCP/IP	Transmission Control Protocol/Internet Protocol
TLI	Transport layer interface
TP	Teleprocessing
TPM	Transaction processing monitor
TSR	Terminate and stay resident
UAE	Unrecoverable application errors
UDP	User datagram protocol
UI	UNIX International Inc.
USL	UNIX System Laboratories
VINES	Virtual Networking System (Banyan)
WAN	Wide area network
Windows NT	Windows New Technology
WPS	WorkPlace Shell (IBM OS/2)
WYSIWYG	"What you see is what you get"
XA	X/Open Resource Manager
XDR	External Data Representation
XPG3	X/Open Portability Guide Issue 3

List of Trademarks

	Trademark or Registered Trademark of
1-2-3	Lotus Development Corp.
1-2-3/G	Lotus Development Corp.
3+Mail	3Com Corp.
3+Open	3Com Corp.
3Com	3Com Corp.
A/UX	Apple Computer, Inc.
Accesspoint	KnowledgeWare, Inc.
Account Resource Management	SunSoft
ACE/Server	Security Dynamics
AD/Cycle	International Business Machines Corp.
ADABAS	Software AG
Advanced Interactive Executive	International Business Machines Corp.
Advanced Peer-to-Peer Networking	International Business Machines Corp.
ADW	KnowledgeWare, Inc.
AIX	International Business Machines Corp.
ALEX	Alex Technologies
ALL-IN-1	Digital Equipment Corp.
ALLBASE/SQL	Hewlett-Packard Corp.
Alpha	Digital Equipment Corp.
Andrews File System	Transarc Corp.
Animator	Micro Focus Inc.
API/SQL	Information Builders Inc.
APPC	International Business Machines Corp.
Apple	Apple Computer, Inc.
AppleTalk	Apple Computer, Inc.
Application Control Architecture	Digital Equipment Corp.
Application Development Workbench	KnowledgeWare, Inc.
Application Environment Specification	Open Software Foundation Inc.
AS/400	International Business Machines Corp.
AT&T	American Telephone and Telegraph
Auspex Performance Monitor	Auspex Systems
Automated Enhanced Security Tool	SunSoft
Banyan	Banyan Systems, Inc.
Berkeley Software Distribution	University of California at Berkeley
BSD	University of California at Berkeley
Btrieve	Novell, Inc.
Builder Xcessory	Integrated Computer Solutions

Trademark or Registered Trademark of

CA-Realia COBOL	Computer Associates International, Inc.
Carbon Copy	Microcom
cc:Mail	Lotus Development Corp.
Character Data Representation Architecture	International Business Machines Corp.
CICS	International Business Machines Corp.
Client/Server Interfaces	Sybase, Inc.
COBOL Workbench	Micro Focus Inc.
CodeCenter	Centerline Software
Common Communications Interface	Micro Focus Inc.
Common User Access	International Business Machines Corp.
Communciation Services Manager	Novell, Inc.
COMPAQ INSIGHT Manager	Compaq Computer Corp.
COMPAQ Server Manager	Compaq Computer Corp.
COMPAQ SystemPro/LT	Compaq Computer Corp.
COMPAQ SystemPro	Compaq Computer Corp.
Cooperative Solutions	Cooperative Solutions, Inc.
Customer Information Control System	International Business Machines Corp.
DAL Server NLM	Apple Computer, Inc.
Data Access Language	Apple Computer, Inc.
Database Gateway	Micro Decisionware Inc.
DataDictionary/Solution	BrownStone Solutions, Inc.
DataLens	Lotus Development Corp.
DB Excel	Reltech Products
DB-Library	Sybase, Inc.
DB2	International Business Machines Corp.
DBC/1012 Data Base Computer	Teradata Corp.
DBC/1012 Model 4 Communications Processor	Teradata Corp.
DCE	Open Software Foundation Inc.
DD/S	BrownStone Solutions, Inc.
DECnet	Digital Equipment Corp.
DECwindows	Digital Equipment Corp.
Demand Protocol Architecture	3Com Corp.
DeskSet	SunSoft
Destiny	UNIX System Laboratories, Inc.
Dialog System	Micro Focus Inc.
Digital	Digital Equipment Corp.
Digital Network Architecture	Digital Equipment Corp.
Direct File System	Novell, Inc.
Distributed Computer Environment	Open Software Foundation Inc.
Distributed Console Access Facility	International Business Machines Corp.
Distributed Data Management Architecture	International Business Machines Corp.

Trademark or Registered Trademark of

Distributed Management Environment	Open Software Foundation Inc.
Distributed Object Management	SunSoft
Distributed Objects Everywhere	Sun Microsystems, Inc.
Distributed Relational Database Architecture	International Business Machines Corp.
DME	Open Software Foundation Inc.
DNA	Digital Equipment Corp.
DR DOS	Digital Research, Inc.
DRDA	International Business Machines Corp.
DualManager	NetLabs, Inc.
Dynamic Data Exchange	Microsoft Corp.
EASEL	Easel Corp.
EASEL Transaction Server Toolkit	Easel Corp.
EASEL Workbench	Easel Corp.
EDA/Data Drivers	Information Builders, Inc.
EDA/Extenders	Information Builders, Inc.
EDA/Link	Information Builders, Inc.
EDA/SQL	Information Builders, Inc.
EDA/SQL SErver	Information Builders, Inc.
Ellipse	Cooperative Solutions, Inc.
Ellipse/DE	Cooperative Solutions, Inc.
Ellipse/PS	Cooperative Solutions, Inc.
Encina	Transarc Corp.
ENFIN	Easel Corp.
Enterprise Data Access/SQL	Information Builders, Inc.
Excel	Microsoft Corp.
Excelerator	Intersolv Inc.
Excelerator II	Intersolv Inc.
Expose	Trellis Inc.
Expose Draw	Trellis Inc.
Expose Network Observer	Trellis Inc.
Expose Network Manager	Trellis Inc.
Express	Information Resources, Inc.
Express Windows	Gupta Technologies, Inc.
Fault-Tolerant System Architecture	Texas Microsystems
FileSecure OverNet	Tallgrass Technologies
Fileshare	Micro Focus Inc.
Flashpoint	KnowledgeWare, Inc.
Forest & Trees	Channel Computing
Formatted Data Object Content Architecture	International Business Machines Corp.
Foundation Classes	Microsoft Corp.
GridPad	GRiD Systems Corp.
Group Manager	International Business Machines Corp.

Trademark or Registered Trademark of

Gupta	Gupta Technologies, Inc.
Hewlett-Packard	Hewlett-Parkard Corp.
High Level Language Application	International Business Machines Corp.
High Performance File System	International Business Machines Corp.
HP	Hewlett-Packard Corp.
HP 9000	Hewlett-Packard Corp.
HP-UX	Hewlett-Packard Corp.
Hub Management Interface	Novell, Inc.
Hypercard	Apple Computer, Inc.
IBM	International Business Machines Corp.
IBM Server 295	International Business Machines Corp.
IDMS	Computer Associates International, Inc.
IEF	Texas Instruments, Inc.
Impromptu	Cognos Inc.
IMS	International Business Machines Corp.
Information Engineering Facility	Texas Instruments, Inc.
Information Warehouse	International Business Machines Corp.
Informix	Informix, Inc.
INFORMIX	Informix, Inc.
INFORMIX Online	Informix, Inc.
InfoSpan	InfoSpan Corp.
INGRES	Ingres Corp.
INGRES Intelligent Database	Ingres Corp.
Intel	Intel Corp.
Intelligent Drive Array	Compaq Computer Corp.
Intelligent Drive Array Controller-2	Compaq Computer Corp.
Interactive UNIX	SunSoft
InterBase	Borland International Inc.
Intersolv LAN Repository	Intersolv Inc.
Kerberos	Massachusetts Institute of Technology
LAN Administration Manager	International Business Machines Corp.
LAN Manager	Microsoft Corp.
LAN Network Manager	International Business Machines Corp.
LAN Server	International Business Machines Corp.
LANalyzer	Novell, Inc.
LANlord	Client Server Technologies (Microcom)
LanProbe II	Hewlett-Packard Corp.
LANtern	Novell, Inc.
LANtern Services Manager	Novell, Inc.
LANVIEW	Cabletron Systems Inc.
LANwatch	FTP Software
LattisNet	SynOptics Communications Inc.
Local Area Transport	Digital Equipment Corp.
Lotus	Lotus Development Corp.

Trademark or Registered Trademark of

Lotus Notes	Lotus Development Corp.
LU6.2	International Business Machines Corp.
Macintosh	Apple Computer, Inc.
MacX	Apple Computer, Inc.
Mail	Microsoft Corp.
Mail Gateways	Microsoft Corp.
MCA	International Business Machines Corp.
MCI Mail	MCI Communications Corp.
Messaging Application Programming Interface	Microsoft Corp.
Micro Channel Architecture	International Business Machines Corp.
Micro Focus Checker	Micro Focus Inc.
Micro Focus COBOL	Micro Focus Inc.
Micro Focus Toolset	Micro Focus Inc.
Microsoft	Microsoft Corp.
Mips	Mips Computers, Inc.
Model 204	Computer Corporation of America
Motif	Open Software Foundation
Motif Window Manager	Open Software Foundation
Motorola	Motorola, Inc.
Mozart	Mozart Systems Corp.
MPE	Hewlett-Packard Corp.
MPE/Ix	Hewlett-Packard Corp.
MS DOS	Microsoft Corp.
MS Windows	Microsoft Corp.
MVS	International Business Machines Corp.
Natural Language	Natural Language Inc.
NetDirector	Ungerman-Bass
NetFrame NF100ES	NetFrame Systems Inc.
NetSecure	Tallgrass Technologies
NetView	International Business Machines Corp.
NetWare	Novell, Inc.
NetWare Asynchronous Communication Services	Novell, Inc.
NetWare Bridge	Novell, Inc.
NetWare Btrieve	Novell, Inc.
NetWare Communication Services Manager	Novell, Inc.
NetWare Connectivity Program	Novell, Inc.
NetWare for UNIX	Novell, Inc.
NetWare for VMS	Novell, Inc.
NetWare Global Messaging	Novell, Inc.
NetWare Loadable Module	Novell, Inc.
NetWare Management System	Novell, Inc.
NetWare Message Handling System	Novell, Inc.

Trademark or Registered Trademark of

NetWare Name Service	Novell, Inc.
NetWare SQL	Novell, Inc.
Network Application Support	Digital Equipment Corp.
Network Archivist	Palindrome Corp.
Network File System	Sun Microsystems, Inc.
Network Information System	Sun Microsystems, Inc.
Network Mangement System	Novell, Inc.
NeWS	Sun Microsystems, Inc.
NeWS Development Environment	Sun Microsystems, Inc.
Newt/OS	Apple Computer, Inc.
NewWave	Hewlett-Parkard Corp.
NeXTStep	NeXT, Inc.
NFS	Sun Microsystems, Inc.
NonStop SQL	Tandem
Novell	Novell, Inc.
Object Component	Borland International Inc.
Object Exchange	Borland International Inc.
Object Linking and Embedding	Microsoft Corp.
Object Management Architecture	Object Management Group
Office Vision	International Business Machines Corp.
ONC ToolTalk	SunSoft
Open Database Connectivity	Microsoft Corp.
Open Interface	Neuron Data Inc.
Open Network Computing	SunSoft
Open Server	Sybase, Inc.
Open Windows Connection	Cogent Data Technologies, Inc.
OpenLook	Sun Microsystems and USL
OpenLook Window Manager	Sun Microsystems and AT&T
OpenSQL	SQL Access Group
OpenView	Hewlett-Packard Corp.
OpenWindows	SunSoft
ORACLE	Oracle Corp.
ORACLE Server for NetWare 386	Oracle Corp.
ORACLE Server	Oracle Corp.
ORACLE Toolkit	Oracle Corp.
OS/2	International Business Machines Corp.
OS/2 Communciations Manager	International Business Machines Corp.
OS/2 Data Base Manager	International Business Machines Corp.
OS/2 EE Data Base Manager	International Business Machines Corp.
OS/2 Extend Edition Data Base Manager	International Business Machines Corp.
OS/2 LAN Server	International Business Machines Corp.
OS/2 Named Pipes	International Business Machines Corp.
OS/400	International Business Machines Corp.

Trademark or Registered Trademark of

OS/400 Database	International Business Machines Corp.
OSF	Open Software Foundation Inc.
OSF/1	Open Software Foundation Inc.
PalmPad	GRiD Systems Corp.
Paradox	Borland International Inc.
PC/Dacs	Pyramid Development Corp.
PC-XView	Spectragraphics Corp.
PenApps	Slate Corp.
PenBasic	Slate Corp.
PenCell	Penware, Inc.
PenPoint	Go Corp.
PerfView	Hewlett-Packard Corp.
POWER	International Business Machines Corp.
PowerBuilder	Powersoft Corp.
PowerFrame 30L	Tricord Systems Inc.
PowerPro Array	Advanced Logic Research, Inc.
PowerScript	Powersoft Corp.
Powersoft	Powersoft Corp.
Presentation Manager	International Business Machines Corp.
ProbeView	Hewlett-Packard Corp.
Professional Office System	International Business Machines Corp.
PROFS	International Business Machines Corp.
PROGRESS	Progress Software Corp.
PS/2	International Business Machines Corp.
Q+E	Pioneer Software
Quest	Gupta Technologies, Inc.
Rdb	Digital Equipment Corp.
Remote Data Access	International Standards Organization
Respository Manager/MVS	International Business Machines Corp.
Retix RD-930	Retix Corp.
Retix TP-920	Retix Corp.
RPC Tool	Netwise, Inc.
RS/6000	International Business Machines Corp.
SA Companion	Sybase, Inc.
SAA	International Business Machines Corp.
SCO UNIX	Santa Cruz Operations, Inc.
Secured Workstation Manager/DOS	International Business Machines Corp.
SecurID Card	Security Dynamics
SequeLink	TECHGnOsIs, Inc.
Server 290 Series	International Business Machines Corp.
SFT III	Novell, Inc.
SNA Management Services	International Business Machines Corp.
Sniffer	Network General Corp.
Solaris	SunSoft
SPARCstations	Sun Microsystems, Inc.

Trademark or Registered Trademark of

SplitSecond RF	Simware Inc.
SQA:Manager	Software Quality Automation
SQA:Robot for Windows	Software Quality Automation
SQL/400	International Business Machines Corp.
SQL Administrator	Microsoft Corp.
SQL Bridge	Microsoft Corp.
SQL/DS	International Business Machines Corp.
SQL Server	Sybase, Inc. and Microsoft Corp.
SQL-Advantage	Sybase, Inc.
SQL-Debug	Sybase, Inc.
SQL*Net	Oracle Corp.
SQLBase	Gupta Technologies, Inc.
SQLBase Server	Gupta Technologies, Inc.
SQLNetwork	Gupta Technologies, Inc.
SQLRouter	Gupta Technologies, Inc.
SQLScope	Novell, Inc.
SQLTalk	Gupta Technologies, Inc.
SQLWindows	Gupta Technologies, Inc.
SQR	Sybase, Inc.
Starbase	Cognos Inc.
Step Multi-Processing Fault-Tolerant 2001	Everex Systems, Inc.
STREAMS	UNIX System Laboratories, Inc.
StreetTalk	Banyan Systems, Inc.
Summit	International Business Machines Corp.
Sun	Sun Microsystems, Inc.
SunOS	Sun Microsystems, Inc.
SUPRe/DAISys	S-Cubed, Inc.
Sybase	Sybase, Inc.
SYBASE Secure SQL Server	Sybase, Inc.
SYBASE Server/Cluster Fault Tolerant	Sybase, Inc.
SYBASE SQL Server	Sybase, Inc.
SYBASE SQL Toolset	Sybase, Inc.
Synchrony	Telepartner International
System 7	Apple Computer, Inc.
System 36	International Business Machines Corp.
System 38	International Business Machines Corp.
System Fault Tolerance Level III	Novell, Inc.
System W	Comshare Inc.
Systems Application Architecture	International Business Machines Corp.
Systems Network Architecture	International Business Machines Corp.
Sytos Plus File Backup Manager	Sytron Corp.
Test for Windows	Microsoft Corp.
ThinkPad	International Business Machines Corp.

Trademark or Registered Trademark of

Toolbook	Asymetrix Corp.
TOP END	NCR Corp.
TPC-A	Transaction Processing Counsel
TPC-B	Transaction Processing Counsel
TPC-C	Transaction Processing Counsel
Transact-SQL	Sybase, Inc.
Transaction Security System	International Business Machines Corp.
Transaction Tracking System	Novell, Inc.
Transport-Independent Remote Procedure Call	SunSoft
Tivoli Management Environment	TIVOLI Systems, Inc.
Tivoli Management Framework	TIVOLI Systems, Inc.
Tivoli/ADE	TIVOLI Systems, Inc.
Tivoli/AEF	TIVOLI Systems, Inc.
Tivoli/Sentry	TIVOLI Systems, Inc.
Tivoli/Works	TIVOLI Systems, Inc.
Tuxedo	UNIX System Laboratories, Inc.
Tuxedo/Host	UNIX System Laboratories, Inc.
Tuxedo/WS	UNIX System Laboratories, Inc.
UI	UNIX International, Inc.
UI-Atlas	UNIX International, Inc.
Ultrix	Digital Equipment Corp.
Ungermann-Bass	Ungermann-Bass
UniKix	Integris
UNIX	UNIX System Laboratories, Inc.
UNIX System V	UNIX System Laboratories, Inc.
VANGuard	Banyan Systems, Inc.
VAX	Digital Equipment Corp.
VINES	Banyan Systems, Inc.
VINES Internet Protocol	Banyan Systems, Inc.
VINES Interprocess Communications Protocol	Banyan Systems, Inc.
VINES SMP	Banyan Systems, Inc.
Virtual Networking System	Banyan Systems, Inc.
Visual Basic	Microsoft Corp.
VM	International Business Machines Corp.
VMS	Digital Equipment Corp.
VSAM	International Business Machines Corp.
VTAM	International Business Machines Corp.
Watchdog PC	Fischer International Systems Corp.
Windows	Microsoft Corp.
Windows Device Driver Kit	Microsoft Corp.
Windows for Pen Computing	Microsoft Corp.
Windows for Workgroups	Microsoft Corp.
Windows New Technology	Microsoft Corp.

	Trademark or Registered Trademark of
Windows NT	Microsoft Corp.
Wingz	Informix, Inc.
Winnet	Microsoft Corp.
WorkPlace Shell	International Business Machines Corp.
X/Open	X/Open Corporation
X Window	Massachusetts Institute of Technology
XDB	XDB Systems, Inc.
XENIX	Microsoft Corp.
Xerox Network Systems	Xerox Corp.
XNS	3Com Corp.
XQLI	Novell, Inc.
Xt+	AT&T
Xtrieve Plus	Novell, Inc.
XView	Sun Microsystems, Inc.
XVT	XVT Software Inc.

Index